Riches *of*

e t e r n i t y

Riches *of*

e t e r n i t y

12 *Fundamental Doctrines from the Doctrine and Covenants*

ASPEN BOOKS
Salt Lake City, Utah

Edited by John K. Challis & John G. Scott

Riches of Eternity

Library of Congress Cataloging-in-Publication Data

Riches of eternity : 12 fundamental doctrines from the Doctrine and
    covenants / edited by John Kevin Challis and John G. Scott.
        p. cm.
    Includes bibliographical references and indexes.
    ISBN 1-56236-210-0
    1. Doctrine and covenants. 2. Church of Jesus Christ of Latter
-Day Saints—Doctrines. 3. Mormon Church—Doctrines. I. Challis,
John Kevin, 1958–   . II. Scott, John G. (John George), 1958–
BX8628.R53 1993
289.3'2—dc20   93-29480
                                                                   CIP

Printed in the United States of America

10   9   8   7   6   5   4   3   2   1

Cover design: Brian Bean

This book is dedicated to our spouses.

Contents

INTRODUCTION

JOHN K. CHALLIS

In 1829 THE Lord said, speaking of his revealed words, "These words are not of men nor of man, but of me" (D&C 18:34). The Doctrine and Covenants of The Church of Jesus Christ of Latter-day Saints, Christ's revealed word to this generation, is of singular importance to members of the Church, inasmuch as the revelations found in it present doctrines of the gospel in a way that modern Saints will understand. The Lord, in fact, has promised us a testimony and doctrine we can comprehend in our own language (see D&C 90:11; 2 Ne. 31:3), and for this reason, we should look to the Doctrine and Covenants for insight into and instruction on matters which relate to the beliefs of Latter-day Saints today.

The need to understand basic gospel doctrines is as pressing today as ever. *Riches of Eternity* is an attempt to bring to light, in twelve doctrinal essays, the fundamental matters outlined in the Explanatory Introduction to the 1981 edition of the Doctrine and Covenants, which reads in part:

> In the revelations the doctrines of the gospel are set forth with explanations about such fundamental matters as the nature of the Godhead, the origin of man, the reality of Satan, the purpose of mortality, the necessity for obedience, the need for repentance, the workings of the Holy Spirit, the ordinances and performances that pertain to salvation, the destiny of the earth, the future conditions of man after the resurrection and the judgment, the eternity of the marriage relationship, and the eternal nature of the family.

The chapters in this volume discuss these most essential matters with an eye to strengthening faith and shoring up foundations.

The first chapter, which discusses *the nature of the Godhead,* serves as a powerful testimony of the Deity we worship. In his usual creative style, Kenneth W. Godfrey unfolds much to us concerning the nature of the Father, the Son, and the Holy Ghost as real beings.

Robert J. Matthews, in chapter two, discusses the often controversial topic of *the origin of man.* Brother Matthews draws upon his experience as a teacher of scripture to present material that offers an enlightening interpretation of what the revealed word says about the beginnings of the human race.

Citing accounts from Latter-day Saint history and revelations contained in the Doctrine and Covenants, John K. Challis seeks to shed light on *the reality of Satan.* In chapter three, Brother Challis begins with the premortal existence when Lucifer became Satan and employs scriptures and the words of the prophets to make clear this "unpleasant" reality.

Chapter four, the research of John G. Scott, outlines *the purpose of mortality.* In it Brother Scott takes a fourfold look at the reasons for this earth life, considering what it is we are to accomplish here and why these things are important.

Robert J. Woodford draws upon years of experience and research to explain *the necessity for obedience.* By juxtaposing obedience with knowledge and agency, Brother Woodford teaches plainly why obedience is necessary in our lives and reminds us of the import of Joseph Smith's great maxim: "I made this my rule: When the Lord commands, do it"!

Philip C. Wightman's essay, chapter six, is a natural outgrowth of the doctrinal matters presented in chapters three, four, and five. Since Satan is real and we are mortal, we are often misled or wilfully disobedient and thus falter. Beginning here, and with an eye to exaltation, Brother Wightman outlines for the reader *the need for repentance.*

Chapter seven, *the workings of the Holy Spirit,* is of solemn importance to the Latter-day Saint. M. Catherine Thomas, in her scripturally based and thoughtful presentation, contributes to our understanding of the Holy Spirit as a personage of spirit and an operative power in the universe.

In chapter eight, *the ordinances and performances that pertain to salvation,* Linda Aukschun discusses the ordinances required for exaltation—ordinances that have been made available again through the Restoration and Priesthood authority.

The destiny of the earth is the doctrinal matter which James A. Carver's chapter illuminates. In this chapter, Brother Carver directs our gospel vision from things past toward things to come, outlining plainly the earth's journey toward its own exaltation.

Richard E. Berrett, illustrating vast doctrinal depth, uses section 76 of the Doctrine and Covenants as the core of chapter ten. According to Brother Barrett, "this great vision of the glories of the eternal realms" is ample foundation for the discussion of *the future conditions of man after the resurrection and the judgment.*

It will come as no surprise to the student of Latter-day Saint history that Danel W. Bachman has written the chapter on *the eternity of the marriage relationship.* Brother Bachman has done extensive research on the doctrines surrounding marriage, plural marriage, and marriage for time and all eternity as revealed in our dispensation.

Finally, Kem T. Cazier's chapter on *the eternal nature of the family* examines the relationship between the family and the eternal gospel, bringing to light the important role the family plays not only in this life but also in the life to come.

These fundamentals of the gospel are eternal in their scope, importance, and doctrinal basis. The twelve essays in this volume illuminate Latter-day Saint belief, and their relationship to the Doctrine and Covenants serves well to teach how comprehensive the restored gospel of Jesus Christ really is. The Doctrine and Covenants of The Church of Jesus Christ of Latter-day Saints is a book of vision and grandeur. Within its pages, one can see far into the future and glimpse the transcendent beauty of the earth in celestial burnings. Or, with equal force, one may glance backward and witness the pivotal moment in the premortal existence when Jesus Christ was chosen to be the Messiah, the Redeemer of the world. The Doctrine and Covenants literally is the Master's; in it are his words. It was the Lord himself who said, "it is my voice which speaketh [these words] unto you; for they are given by my Spirit unto you...; Wherefore, you can testify that you have heard my voice, and know my words" (see D&C 18:35–36).

This book is the production of various religious educators who recognize the powerful message which the twelve fundamental matters of the Doctrine and Covenants present. It is the work of individual members of The Church of Jesus Christ of Latter-day Saints who have a testimony of the restored gospel and a love for the scriptures and the Lord, members who teach the gospel at numerous institutions and are faithful and committed to the Church and the Savior. The ideas and doctrines discussed in this edited volume are the sole responsibility of the various authors and editors. They are not to be considered a primary source of doctrinal statements regarding The Church of Jesus Christ of Latter-day Saints. Only the Prophet and the presiding councils of the Church can reveal or speak for the Lord in relation to things of doctrine. If there are errors, they are only the manifestations of human limitations and are the responsibility of the writers of this volume.

ACKNOWLEDGEMENTS

THERE ARE MANY people who have contributed graciously to this book in one form or another. We first want to thank all of the authors who have spent so many hours pouring over the scriptures and the words of the prophets. The fine scholarship that they have presented in this volume will make this book an important contribution to LDS education and thought on the Doctrine and Covenants.

Additionally, we want to extend thanks to Delynn Halford, Larry Raymond, Julie Challis, and Valene Scott, who put in countless hours proofreading and double checking the material. We also thank Gary Astle of Compu-Aid, and Lynn Hopkins for their technical advice and help. Appreciation needs to be expressed to our colleagues at the Star Valley Institute and Seminary for their confidence and support, to Robert J. Matthews and Richard Draper for encouragement and advice during critical times, and to Danel W. Bachman for his inspiration in selection of the title. We are also grateful to the wonderful people at Aspen Books, namely, Stan Zenk, who saw immediately the value of this work, and Paul Rawlins, who oversaw production of the book.

Our spouses, who sacrificed our not being at home so many nights, deserve much of the credit for this volume. Without their enduring support we could not have accomplished the writing and editing of this book. Their patience far exceeded the normal bounds of loving spouses, as did that of our children. Thank you.

THE NATURE OF THE GODHEAD

KENNETH W. GODFREY

DEFINING *NATURE* IN *Webster's Third New Unabridged International Dictionary* requires a full column.[1] There are at least fifteen major meanings for this word, and accompanying each definition are more than a few synonyms. These include normal, characteristic, essential character, essence, fundamental disposition, temperament, and total reality. Thus an essay titled "The Nature of the Godhead" requires explications involving the essential character of the Father, the Son, and the Holy Ghost, as well as their essence, fundamental disposition, temperament, and total reality. At the outset it should be apparent to every reader that to fulfill such a task, because of the "nature" of the subject matter, indubitably is impossible. This essay, therefore, will attempt to describe the nature of the Godhead in a limited way as depicted in the Doctrine and Covenants.

Growing up, I sometimes encountered a theology that seemed to exacerbate both humankind's natural meanness and God's wrath. This theology, when coupled with rampant rumors regarding the horrors associated with the second advent of the Savior, caused fear to find a home deep within my soul. Just what sort of personages, I wondered, constituted the Godhead? Reading the Doctrine and Covenants at first did little to ease my anguish or calm my anxiety. Though I never really doubted that a God existed somewhere, my real interest was in trying to fathom just what was his fundamental character, disposition, and temperament. Passages of scripture vividly describing his anger, wrath, indignation, chastening hand, and distaste for sin seemed to portray a deity less than approachable, and one that I certainly did not look forward to meeting.

Other attributes he seemed to possess were also troublesome. Having had to kindle and then light a stove on many cold winter mornings left me with little to imagine when I read of God's anger being "kindled" against the wicked. In many sections of the Doctrine and Covenants, both God and Christ sound out of sorts and even mean. Section 133:51, for example, displays a deity trampling on the wicked in his fury. While still a boy I became almost convinced that unlike myself, God was not sorry when he became angry. Losing my temper, becoming filled with wrath, caused me to feel silly, dirty, and unclean after the fury had passed. Why was God so different from me, I thought? Yet in the following verse we learn that those who survive the second coming "shall mention the loving kindness of their Lord" (D&C 132:52). Perhaps Deity's love transcends and overshadows his wrath, and his anger is an aberration? I wondered.

Many of God's attributes seemed unique, unfathomable, foreign, or strange when viewed by a small-town farm boy. Deity, I read, possessed all power (D&C 20:24), was unchangeable, and had a course described as one eternal round (D&C 35:1). Everything, the scriptures declare, including myself, exists in his eternal presence, and he comprehends everything (D&C 88:40, 67), or all that is, can, or will be. While commanding me to completely forgive others, God's own judgment is swift, quick, sure, and ubiquitous. Angels, continually before him, praise him forever, and "intelligence" is his glory (D&C 93:36). Attributes of judgment, knowledge, power, intelligence, glory, and blinding light seemed to be his essence. Surely, I, being so totally different, could not have been made in his image.

Just as my discouragement and bewilderment reached its zenith, I usually stumbled on a contrary nature for the God of my fathers. In the Doctrine and Covenants, God tells members of the early Church to "be of good cheer, little children" (D&C 61:36). Knowing how my own father and mother treated me, I felt a small fire of hope and love ignite (or "kindle") within my soul. God's calling the Church members his "little flock" (D&C 6:34) reminded me of our old mother hen and the way she stayed alert when the chicks pecked wheat in the yard. With the approach of a hawk, she quickly had the brood under her wings, eyes flashing, claws poised, ready, just daring the predator to attack and attempt to devour one of her chicks. Was God my protector, I wondered?

Reading that he blesses us, calls the dead from their graves, succors those who are tempted, is merciful, saves all except sons of perdition, and calls me his friend filled my heart with expectation. Discovering that his bowels brim with compassion, that his voice is one of mercy and gladness, and that he is filled with love almost filled my heart of faith.

His voice, he assures the faithful, is one of gladness as he sends the Holy Ghost to comfort and succor us. Christ, I am assured, is my advocate with the Father. But why, I postulate, if he is my father and filled with compassion, do I need an advocate? Why, if he encircles me in "the arms of [his] love" (D&C 6:20), did Christ have to give his own life so that as many as will believe might become the sons and daughters of God (D&C 34:3)? Are we not told that we are his offspring (D&C 25:1)? Why cannot a natural man abide the presence of God, his father (D&C 67:12)? Then I learned that men and women become sensual and devilish by transgressing holy laws; they are not born that way (D&C 20:20). Still I needed help in answering my other questions.

Surely the revelations given to Joseph Smith provide great insights into the nature of the Godhead. However, I found in studying the Doctrine and Covenants that each member of the Godhead can be rightly called the great comprehender, the placer of truth, and the possessor of all intelligence. They individually and collectively both give and allow freedom, and yet their purposes cannot be frustrated (D&C 3:1). Though billions of God's children abide on this planet called earth, he has the capacity to hear each prayer as if that were the only one being uttered, something impossible for man to comprehend (D&C 96:6). Still confused, I resolved anew to study more diligently the sections of the

Doctrine and Covenants for answers about the characteristics and nature of the Godhead.

The Nature of God, the Father

Our Heavenly Father "has a body of flesh and bones as tangible as man's" (D&C 130:22). In 1844, the Prophet Joseph Smith declared that he had always taught that "God [is] a distinct personage."[2] Thus we know that personhood and distinctness are part of God's nature. He is unique in appearance, and his personality is recognizable, different in some ways from all that has been begotten and created. When we meet him again, we will recognize him and know who he is, partly because of his distinctive, even unique, features.

God is a personage whose nature also includes fatherhood.[3] Brigham Young once said, "He is the father of our spirits; and if we could know, understand and do His will, every soul would be prepared to return back into His presence, and when they get there they would see that they had formerly lived there.... And they would embrace their father and He would embrace them and say, My son, My daughter, I have you again; and they would say, O, My Father, My Father, I am home again."[4] In this sermon, Brigham Young encapsulates perhaps the best, the most appealing, endearing aspect of God's nature. Men and women can go home again; and what is more, they will find a father waiting there.

Though he is a distinct personage, God's nature has the quality of sameness (D&C 20:12). What he is today corresponds with what he was and will be. Varying not, God's course is described as "one eternal round" (D&C 3:2; 35:1) and his character as unchangeable (D&C 20:17). "All things," he tells us, "are present before mine eyes" (D&C 38:2). For Deity, time is one eternal now. If God's nature personifies sameness, and if all that is or will be makes up his present, then he must exist "outside of time and all time is spread out before Him as eternally present."[5] Does this attribute imply that time for us is "some kind of trick, a cosmic illusion?"[6] Even as we believe that time is absolutely significant and that we are free, does God's knowledge imply, too, that we are "absolutely knowable, predictable, . . . absolute mechanism"?[7] How can a being escape infinite boredom when everything is "present and the same," I ask myself.

At this stage of our existence, it becomes apparent that we are not capable of understanding what God's attribute of sameness fully implies. However, we are told, without equivocation, that God makes us free and that we are free indeed (D&C 98:8). Thus we believe that what we think, plan, and act out in time has significance. It is possible, moreover, that knowing something will happen or knowing that someone is going to do something does not necessarily cause the event or the action. God's nature, it seems, allows freedom, allows us to think in terms of past, present, and future without encroaching upon or eroding our moral agency (D&C 101:78).

That God is constant has the advantage, moreover, of allowing faith that what is right and wrong for one generation will generally be right and wrong for the next. Possessing a nature that envelopes sameness and transcends time has the advantage, too, of ensuring that the "works, and the designs, and the purposes of God cannot be frustrated" (D&C 3:1). God is never surprised and even events hundreds of years in the future that appear at first to frustrate his plans have contingencies already in place, as the account of the lost manuscript of the Book of Mormon bears out.[8]

This attribute of sameness also means, as we are told in the Doctrine and Covenants, that "God doth not walk in crooked paths, neither doth he turn to the right hand nor to the left, neither doth he vary from that which he hath said . . . and his course is one eternal round" (D&C 3:2). God's essence includes steadiness, sureness, and certainty. What he says, he means, and to his commandments we can anchor our souls.

Not only are all things present before God's eyes, but he also knows all things. He calls each of us by name, knows our hopes, dreams, and the desires of our hearts. Knowing who we are and from whence we came, he is aware, too, of our destiny. Such all-inclusive knowledge makes it possible for God to stay aware of even the sparrows in the field, as well as the kings on their thrones. No thing escapes his notice. Moreover, he not only knows us but also comprehends us (D&C 88:6). While at times we seem not to know ourselves nor comprehend why we do what we do, feel what we feel, and think what we think, God comprehends "all things" (D&C 88:41). He knows.

Even the "bad," we are told, is included in God's knowledge. He is conscious, aware, cognizant of all that is evil in the world. That his knowledge of evil does not affect his goodness should provide solace to our own souls. We, too, while remaining aware of much of the bad that often seems ready to engulf us, can maintain our own attribute of goodness (D&C 127:2).

Over and over again, the Doctrine and Covenants proclaims that God's nature includes power. He reigns with almighty power (D&C 20:24) and gives man the power to prophesy (D&C 34:10), power to overcome evil (D&C 50:32), power to understand his mysteries (D&C 76:116; 107:19), and the power of priesthood (D&C 113:8). Frequently God declares that he has all power (D&C 109:77). Does this mean he possesses the might to do anything? Or does it mean that all that can be done, God can do, as B. H. Roberts suggests.[9] Word games are at times used to disparage God's attribute of power. Can God, for example, create a rock so large he cannot lift it? Can he make a valley without a mountain on each side? Regardless of how we answer such questions, God's power has been restricted. I prefer to believe that God possesses the power to exalt his children if they will but heed his voice and follow the path laid out from the very beginning. Then, even as we dwell with him, we can ask him, if we are still so inclined, whether or not he can do anything. We should remain cognizant that nowhere in scripture does God suggest limits to his power, except that intelligence cannot be created or made (D&C 93:29), we cannot be saved in ignorance (D&C 131:6) nor in our sins, and blessings are predicated upon obedience to law (D&C 130:20). God, moreover, cannot lie. He is a God of truth. God's nature, then, includes the attribute of power with very few restrictions.

Deity's essential character encompasses, too, the attributes of love, compassion, and caring. Each soul is great in his sight, and all are encircled in the arms of his love. He gives liberally (D&C 46:7), commands love (D&C 59:5), and is full of mercy (D&C 84:102). Nothing brings him the same quality of joy as when a sinner repents and returns to the flock (D&C 18:13). Even the heavens experience true happiness when this happens.

Foreverness is still another part of God's nature. He is infinite, eternal, everlasting. Neither his works, nor his glory, nor his essential being ever end. Anything that characterizes his person has always existed, and he, too, "abideth forever," to borrow a scriptural phrase. He is immortal. If we are to become like him, we had better learn to like ourselves because we, too, will exist eternally. We cannot escape, even if we wanted to, from ourselves.

Furthermore, God possesses glory. Light surrounds his countenance. In fact, his glory is such that mortals, in the absence of the priesthood, cannot abide his presence unless quickened by the Spirit of God (D&C 67:11–12; 84:22). Light proceeding from the presence of God fills the immensity of space (D&C 88:6–14). Good people "shall be crowned with glory" and live forever in the presence of God the Father (D&C 88:19). At least a portion of God's glory is intelligence (D&C 93:36). Even if one equivocates a bit, we can be certain that all that is known, God knows. His intelligence, some attest, is greater than the combined knowledge of all others that exist.[10] Not only is his knowledge all-inclusive, but his character is flawless. Such attributes as love, long-suffering, humility, patience, kindness, easiness to be entreated, charity, and faith dwell in him perfectly. His work and glory is to bring to pass the eternal life of his children.

The eighty-fourth section of the Doctrine and Covenants declares that glory, power, mercy, justice, grace, truth, and peace can be ascribed to our God (D&C 84:102). Perhaps the order in which this list of attributes is rendered means that God's justice is tempered by his mercy; the truth is cushioned by his grace; and his glory, honor, and power are softened by his peace. His nature is such that our Father delights when his children pass the mortality test and, endowed with his grace and mercy, are able to inherit eternal life. However, those who refuse his pleadings and turn away are reminded more than a score of times in the pages of the Doctrine and Covenants that a just punishment will surely occur (D&C 3:4). There comes, moreover, a day when "the wrath of God shall be poured out upon the wicked without measure" (D&C 1:9). Those who march their own path shall perish (D&C 1:16), and those who give way to carnal desires will one day pay dearly for their sins (D&C 3:4). When the world ripens in iniquity, God will send flies upon the earth to take "hold of the inhabitants thereof," and maggots shall come upon them (D&C 29:18). The great tragedy of the Second Coming of the Master is that too many will, inasmuch as they have failed to respond to God's pleadings, be destroyed in their sins because they refuse to repent (D&C 29:17–18).

While it may not be right to harbor such feelings, almost everyone, for at least a moment, senses some exhilaration when in a movie or on the TV screen or in a novel or on the stage, the bad guy, the bully, the villain pays his dues and is wasted by the good guy. When I was a seventh grader, an eighth-grade bully terrorized our days. Afraid of his catching one of us alone, we moved from classroom to classroom in large groups. Our days were nightmares and our nights consisted of dreams of the next day's humiliations, which usually came to pass. The toughest boy in the seventh grade one day took ten or twelve of us aside to a dark corner of the junior high school and unveiled a plan of not only justice but also revenge. We surrounded the bully on the playground. Arrogantly, sarcastically, and with a sinister tone in his voice, he utterly refused to promise to desist or even reduce the number of his attacks on the weak. We tightened our circle each time he denied our request, and he confidently called on some eighth-graders for help. Smiling, they moved farther away, rejecting his pleas. At a predetermined signal, we all rushed the bully, wrestled him to the ground, and I quickly took off his pants and ran them up the flagpole. That night, even while praying, I felt a strange exhilaration, a peace, that what we had done was just. There does come a time when God's very nature demands that those who refuse to heed must pay. God is just, as well as merciful and long-suffering. We are assured, however, that justice only "kicks in" after we have been entreated, pleaded with, and given numerous chances to come into the fold.

The Nature of Jesus Christ

The essential characteristic of Jesus Christ is sonship. Over and over again in the pages of the Doctrine and Covenants he declares that he is the Son of God.[11] He has a resurrected body of flesh and bones and is a separate and distinct personage from God, his Father, and Christ is the only begotten of his Father in the flesh.

Like his Father, Christ has all power and is a God of judgment who will one day weigh all people in the balance (D&C 19:3). Endless and Eternal are two of his names, and he has suffered for all of us that we might not suffer if we fully repent (D&C 19:16). His suffering was so severe that it caused him to tremble, bleed from every pore, and to "suffer both body and spirit" (D&C 19:18). Thus one aspect of Christ's character is that he has the ability to feel infinite pain and to suffer even as we will if we do not repent (D&C 19:17).

While he was subject to temptations, he, unlike his brothers and sisters, gave them no heed (D&C 20:22). Because he committed no sin, was foreordained, and was like unto God, he was worthy to perform the Atonement and become our Savior (D&C 15:1; 16:1). Christ, by nature then, is the Redeemer. His sacrifice fills the demands of justice and enables repentant sinners to become clean and return home to God the Father.

Christ, his Father, and the Holy Ghost are a Godhead of unity (D&C 20:28). Not only are they unified and one with each other, but they are also whole themselves. Christ declares, "If ye are not one ye are not mine" (D&C 38:27). As we sin, seek our own, fail in patience, long-suffering, and humility, we negate our wholeness. Only as we attain the attributes of God do we become one, unified with our own selves and in harmony with Deity. Christ is at peace with who he is, what he is, why he is, and even how he is. Thus he is free to be one with God and the Holy Ghost.

The nature of Christ is also that of pleader (D&C 38:4). He speaks for us before the Father and is our advocate (D&C 62:1). By his grace we are both justified and sanctified (D&C 20:30–31). He is indeed the Savior of the world (D&C 42:1). Knowing the weaknesses of men and women, he succors those who are tempted (D&C 62:1), stands by us in tribulations, and exhorts us to be of good cheer (D&C 68:6). The Christ revealed in the Doctrine and Covenants sides with us, encourages repentance, and provides those who stumble with solace and hope. He seems to understand that earth life is a time of mistakes and knows that we, like employees of a chicken farmer, will break some eggs. As we do, all Christ asks is that we admit our mistakes, make restitution if we can, try harder, and rely on his help and grace. Through that assistance, he carefully pilots us home. Only those who refuse his aid, reject his atonement, and rebel against walking the path of salvation, turning deaf ears to his pleadings, will one day pay the full consequences for their choices.

Like his Father, Christ possesses all things (D&C 50:27), comprehends all things (D&C 88:6), created worlds without number (D&C 76:23-24), and has prepared for us "a crown of immortality and eternal life" (D&C 81:6). It is the light of Christ given to all men and women that is sometimes defined in other scripture as a conscience (Moro. 7:13, 16–19). Through this medium all those accountable who come to earth know the difference between right and wrong (D&C 84:44–46). While the content of different people's moral codes may not be exact duplicates of each other, still each person born into any cultural milieu, with the help of the light of Christ, learns his or her own taboos. Christ, then, is the "true light that lighteth every man that cometh into the world" (D&C 93:2). While this light may burn low at times, it is seldom, in any person, completely extinguished.

It becomes apparent that the Doctrine and Covenants depicts a Christ whose very nature is one of "Helpful Redeemer." He is an encourager, a pleader, a second comforter, an advocate, and even his bowels are filled with compassion (D&C 101:9). He died for all the sins that have been and ever will be committed. He administers salvation (D&C 109:4), and he is a resurrected being even as we one day will be (D&C 130:22). With his help, by heeding his pleadings and coming into his outstretched arms, men and women can achieve eternal life, the greatest of all the gifts of God (D&C 6:7, 13).

Perhaps some wonder just why a god whose very nature personifies fatherhood requires that a beloved, only begotten son plead the cause of the other children and atone for their sins. God certainly has the power alone to encircle us in the arms of his love. Perhaps he sends Christ so that we all might be taught the value of service, the importance of helping each other. Christ by nature is a servant, a shepherd, a helper, an encourager who sees the good and assures us that it can, and will, transcend and overcome the bad. We, too, as children of God and brothers and sisters of Christ, can, in a lesser yet still significant way, encourage, serve, help, and provide hope for others stumbling along the straight yet narrow path leading home. Christ certainly encourages us to extend the invitation.

The Atonement itself, the most important gospel doctrine, also has symbolic significance. Even as Christ suffered and agonized for us, we can help each other bear the burdens of unwise choices. Our own agony when family, friends, and associates stumble immeasurably helps them heal and again become strong. When we have suffered enough, Christ forgives us, implying that we should, as well, be willing to forgive ourselves and everyone else and then get on with our lives. Christ's sacrifice is a compelling example of love, caring, and willingness to give everything on behalf of God's sons and daughters.

The Nature of the Holy Ghost

The Holy Ghost does not have a body of flesh and bones, but is a male personage of spirit (D&C 130:22). We learn, too, from the Doctrine and Covenants that all spirit is matter, only more pure and fine than the elements of this earth (D&C 131:7). Thus, even though lacking a physical body, the Holy Ghost, being a personage of spirit, has form and shape and is recognizable. He can speak, hear, move, and communicate with men and women. Like the Father and the Son, the Holy Ghost is infinite, eternal, and without end (D&C 20:28).

Again, even as the Father and the Son, the Holy Ghost "knows all things" (D&C 35:19; 42:17). Possessing all knowledge allows the Holy Ghost to inspire prophets (D&C 34:10), to give men utterance (D&C 14:8), show all things (D&C 39:6), and teach us the truth (D&C 50:14). That he knows what was, is and will be means that he does not err, nor does he lie, but always speaks the truth in love (D&C 39:6; 50:17).

The Holy Ghost is often called by the Father "the Spirit of truth" (D&C 50:17). Because the Holy Ghost possesses so perfectly the attribute of truth, the words, thoughts, and feelings he conveys to humankind are accompanied by the absolute assurance that the message is in every way valid. The Holy Ghost, God declares, is truth, having no end, and has the ability to make the truth abound in us (D&C 88:66). However, we learn from the Book of Mormon that he only conveys the truth "unto the hearts and minds of the children of men" (2 Ne. 33:1; Enos 1:10). We then, as agents, must invite him into our hearts.

The power of truth which exudes from the Holy Ghost's nature carries with it its own solace. We are told that he teaches us "the peaceable things of the kingdom" (D&C 36:2). This implies that his nature encompasses peace. Oliver Cowdery was reminded, even before the Church was organized, of a time when the Holy Ghost spoke peace to his mind (D&C 6:23). There is, as the writer can testify, a peace that accompanies revelation received from this source.

Frequently in the Doctrine and Covenants the Holy Ghost is referred to as the "Holy Spirit of promise" (D&C 76:53). It is the Holy Ghost who ensures that all religioius promises, contracts, and covenants entered into by righteous men and women, by proper priesthood authority, will be fulfilled in every way. Those who are unworthy, unless they repent, do not have these holy ordinances "sealed by the Holy Spirit of promise" (D&C 76:53). Knowing that we cannot be saved in our sins and being a conveyor of truth, the Holy Ghost cannot lie and seal any gospel ordinances for the unworthy.

Still another aspect of the Holy Ghost's nature is that of comforter (D&C 21:9). The Comforter assures us that Jesus is the

Christ, confirms that the revelations and commandments are true, and teaches us all things that are expedient for us to know (D&C 75:10). This Comforter, the Holy Spirit of Promise, also assures worthy Saints of eternal life (D&C 88:4).

The Godhead

A perusal of the Doctrine and Covenants provides striking evidence that the Godhead concern themselves with minute details regarding our sojourn on this earth. They command the Saints to build a hotel in Nauvoo, detailing the wood to be used in the construction thereof and the amount of stock one man can own. They direct where and when the brethren shall serve missions. It is important to them that the Twelve depart for their mission to England from Far West, not Nauvoo, where they resided in 1839. God knows that Martin Harris and William E. McLellin are tempted to commit adultery, that Hyrum Smith's family will be important to the Church, that Emma Smith has murmured because of what she has not seen (D&C 25:4), that John Whitmer and Philip Burroughs should be missionary companions, that Isaac Morley will not be tempted more than he can bear (D&C 64:20), and even declares that there was joy in heaven when Warren Cowdery changed occupations (D&C 106:6). God is displeased when Sidney Rigdon writes an inadequate description regarding Jackson County, Missouri, and requires a rewrite of his essay (D&C 63:56). There seems to be no end to the Godhead's concern for the Father's earthly children.

Why all this attention to minutiae and detail? Perhaps it is the nature of the Godhead to know that by small and simple things great things are brought to pass (D&C 64:33). When we do the little things, greater things follow. Disclosing that it is his will that the widow, Vienna Jaques, should receive money to bear her expenses to Zion (D&C 90:28) just might inspire us to pay more attention to the needs of widows in our own wards and stakes. Knowing that God possesses the attribute of consistency makes us cognizant that his will today would be that our own Vienna Jaques be cared for and looked after. You, my children, God seems to be saying, need to give attention to small things like a cross word, how you conduct your business affairs, what your homes are like, your environment, and how you treat each other. This obsession for detail, when balanced against the cosmic, apocalyptic, majestic declarations found in the Doctrine and Covenants, provides evidence of the grandeur and the purpose that is embedded in the universe, as well as the love that envelops the Godhead.

There is much we still do not understand about God and his nature. How can all things that have, can be, and will be, be present before him? If he absolutely knows everything, how can men and women be free? If he has all power, why does evil exist? If he is our Father, why does he often, for so long, leave some of us alone, our prayers unanswered? Why does he often sound angry in the Doctrine and Covenants? There is much to ponder, study, and pray about. But with these and other questions still sounding in our ears, let us now draw a few conclusions.

Conclusions

The Godhead, we are assured in the Doctrine and Covenants, is composed of three separate and distinct male personages. They each know everything and possess all power. While they allow evil to exist, good will triumph in the end. Satan will be bound and earth life will seem to have been but a moment. God is our Father; Christ, our Redeemer and Brother; and the Holy Ghost, our Comforter and Conveyor of Truth, the Great Testifier. Being Gods of truth, they can be trusted and depended upon. They love everyone without exception and desire that all inherit eternal life. Yet men and women cannot be saved while still in their sins.

The anger, the harsh sounding voice of the Godhead, seems directed, for the most part, to those who choose not to hear their quiet pleadings. Their wrath, too, is for those who reject divine counsel and engage in wickedness. We are assured over and over again that though God is merciful, he is also just. There does come a time when wickedness brings its own pain, its own sorrow, its own anguish, its own reward, and even God cannot change that. Bad loses, evil men and women eventually pay in an unpleasant way for their sins. It appears that these people's conduct has somehow impaired not only their sight but their hearing as well. Their desensitized feelings are so callous that only the harsh, angry, loud voice of Deity attracts their attention (D&C 43:25). Thus God loudly calls upon them to repent, like a certain trumpet or even a brass band, lest they encounter a wrath that is sure.

In contrast, the humble, the righteous, those easily entreated who try hard to do right, whose hearing is sensitive and sure and whose sight is eternal, they hear the pleadings of a gentle parent asking that they come to Christ and have joy. Encircled in the arms of his love, he refers to them as his "little flock" in endearing tones. We, all God's children, are free to choose by our conduct, our desires, our motivations, which voice we hear because it is the nature of the Godhead to allow men and women to be agents, hopefully both free and moral. I only pray that my conduct, my character, and my spirituality are such that the only God I encounter is the gentle, loving Father whose only desire is to encircle me in the arms of his love. Like Enos and Moroni, I long with pleasure to see his face (Enos 1:27; Moro. 10:34).

NOTES

CHAPTER ONE

1. The 1828 Webster's *Dictionary* states that *nature* means a principle of action, species, or that which we are born with.

2. Joseph Smith, *History of The Church of Jesus Christ of Latter-day Saints*, 2d ed. rev. (Salt Lake City: Deseret Book Co., 1980), 6:474.

3. D&C 18:23; 25:1; 38:4; 42:17; 61:36.

4. Brigham Young, in *Journal of Discourses* (Liverpool, England: Latter-Day Saints' Book Depot, 1854–86), 4:268.

5. Marden J. Clark, *Liberating Form* (Salt Lake City: Aspen Books, 1992), 36.

6. Ibid.

7. Ibid.

8. D&C 3 and 10.

9. B.H. Roberts, *The Seventy's Course in Theology, Fourth Year: The Atonement* (Salt Lake City: The Deseret News, 1911), 70.

10. Neal A. Maxwell, *Ensign*, November 1981, 8–10.

11. D&C 6:21; 10:57; 11:28; 14:9.

Chapter Two

THE ORIGIN OF MAN

Robert J. Matthews

WE ARE THE literal offspring of God. This is the declaration of both ancient and latter-day scripture. God is our Father. We are his children. Since the revelations inform us that the Father is a personage with a body of flesh and bone, there is no difficulty understanding that mankind is created in the image of God's person. But the children of God are dual beings—they are both spirit and flesh—and the Lord has revealed through his prophets and their writings that we are the children of God as to both our spirit and our flesh.

The focus of this book is the Doctrine and Covenants. However, the revelations and utterances contained therein were not received in a vacuum and were given with the presumption that the Church was already somewhat acquainted with earlier scripture found in the Bible and the Book of Mormon. Hence, the revelations contain many allusions to biblical events, biblical characters, and biblical doctrines. But the revelations in the Doctrine and Covenants clarify and extend our understanding further, beyond the preliminary biblical account. This is evident in several subject areas in addition to the topic of mankind's origin. The extra help and clarification is especially necessary since the doctrinal content of our present Bible has been diminished through the many plain and precious truths that have been deleted from the Bible. For these reasons the treatment of the origin of mankind in this chapter will draw upon the Bible, the Book of Mormon, and the Pearl of Great Price, as well as the

Doctrine and Covenants.[1] These will be supplemented occasionally by statements of various General Authorities of The Church of Jesus Christ of Latter-day Saints.

The Spirit Body

Human beings are individual, intelligent, thinking, accountable spirit personages. Some spirits are female, others are male. Spirits are capable of love, hate, joy, sorrow, obedience, disobedience, loyalty, rebellion, and many other character traits and attributes. Spirits are immortal—they never die. They were begotten by our Heavenly Parents.

The human spirit is a personage that resembles the physical body. Spirit substance is real matter, but is considerably more refined than the physical substance of the mortal, fallen, temporal world of earth life.

Biblical passages that refer to the human spirit include the following:

Genesis 25:8, "Then Abraham gave up the ghost, and died."
Numbers 16:22, "O God, the God of the spirits of all flesh" (compare Num. 27:16).
1 Kings 17:21, "let this child's soul come into him again."
Zechariah 12:1, "the Lord ... formeth the spirit of man within him."
Luke 24:39, "a spirit hath not flesh and bones."
Acts 7:59, "Lord Jesus, receive my spirit."
Hebrews 12:9, "shall we not ... be in subjection unto the Father of spirits."
James 2:26, "the body without the spirit is dead."
See also Job 32:8; Ecclesiastes 12:7; 1 Peter 3:19.

Book of Mormon references to the spirit are often clearer and more distinct than those in the Bible and include these:

1 Nephi 11:11, "I spake unto him as a man speaketh; for I beheld that he was in the form of a man, nevertheless, I knew that it was the spirit of the Lord."

Mosiah 2:28, "I am about to go down to my grave . . . [and I desire that] my immortal spirit may join the choirs above."

Alma 40:11, "the spirits of all men, as soon as they are departed from this mortal body, . . . are taken home to that God who gave them life."

Moroni 10:34, "I soon go to rest in the paradise of God, until my spirit and body shall again reunite."

See also 2 Nephi 9:8–14; Alma 11:43–45; 42:9; Ether 3:15–16.

Passages found in the Pearl of Great Price include the following:

Moses 6:36, "And he [Enoch] beheld the spirits that God had created."

Moses 7:57, "And as many of the spirits as were in prison came forth and stood on the right hand of God."

Abraham 3:18–19, If there are two spirits, and one is above the other in intelligence, there will be a third above it.

Abraham 3:22–26, Abraham is shown the spirits (intelligences) that existed before the world was, and he sees that there were some more intelligent than the others. The greater spirits were foreordained to become rulers in God's kingdom.

Having established from the other scriptures that the spirit children of God are intelligent and accountable personages, we can find confirmation and extended information regarding the spirit children of God in the Doctrine and Covenants.

In the vision of the degrees of glory identified as section 76, we learn that the Prophet Joseph Smith and Sidney Rigdon saw not only the postmortal worlds but also the doings of spirits in the premortal existence.

By the power of the Spirit our eyes were opened and our understandings were enlightened, so as to see and understand the things of God—

Even those things which were from the beginning before the world was, which were ordained of the Father, through his Only Begotten Son, who was in the bosom of the Father, even from the beginning;

Of whom we bear record; and the record which we bear is the fulness of the gospel of Jesus Christ, who is the Son, whom we saw and with whom we conversed in the heavenly vision. . . .

. . . And this we saw also, and bear record, that an angel of God who was in authority in the presence of God, who rebelled against the Only Begotten Son whom the Father loved and who was in the bosom of the Father, was thrust down from the presence of God and the Son,

And was called Perdition, for the heavens wept over him—he was Lucifer, a son of the morning.

And we beheld, and lo, he is fallen! is fallen, even a son of the morning!

And while we were yet in the Spirit, the Lord commanded us that we should write the vision; for we beheld Satan, that old serpent, even the devil, who rebelled against God, and sought to take the kingdom of our God and his Christ—

Wherefore, he maketh war with the saints of God, and encompasseth them round about. (D&C 76:12–14, 25–29)

The rebellion of Lucifer, a spirit being, is clearly depicted in the foregoing passage. Doctrine and Covenants 29:36 adds (clarifying Rev. 12:4) that there were many spirits who followed Lucifer in his rebellion. The Prophet Joseph Smith explained that the devil's punishment is to never receive a physical body.[2] Thus the devil and his spirit-being "angels" will remain spirits throughout eternity, never to receive a physical body.

Of the nature of spirits the Prophet Joseph Smith has written that

the spirit is a substance; that it is material, but that it is more pure, elastic and refined matter than the body; that it existed before the body, can exist in the body; and will exist separate from the body, when the body will be mouldering in the dust; and will in the resurrection, be again united with it.[3]

Spirit bodies resemble bodies of flesh and bone. This is evident from the experience of the Brother of Jared with the premortal Jesus, recorded in Ether 3. This event occurred 2000 or more years B.C.

> Behold, this body, which ye now behold, is the body of my spirit; and man have I created after the body of my spirit; and even as I appear unto thee to be in the spirit will I appear unto my people in the flesh. (Ether 3:16)

The form and visual appearance of human spirits (and animal spirits also) resemble their earthly bodies, as recorded in Doctrine and Covenants 77:2.

> That which is spiritual being in the likeness of that which is temporal; and that which is temporal in the likeness of that which is spiritual; the spirit of man in the likeness of his person, as also the spirit of the beast, and every other creature which God has created.

There is a great variety of intelligence and capacity among spirits. Since all spirits had agency in premortality, variety and gradation soon became apparent. Some spirits became noble and great in knowledge and in character. Likewise, some did not. The greatest of all, of course, is he whom we know as Jehovah, or later as Jesus Christ. Another, among the mightiest and most accomplished, was the spirit known as Michael, the archangel. *Michael* means "who is like God" (a statement—not a question). Michael is the only one designated as an archangel in the scriptures. More will be spoken about him later in this chapter.

Other spirits who obtained noble status in the premortal existence are those who would become prophets and leaders of the Church on the earth. This is explained in Doctrine and Covenants 138:53–56, wherein President Joseph F. Smith declared:

> The Prophet Joseph Smith, and my father, Hyrum Smith, Brigham Young, John Taylor, Wilford Woodruff, and other

choice spirits who were reserved to come forth in the fulness
of times to take part in laying the foundations of the great
latter-day work,

Including the building of the temples and the performance of ordinances therein for the redemption of the dead,
were also in the spirit world.

I observed that they were also among the noble and great
ones who were chosen in the beginning to be rulers in the
Church of God.

Even before they were born, they, with many others,
received their first lessons in the world of spirits and were
prepared to come forth in the due time of the Lord to labor
in his vineyard for the salvation of the souls of men.

From the foregoing and other passages, we perceive that
there is instruction in the premortal existence and that obedience to gospel principles makes for spiritual progress. Although
only men are spoken of in the foregoing passage, we may rest
assured that female spirits were and are among the noble and
great ones.

The premortal spirit existence is alluded to also in Doctrine
and Covenants 49:17 and in 93:38.

The Physical Body

An account of the creation of the physical bodies of Adam and
Eve is given in the book of Genesis and also in the Book of Moses
and the Book of Abraham. All of the details, of course, are not
made plain, but the underlying truth is apparent that our physical
creation (as with our spirit creation) was intentional, deliberate,
purposeful, and nonaccidental. Our creation in both spirit and
body was a deliberate design and act of God. Our bodies were
created in part to become a tabernacle for our spirits to live in
while on earth.

Another purpose of the physical body is to provide an eternal
tabernacle for the spirit after the resurrection. We read in
Doctrine and Covenants 93:33–34 that a spirit without a body cannot have a fulness of joy, and even with a body, a fulness of joy

can be obtained only when the spirit and body are "inseparably connected," that is, when resurrected (cp. Alma 11:45). Thus the physical body is designed and prepared as a tabernacle of the spirit not for mortality alone, but for eternity. These factors give us a clue as to why the spirits of the dead feel that a long separation from their physical bodies is a type of bondage (D&C 45:17; 138:50).

The Prophet Joseph enlarged on this theme as follows:

We came to this earth that we might have a body and present it pure before God in the celestial kingdom. The great principle of happiness consists in having a body. The devil has no body, and herein is his punishment.[4]

Adam's body is said to have been created from the dust of the earth (Gen. 2:7; Moses 3:7; Abr. 5:7; D&C 77:12), meaning that it was created or made from the elements of the earth. The book of Moses offers further insight into this matter by stating that Adam's children were also created from the dust of the earth (Moses 6:59). The same expression is used to describe the bodily "creation" of Adam's children as was used to describe the creation of Adam's body. Does this not suggest the same process was used? Adam is also spoken of as being the "son of God" (Moses 6:22).

In the gospel of Jesus Christ the human family is at the pinnacle of dignity, because the first man and the first woman—Adam and Eve—were the direct and first-generation literal offspring of Heavenly Parents both in the spirit body and in the physical body. The human family is literally, in every sense, the offspring of God. This is according to divine law, for the scriptural accounts state that living things reproduce and bring forth "after their kind," and that the "seed could only bring forth the same in itself, after his kind" (see Abr. 4:11, 12, 21, 24–25). Mankind, both male and female, was created in the "image" and the "likeness" of "the Gods" (Abr. 4:26–27).

The writings of Moses, revealed to Joseph Smith, quote from "the book of the generations of Adam," saying that the bodies of men and women, in the beginning on the earth, were made "in the likeness" and the "image of [God's] own body" (see Moses 6:8–9). There follows a detailed listing of Adam's earthly family from generation to generation—not a pedigree of the spirits of men but of the physical body—and it lists Adam, Seth, Enos, etc., for seven generations down to Enoch (Moses 6:10–21). It is precisely stated that Adam begat a son "in his own likeness, after his own image, and called his name Seth" (Moses 6:10). This is the precise and identical language by which Adam's own physical creation is spoken of. Since we know how Adam and Eve begat Seth's body, does this not imply that the same process also applies to the way Adam's body was formed? This conclusion is reinforced by the next verse, which reads: "And this is the genealogy of the sons of Adam, who was the son of God" (Moses 6:22).

Since these statements are in the context of fathers begetting the bodies of children on the earth, the consistent and plain reading of the scripture conveys the idea that just as Seth is the son of Adam and Eve, so also are Adam and Eve, in the physical body, the physical offspring of Heavenly Parents. Any other reading would be strained and artificial. This is a demonstration of the law that living things, including the Gods, reproduce "after their kind." Thus the terms "fatherhood of God" and "brotherhood of man" are not simply figures of speech, but are literal expressions when seen through the lens of latter-day revelation.

There is something comforting and reassuring in searching holy writ and knowing that the human family's pedigree chart runs back to God and not to the animals. The foregoing passages make it quite easy and natural for us to realize that Adam and Eve were not the products of organic evolution, up from the ape, but rather that human beings have a divine origin in both body and spirit.

The First Presidency of the Church in 1909 confirmed the divine origin of mankind in both body and spirit. Following is an excerpt from the document. Please note that it deals specifically with the spirit and the body, comparing Adam and Jesus Christ, as well as dealing generally with all mankind:

All men and women are in the similitude of the universal Father and Mother, and are literally the sons and daughters of Deity....

Adam, our great progenitor, "the first man," was, like Christ, a pre-existent spirit, and like Christ he took upon him an appropriate body, the body of a man, and so became a living soul.... [A]ll men existed in the spirit before any man existed in the flesh, *and . . . all who have inhabited the earth since Adam have taken bodies and become souls in like manner.*

It is held by some that Adam was not the first man upon this earth, and that the original human being was a development from lower orders of the animal creation. These, however, are the theories of men. The word of the Lord declares that Adam was "the first man of all men" (Moses 1:34), and we are therefore in duty bound to regard him as the primal parent of our race. It was shown to the brother of Jared that all men were created in the *beginning* after the image of God; and whether we take this to mean the spirit or the body, or both, it commits us to the same conclusion: Man began life as a human being, in the likeness of our Heavenly Father. (emphasis added in the first instance)[5]

Some may wonder how Jesus could be the Only Begotten of the Father in the flesh if Adam also was thus begotten. Elder Bruce R. McConkie expressed his understanding of the creation of Adam in these words, while discussing the meaning of Luke 3:38 which says Adam is the son of God:

This statement, found also in Moses 6:22, has a deep and profound significance and also means what it says. Father Adam came, as indicated, to this sphere, gaining an immortal body, because death had not yet entered the world (2 Ne. 2:22). Jesus, on the other hand, was the Only Begotten in the flesh, meaning into a world of mortality where death already reigned.[6]

It is in the light of the foregoing statements that Doctrine and Covenants 20:17-25 can be most fully and literally understood:

By these things we know that there is a God in heaven, who is infinite and eternal, from everlasting to everlasting the same unchangeable God, the framer of heaven and earth, and all things which are in them;

And that he created man, male and female, after his own image and in his own likeness, created he them;

And gave unto them commandments that they should love and serve him, the only living and true God, and that he should be the only being whom they should worship.

But by the transgression of these holy laws man became sensual and devilish, and became fallen man.

Wherefore, the Almighty God gave his Only Begotten Son, as it is written in those scriptures which have been given of him.

He suffered temptations but gave no heed unto them.

He was crucified, died, and rose again the third day;

And ascended into heaven, to sit down on the right hand of the Father, to reign with almighty power according to the will of the Father;

That as many as would believe and be baptized in his holy name, and endure in faith to the end, should be saved—

It is certain that the first man and the first woman were highly intelligent and capable, for they had a pure language which was both written and spoken, as we read in Moses 6:5-6.

And a book of remembrance was kept, in the which was recorded, in the language of Adam, for it was given unto as many as called upon God to write by the spirit of inspiration;

And by them their children were taught to read and write, having a language which was pure and undefiled.

Enoch also kept a record of the gathering at Adam-ondi-Ahman which was held three years before Adam's death as noted in Doctrine and Covenants 107:57, a record we will eventually have access to for our learning.

Furthermore, the earliest generations on the earth were excellent physical specimens and were not just one step away from the caveman or the ape. We find the following in Doctrine and Covenants 107:42–43 concerning the physical appearance of Adam and his son Seth:

> From Adam to Seth, who was ordained by Adam at the age of sixty-nine years, and was blessed by him three years previous to his (Adam's) death, and received the promise of God by his father, that his posterity should be the chosen of the Lord, and that they should be preserved unto the end of the earth;
>
> Because he (Seth) was a perfect man, and his likeness was the express likeness of his father, insomuch that he seemed to be like unto his father in all things, and could be distinguished from him only by his age.

The inference is that both Adam and Seth were fine looking, perfect men. But by whose standards? Beauty is in the eye of the beholder and is a very subjective thing. However, the Prophet Joseph compared the physical beauty of Adam and Seth to his own brother Alvin who had passed away in 1823 at the age of 26. The Prophet was very fond of Alvin, and he spoke of him tenderly, calling him "one of the noblest of the sons of men."[7] Later Joseph said of Alvin, "He was a very handsome man, surpassed by none but Adam and Seth, and of great strength."[8] The members of the Smith family were tall, lean, and long limbed. If that is the standard by which Joseph Smith judged handsomeness, then it bodes well for Adam and Seth being not anything at all like the images of the traditional "early man" of the evolutionists. The Prophet Joseph is also reported to have described Adam as a "'perfect man'" who "'never stumbled or fell a joint [sic] to the ground'."[9]

Adam's physical body was the tabernacle of the great and majestic Michael the archangel. When the premortal spirit known as Michael came to earth and obtained a physical tabernacle, he was known as Adam (D&C 27:11). It is fitting that such a noble spirit be tabernacled in a body that was the literal offspring of God, rather than in the body of an animal.

Thus from Adam and Eve, our first parents on the earth, has come the family of all the earth (2 Ne. 2:20). And within the physical body of each person, sons and daughters of Adam and Eve, there dwells an immortal spirit. When Adam and Eve were placed in the Garden of Eden they were deathless. Being the children of immortal, celestial, exalted parents, they (Adam and Eve) were also without death. When Adam and Eve partook of the forbidden fruit they became mortal, or fallen, and capable of producing mortal children, that is, the human family of all the earth. Hence, the human race shares a common origin, with the Parents of our spirits residing in the heavens and the parents of our flesh being the first mortal flesh on the earth (see Moses 3:7).

NOTES

CHAPTER TWO

1. Of necessity, only the major references dealing with the origin of mankind could be cited in this chapter. The diligent student is invited to use the Topical Guide in the LDS edition of the Bible and the Index to the triple combination for a more extensive presentation of scriptures on the subject. The Bible Dictionary in the LDS edition of the Bible also provides a listing of pertinent scriptures, as well as discussion, on these topics.

2. Joseph Smith, *Teachings of the Prophet Joseph Smith*, comp. Joseph Fielding Smith (Salt Lake City: Deseret Book Co., 1976), 181, 297.

3. Ibid., 207.

4. Ibid., 181.

5. "The Origin of Man," *Improvement Era* 13 (1909): 75-81; see also *Encyclopedia of Mormonism*, ed. Daniel H. Ludlow (New York: Macmillan Publishing Co., 1992), 4:1667–68; Bruce R. McConkie, *Mormon Doctrine*, 2d ed. (Salt Lake City: Bookcraft, 1966), 16–18.

6. Bruce R. McConkie, *Doctrinal New Testament Commentary* (Salt Lake City: Bookcraft, 1973), 1:95.

7. Joseph Smith, *History of The Church of Jesus Christ of Latter-day Saints* (Salt Lake City: Deseret Book Co., 1980), 5:126.

8. Ibid., 5:247.

9. Diary of Oliver B. Huntington, in Hyrum L. Andrus, *Joseph Smith, the Man and the Seer* (Salt Lake City: Deseret Book Co., 1960), 92.

THE REALITY OF SATAN

JOHN K. CHALLIS

It reminds me of an anecdote of a man who was travelling. He saw a devil as he was travelling, and the devil was asleep; and he was asked the reason, and the answer was, the people were asleep. When he came back, the devil was running. He inquired what was the matter, and the answer was, the people [have awakened]. It has been precisely so from the time that Joseph Smith found the plates: the Devil has been after him, and after this people to the present.

—Joseph Young[1]

TO THE PROPHET Joseph Smith the Lord said, "Behold, thou wast called and chosen...to my ministry." These words opened a revelation intended to strengthen and encourage Joseph. As the leader of a new dispensation, he needed assurance and encouragement from time to time. The Lord, understanding this, continued the revelation now known as section 24 of the Doctrine and Covenants by saying: "I have lifted thee up out of thine afflictions, and have counseled thee, that thou hast been delivered from all thine enemies, and thou hast been delivered from the powers of Satan and from darkness!" (v. 1)[2]

The last phrase of this July 1830 revelation carries with it a sense of victory—an affirmation of liberty from a force desiring to take Joseph captive and lead him down to destruction (Alma 12:11). This force is Satan, or the devil.

The Savior, by direct revelation, has clearly taught that Satan is not to be trifled with. In the meridian of time, for example, the Lord counseled his disciples to "fear not them which kill the body, but are not able to kill the soul: but rather *fear him which is able to destroy* both soul and body in Hell" (Matt. 10:28; emphasis added).[3] Along these same lines, President Spencer W. Kimball has taught that an "*awareness* of the existence, the power, and the plans of Satan" can help in our overcoming the world and conquering the adversary (emphasis added; see also Rev. 3:12; D&C 10:5).[4] The goal of this chapter is to use teachings of the prophets and scripture to demonstrate the reality of Satan. In light of Christ's teachings to his disciples and the words of President Kimball, this topic should be considered by every Latter-day Saint.

Before proceeding further, it is important to point out that despite Satan's reality, he—the devil—is still in subjection to God. Joseph Smith emphasized this fact by calling upon the "Lord God Almighty... who *controllest and subjectest the devil*," while he and his companions were in Liberty Jail (D&C 121:4; emphasis added).

Additionally, to maintain perspective and to avoid too much aggrandizement of Satan, it is helpful to note that his role as he "who opposeth" (2 Thes. 2:1–4) is what we might call a "necessary evil." The doctrine of agency makes the reality of Satan a necessity. However, not all of the blame for the sins and errors of God's children can be placed on the devil. The Prophet Joseph made this clear when he taught

> that Satan was *generally blamed for the evils which we did*, but if he was the cause of all our wickedness, men could not be condemned. The devil *could not compel mankind to do evil*; all was voluntary. Those who resisted the Spirit of God, would be liable to be led into temptation, and then the association of heaven would be withdrawn from those who refused to be made partakers of such great glory. God would not exert any compulsory means, and the devil could not; and such ideas as were entertained [on these subjects] by many were absurd. (emphasis added; brackets in original)[5]

These teachings regarding agency are reinforced in the Doctrine and Covenants. In section 29, the Lord has revealed that "it must needs be that the devil should tempt the children of men, or they could not be agents unto themselves; for if they never should have bitter they could not know the sweet" (v. 39).[6]

The Prophet's comments emphasize the idea that Satan can not compel us to do evil. This is one of the great assurances of the gospel of Jesus Christ. Elder James E. Faust of the Council of the Twelve, in an address in which he refers to Satan as "The Great Imitator," has said, "Certainly he [the devil] can tempt and he can deceive, but *he has no authority over us which we do not give him*" (emphasis added).[7]

Thus Satan, though real, possesses limited power. He is not allowed to tempt little children, for example, and he can not conquer us if we pray always (see D&C 10:5; 29:47). Though Satan's power is strong, it is comforting to know that the Lord has made provisions for our safety—if we choose that which is good. Any other choice is full of hazard (see Alma 34:31–35; Moro. 7:12).

In order to obtain a clear understanding of Satan's reality, it is important to discuss, first, how Satan came to be; second, the reality of Satan in latter-day events; and third, what latter-day prophets have said of Satan's reality and power.

How Satan Came to Be: His Premortal Existence and Rebellion

On the 16th day of February 1832, Joseph Smith and Sydney Rigdon received what is sometimes referred to as "The Vision,"[8] now recorded in section 76 of the Doctrine and Covenants. In a series of visions, Joseph and Sidney were shown "even those things which were from the beginning before the world was" (76:13). In what was to be the first of these visions[9] they saw, through the eyes of their understandings, "the Son, on the right hand of the Father" and holy angels; they heard the voice of the Father bear witness of his Son; and, in the midst of this panorama, they came to know that Jesus Christ is the Creator of this and other worlds (vv. 19–24).

Suddenly, and in stark contrast, Joseph and Sidney received a vision of Satan. This second vision, starting in verse 25, reveals the reality of Satan. It teaches us, first, that Satan was known as Lucifer in the premortal existence, and, second, that this same Lucifer was an "angel of God who was in authority in the presence of God" (v. 25). He "rebelled against the Only Begotten Son whom the Father loved" (v. 25), and because of his desire to rebel, the Prophet said he "sought for things which were unlawful. Hence he was sent down."[10] Moses, a prophet who knew firsthand of Satan's reality (Moses 1:12–22), writes that Lucifer then *"became Satan, yea, even the devil, the father of all lies"* (Moses 4:4; emphasis added).

By rebelling he became Perdition, never again to be forgiven,[11] and "the heavens wept over him—he *was Lucifer, a son of the morning"* (D&C 76:26; emphasis added). Notice the feeling of sadness, loss, and regret conveyed in that verse through the use of the past tense. But Satan's choice had been made; he had sought for his own glory over our Heavenly Father's plan of salvation and had, according to Joseph Smith, "stood up *as a Savior"* (emphasis added).[12]

The reality of this event was matter-of-fact to many of the early Saints who had been tutored by Joseph and his prophetic insight. One such individual, Orson F. Whitney, had let the words of the scriptures and the teachings of Joseph distill into him and chose poetry to express his feelings. With themes reflecting the Prophet's teachings[13] about Lucifer's rebellion, Brother Whitney wrote "Elect of Elohim" as part of his *Elias: An Epic of the Ages.* This poem vividly recreates that moment in premortality when "One was choice of Elohim / O'er one who fighting fell:"

> In solemn council sat the Gods; . . .
>
> Silence self-spelled; the hour was one
>   When thought doth most avail;
> Of worlds unborn the destiny
>   Hung trembling in the scale.
> Silence o'er all, and there arose,

Those kings and priests among,
A Power sublime, than whom appeared
None nobler 'mid the throng.

A stature mingling strength with grace,
Of meek though Godlike mien,
The love-revealing countenance
Lustrous as lightning sheen;
Whiter his hair than ocean spray,
Or frost of alpine hill.
He spake;—attention grew more grave,
The stillness e'en more still.

"Father!"—the voice like music fell,
Clear as the murmuring flow
Of mountain streamlet trickling down
From heights of virgin snow.
"Father," it said, "since one must die,
Thy children to redeem,
Whilst earth, as yet unformed and void,
With pulsing life shall teem;

"And thou, great Michael, foremost fall,
That mortal man may be,
And chosen Saviour yet must send,
Lo, here am I—send me!
I ask, I seek no recompense,
Save that which then were mine;
Mine by the willing sacrifice,
The endless glory, Thine! ... "

Silence once more. Then sudden rose
Aloft a towering form,
Proudly erect as lowering peak
'Lumed by the gathering storm;
A presence bright and beautiful,
With eye of flashing fire,

A lip whose haughty curl bespoke
    A sense of inward ire.

"Give me to go!" thus boldly cried,
    With scarce concealed disdain;
"And hence shall none, from heaven to earth,
    That shall not rise again.
My saving plan exception scorns;
    Man's agency unknown;
As recompense, I claim the right
    To sit on yonder throne!"

Ceased Lucifer. The breathless hush
    Resumed and denser grew.
All eyes were turned; the general gaze
    One common magnet drew.
A moment there was solemn pause;
    Then, like the thunder-burst,
Rolled forth from lips omnipotent—
    From Him both last and first:

"Immanuel! thou my Messenger,
    Till time's probation end.
And one shall go thy face before,
    While twelve thy steps attend.
And many more, on that far shore,
    The pathway shall prepare,
That I, the First, the last may come,
    And earth my glory share...."

'T was done. From congregation vast
    Tumultuous murmurs rose;
Waves of conflicting sound, as when
    Two meeting seas oppose.
'T was finished. But the heavens wept;
    And still their annals tell
How one was choice of Elohim,
    O'er one who fighting fell.[14]

Lucifer's rebellion literally led to his downfall, "for," said the Lord, "he rebelled against me, saying, Give me thine honor, which is my power; and also a third part of the hosts of heaven turned he away from me because of their agency; And they were thrust down, and thus came the devil and his angels" (D&C 29:36–37).

The Reality of Satan in Two Latter-day Events

President Marion G. Romney said, "At the opening of every dispensation [Satan] has made a *frontal attack against the advent of truth*" (emphasis added).[15] Since the first days of this dispensation, the Latter-day Saints have witnessed the reality of Satan. John the Revelator has given us some insight as to why this may be so. He said that "the devil is come down...[to earth] having great wrath, because he knoweth that he hath but a short time" (Rev. 12:12). And since Satan knows that his time is short, and because he is the "enemy to all righteousness" (see Mosiah 4:14–15), he vented his wrath upon a fourteen-year-old boy in the spring of 1820.

The First Vision teaches the reality of Satan

With prophetic hindsight Joseph Smith said:

> It seems as though the adversary was aware, at a very early period of my life, that I was destined to prove a disturber and an annoyer of his kingdom; else why should the powers of darkness combine against me? Why the opposition and persecution that arose against me, almost in my infancy. (JS–H 1:20)

However, it is unlikely that young Joseph Smith thought there was "some actual being from the unseen world" (JS–H 1:16) waiting in a stand of trees on that "beautiful, clear day, early in the spring of eighteen hundred and twenty" when Joseph went to seek wisdom from God (JS–H 1:14).

In two of the four published recitals of the First Vision[16] (the 1835 account and the 1838 account, which is now JS–H 1:5–20), the attack of a powerful "unseen" being is recorded. Elder Neal A. Maxwell, with depth and insight, has said that "for the faithful, our finest hours are sometimes during or just following our darkest hours."[17] This was absolutely true for Joseph Smith. His glorious theophany came *after* his being seized and overcome for a time by Satan. The attack was a powerful one. Joseph said in 1835 that

> my toung [*sic*] seemed to be swolen [*sic*] in my mouth, so that I could not utter, I heard a noise behind me like some person walking towards me, I strove again to pray, but could not, the noise of walking seemed to draw nearer, I sprung up on my feet, . . . and looked around, but saw no person or thing.[18]

In his 1838 recital of the events, Joseph spoke of "a thick darkness" gathering around him and said that it seemed for a time he was "doomed to sudden destruction" (JS–H 1:15). In this moment of deepest despair, when he felt he would be destroyed (see JS–H 1:15-16), he was delivered. Of this deliverance the Prophet said, in 1835 and 1838 respectively, "my mouth was opened and my toung [sic] liberated," and a "pillar of fire appeared above my head . . . and filled me with Joy unspeakable."[19] In this light, Joseph said he saw, "two Personages, whose brightness and glory defy all description, standing above me in the air. One of them spake unto me, calling me by name and said, pointing to the other—*This is My Beloved Son. Hear Him!*" (JS–H 1:17).

Thus, in a matter of minutes, through the experience of the First Vision, Joseph learned that the Father and the Son are real and that Satan is real, as well. There are few experiences which could rival this one for its powerful demonstration of the ultimate contrast between God and Satan.[20]

The episode of the lost 116 pages and the reality of Satan

The Doctrine and Covenants sheds further light on the reality of Satan in the sections dealing with the lost manuscript pages of the Book of Mormon. Sections 3 and 10 openly treat the "evil one" (D&C 93:37). In section 3 the Lord says, "The works, and the designs, and the purposes of God cannot be frustrated, neither can they come to naught" (D&C 3:1). The Lord also taught that he does not walk in crooked paths, that his paths are straight, and "his course is one eternal round" (3:2). And in words of counsel to Joseph, the Lord says, "Remember, remember that it is not the work of God that is frustrated, but the work of men" (3:3). These words came after the Prophet and his scribe Martin Harris had lost the 116 pages of manuscript for the book of Lehi. This book, intended to be the first book in the Book of Mormon, was translated by Joseph from the plates entrusted to him by the angel Moroni. Martin Harris's wife harbored strong feelings about her husband's involvement in the project and demanded to see proof. Martin was granted the opportunity to take the manuscript to show to his wife, and while in his care, it disappeared. [21]

Section 10 also gives insight into events surrounding the loss of the manuscript. Verse 2 points out that Joseph lost his gift of translating for his part in the incident, and the verse also states frankly that Joseph's mind had become darkened. Darkness is symbolically linked with the devil in scripture. Joseph Smith was involved in the creative process with God in bringing forth the Book of Mormon. This being the case, the battle lines were drawn and Satan immediately started aiming his wrath at the Prophet. The Lord was using Joseph to create, and Satan, through Harris's wife and others, was trying to destroy or stifle the Lord's plans.

Brigham Young has given us a clear example of this concept in an address given at the Salt Lake Tabernacle:

I frequently think of the difference between the power of God and the power of the devil. To illustrate, here is a structure in which we can be seated comfortably, protected from the heat of summer or the cold of winter. Now, it required labour, mechanical skill and ingenuity and faithfulness and diligence to erect this building, but any poor, miserable fool or devil can set fire to it and destroy it. That is just what the devil can do, but he never can build anything. The difference between God and the devil is that God creates and organizes, while the whole study of the devil is to destroy. [22]

One reason Satan cannot frustrate the work of God is that he simply does not know the mind of God (see Moses 4:6). The Lord told Joseph that "the devil has sought to lay a cunning plan, that he may destroy this work" (D&C 10:12). The plan was that the lost 116-page manuscript be altered. When Joseph retranslated it, the altered original manuscript would surface, the two works would be examined, differences would be noted, and Joseph would be labeled a fraud. In section 10, the Lord says of Satan and those who laid this plan, "Satan has great hold upon their hearts;... they love darkness rather than light, because their deeds are evil;...Yea, he stirreth up their hearts to anger against this work" (see vv.14-24). In surmising Satan's plan, the Lord said, "Thus Satan thinketh to overpower your testimony in this generation, that the work may not come forth" (10:33). However, as Brigham Young would later testify, "The power of the devil is limited; the power of God is unlimited." [23]

God, in his wisdom and power, had foreseen Satan's designs, and had prepared an alternate plan. Through the use of his prophets, the Lord had a backup record prepared and placed into the plates long before the latter-day Prophet received them. Thus, the record lost in the 116 pages was restored in the form of 1 Nephi through Omni.[24] Once again the attempts of Satan to fight against God were thwarted, and within the body of revelation given to us concerning this event much has been added to our understanding of Satan's techniques, as well. Section 10 teaches us that Satan leads people's souls to destruction (v. 22, 27), and he does this by leading them to lie, to harden their hearts, to attempt to overpower the elders' testimonies, and by stirring up their hearts to contention (v. 25-63).

The First Vision and the lost manuscript episode add insight into Satan's work. The first illustrates an open confrontation by the devil. The second illuminates how he who "doth carry on his works of darkness" (Hel. 6:30) schemes in the shadows, and behind closed doors (see Hel. 6:28-30; D&C 38:11-13, 28). Both bear powerful testimony to the Latter-day Saint, however, that Jesus Christ is in control. Through these examples, the Lord reassures us today, as in days of old, "Let not your heart be troubled: ye believe in God, believe also in me" (John 14:1).

Prophets Testify of Satan's Reality

Prophets have always been open about the reality of Satan, and the war between Satan and the Father and Son has been no mystery through the ages. President Gordon B. Hinckley in a general conference address taught the Saints concerning this war. After lamenting over wars in the world and the "terrible waste of human life and natural resources" they bring, President Hinckley cautioned that "there is another war." He said that this is a war which has "gone on since before the world was created and which is likely to continue for a long time yet to come." After using the scriptures to recite the story of the war in heaven, President Hinckley continued:

> That war, so bitter, so intense, has gone on, and it has never ceased. It is the war between truth and error, between agency and compulsion, between the followers of Christ and those who have denied Him. His enemies have used every stratagem in that conflict. They've indulged in lying and deceit. They've employed money and wealth. They've tricked the minds of men. They've murdered and destroyed and engaged in every other unholy and impure practice to thwart the work of Christ.[25]

In this powerful address, President Hinckley, like so many other prophets and apostles, speaks plainly of the tools of the devil and the reality of his unholy work. Counsel from a prophet or apostle concerning any gospel principle is of profound importance, including counsel on the principle of interest in this chapter—the reality of Satan. Joseph Smith, Brigham Young, Wilford Woodruff, Spencer W. Kimball, and Ezra Taft Benson have each left us prophetic discourses concerning Satan. The following is a compilation of teachings about him from each of these great leaders in this dispensation.

Joseph Smith

The Reality of Satan—Joseph Smith taught that Satan was a real, spatial being, saying on one occasion, "I saw Satan fall from heaven, and the way they [Satan and his angels] ran was a caution."[26] He said also, "Lying spirits are going forth in the earth. There will be great manifestations of spirits, both false and true."[27] "Satan will rage, and the spirit of the devil is now enraged."[28] He taught that those who falsely accuse their ecclesiastical elders place "themselves in the seat of Satan, who is emphatically called 'the accuser of the brethren.'"[29] And, in an important teaching concerning Satan and his role as opposer, Joseph used the betrayal of Jesus by Judas Iscariot as an example, noting that "Satan entered into him," and Judas's heart no longer belonged to the Lord. What light he had received from the Master was taken from him. This is the case for all who turn from the Lord, according to Joseph Smith:

> When once that light which was in them is taken from them, they become as much darkened as they were previously enlightened, and then, no marvel, if all their power should be enlisted against the truth, and they, Judas like, seek the destruction of those who were their greatest benefactors.[30]

The Prophet was illustrating the fact that those who do not take Satan seriously will gradually fall into his hands and lose their light (cf. Alma 24:30; D&C 93:39).

Brigham Young

Lucifrer and His Opposition to the Work of God—"There was a Devil in heaven, and he strove to possess the birthright of the Saviour. He was a liar from the beginning, and loves those who love and make lies, as do his imps and followers here on the earth."[31]

"Show me one principle that has originated by the power of the devil. You cannot do it. I call evil inverted good, or a correct principle made an evil use of."[32] "The Devil's forces are particularly marshalled against us."[33] "As it has always been, and will be yet for some time, when the sons of God assemble together, Satan will be on hand as an accuser of the brethren, to find fault with those who are trying to do good."[34]

Wilford Woodruff

Lucifer's Operations and Labors—"The world has sought our overthrow from the beginning, and the devil does not like us very well. Lucifer, the Son of Morning, does not like the idea of revelation to the Saints of God."[35] "This arch enemy of God and man, called the devil...who dwells here on the earth, is a personage of great power; he has great influence and knowledge. He understands that if this kingdom, which he rebelled against in heaven, prevails on the earth, there will be no dominion here for him. He has great influence over the children of men; he labors continually to destroy the works of God in heaven, and he had to be cast out. *He is here, mighty among the children of men"* (emphasis added).[36]

Spencer W. Kimball

Satan's Reality and Temptations—"The adversary is so smart and subtle that he takes every man in his own game...Lucifer is real. He is subtle. He is convincing. He is powerful."[37] "The adversary ...knows that he cannot induce good men and women immediately to do major evils so he moves slyly, whispering half- truths until he has his intended victims following him, and finally he clamps his chains upon them and fetters them tight, and then he laughs at their discomfiture and their misery."[38] "The powerful Lucifer has his day. He whispers into every man's ears. Some reject his enticing offers, others yield. Satan whispers, 'this is no sin. You are no transgressor. I am no devil. There is no evil one. There is no black. All is white.'"[39]

Ezra Taft Benson

Satan's Intentions—"We live today in a wicked world. Never in our memory have the forces of evil been arrayed in such a deadly formation. The devil is well organized and has many emissaries working for him. His satanic majesty has proclaimed his intention to destroy our young people, to weaken the home and family, and to defeat the purposes of the Lord Jesus Christ through His great Church."[40] "I realize that the devil is alert. He is the enemy of the work. He is the enemy of all righteousness, and I know that he is clever, that he never takes a holiday. He works overtime. He is ingenious. I am confident he will devise new ways to fight this work. We may not know just what form those schemes will take, but we must be vigilant."[41]

Conclusion:
Becoming like Christ Despite Satan's Opposition

Satan is real. That is one gospel principle which is unpleasant, but vital to comprehend. As has been illustrated in this chapter, Lucifer was a great and powerful being in the premortal existence. President Benson wrote that Lucifer "presented a counterplan to the gospel of our Lord . . . a plan of force that would have robbed man of his freedom of choice."[42] However, this plan was rejected and he became Satan. By so doing he, through his own agency, became the leading factor in our agency. For agency to have meaning there needs to be opposition (see 2 Ne. 2). The presence of opposition gives those in mortality freedom to chose between opposing forces. "Satan," President Benson has also said, "advocated absolute eternal security at the sacrifice of our freedom."[43]

Satan has placed himself eternally at odds with the Savior and "desires that all men might be miserable like unto himself" (2 Ne. 2:27). In the final analysis, Satan wants us to be like him. Upon recognizing this, and also understanding that the devil is subtle in his approach, an awareness that he is always there becomes important. Thankfully, the Savior is always there as well. The Savior has said, "Behold, I stand at the door, and knock: if any man hear my voice, *and open the door*, I will come in to him, and will sup with him, and he with me" (Rev. 3:20; emphasis added). The Savior knocks on the door, giving us the *opportunity to choose* to open it and invite him into our lives. By inviting the Lord into our lives, we can overcome Satan, and his world, and through faithfulness sit in glory with the Savior in his throne (Rev. 3:20–21).

The devil, on the other hand, crashes the door down or steals in uninvited and through lies and cunning attempts to induce us to do evil. The prophet Lehi, commenting on Satan's attempts, taught that if we choose evil this will give the "spirit of the devil power to captivate, to bring [us] down to hell, that *he may reign over [us] in his own kingdom"* (2 Ne. 2:29). It is simple. The Savior reigns *with us*, Satan would *reign over us*.

Words from scripture and the words of the prophets and apostles provide us with invaluable instruction about the reality of Satan. To these instructions, I would add my belief that Satan's biggest personal setback has been his jealousy of Jesus Christ. With bitterness, Satan cried with "a loud voice" unto Moses "and ranted upon the earth, and commanded, saying: I am the Only Begotten, worship me" (Moses 1:19). Inherent in our Heavenly Father's plan is the principle of becoming like Jesus and the Father (cf. Matt. 5:48; 3 Ne. 12:48). Satan's pride and selfishness would not allow him to accept this. He wanted to replace God, not to become like him. But, according to President Ezra Taft Benson, there is nothing greater than becoming like Jesus:

> The only measure of true greatness is how close a man can become like Jesus. *That man is greatest who is most like Him, and those who love Him most will be most like Him.* How, then, does a man imitate God, follow His steps, and walk as He walked, which we are commanded to do? (See 3 Ne. 27:27; 1 Pet. 2:21; 1 John 2:6.) We must study the life of Christ, learn his commandments and do them.[44]

This is the great choice in life: who we will choose to call Master, who's works we will choose to do, who, ultimately, we will choose to become like for eternity.

Notes

Chapter Three

1. Joseph Young, in *Journal of Discourses* (Liverpool, England: Latter-Day Saints' Book Depot, 1854-86) 6:208; hereafter cited as *JD*.

2. This revelation was received in a period of time when there were three branches of the Church: Manchester, Fayette, and Colesville. Additionally, between the time of the first conference of the Church on 9 June 1830 and the Prophet's receiving section 24 in July 1830, Joseph had been arrested twice. Each arrest was for "disorderly" preaching. He was acquitted both times and escaped his enemies. It is illustrative of the persecution which was beginning to rage against the infant Church. See also Lyndon W. Cook, *The Revelations of the Prophet Joseph Smith* (Salt Lake City: Deseret Book Co., 1985), 35; and Joseph Smith, *History of The Church of Jesus Christ of Latter-day Saints* (Salt Lake City: Deseret Book Co., 1965-68), 1:89-96; hereafter cited as *HC*.

3. For a discussion on physical and spiritual death see "Spiritual Death," in Bruce R. McConkie, *Mormon Doctrine,* 2d ed. (Salt Lake City: Bookcraft, 1966), 756-59. It is assumed that Satan can kill the body through utilizing wicked men; e.g., Cain and Able (see Moses 5:18-35). The Lord seems to be teaching that spiritual death is much more to be feared than physical death.

4. Spencer W. Kimball, cited in Elray L. Christiansen, *Ensign,* November 1974, 24. Elder Christiansen also quotes President Harold B. Lee as warning us to "'make no mistake about his [Satan's] reality as a personality, even though he does not possess a physical body,'" 23.

5. Joseph Smith, *Teachings of the Prophet Joseph Smith,* comp. Joseph Fielding Smith (Salt Lake City: Deseret Book Co., 1977), 187; hereafter cited as *TPJS*.

6. Elder Dallin H. Oaks has said of agency: "Free agency cannot be exercised unless there is opposition in all things. That opposition is provided by Satan, who once sought to destroy our free agency. His effort continues. He tries to persuade us to do evil and to make

those choices that will finally give him the mastery he was denied in the preexistence—to have all power over us, to lead us captive at his will." In *The Book Of Mormon: Second Nephi, The Doctrinal Structure*, ed. Monte S. Nyman and Charles D. Tate, Jr. (Provo, Utah: Religious Studies Center, 1989), 9.

7. James E. Faust, *Ensign,* November 1987, 35. See also *TPJS,* 181 for additional commentary.

8. According to Lyndon Cook, the early Saints did not confuse "The Vision" with the First Vision of 1820. This was due to limited public knowledge of Joseph's theophany until 1842. See Cook, *Revelations,* 311 n.1.

9. There is some variety when it comes to the actual numbering of these visions as they are broken into verses. For instance, I break section 76 out into six visions, while Larry E. Dahl, for example, lists five (see "The Vision of the Glories," in *Studies in Scripture, Vol. One, The Doctrine and Covenants,* ed. Robert L. Millet and Kent P. Jackson [Salt Lake City: Randall Book Co., 1984], 282–83). Confusion is removed, in part, when we remember that "the seer is caught up in vision and sees things from God's perspective." This insight, from Stephen E. Robinson, points out that "time ceases to be an important element; this is one reason the chronology in [the book of] Revelation at times seems to be scrambled: with God there is no time as we reckon it. (See Alma 40:8)." (Stephen E. Robinson, "Warring against the Saints of God," *Ensign,* January 1988, 36.) Joseph and Sidney's codification of "The Vision" may be one reason—aside from the narrative style—why the visions are spread throughout or seem mixed in section 76. For a discussion of section 76, see Richard Berrett's chapter in this volume, "The Future Conditions of Man after the Resurrection and the Judgment."

10. *HC,* 5:388.

11. *TPJS,* 358, 361. Sons of perdition, or those who are Perdition, have sinned against the Holy Ghost and cannot be forgiven. See also, Joseph Fielding Smith, *Doctrines of Salvation,* comp. Bruce R. McConkie (Salt Lake City: Bookcraft, 1955), 2:134.

12. *HC,* 6:314. This statement, from Joseph Smith's King Follet Discourse, is also recorded in *TPJS,* 357. The Prophet's remark concerning Jesus Christ and Satan presenting themselves as saviors

is mentioned in at least two other journal records of this address. Willard Richards quotes the Prophet as saying, "The plans the devil laid to *save* the world.—Devil said he *could save them all*—Lot fell on Jesus." In Andrew F. Ehat and Lyndon W. Cook, comps., *The Words of Joseph Smith* (Provo, Utah: Religious Studies Center, 1981), 342; emphasis added. Wilford Woodruff's record of the King Follett Discourse reads, "All will suffer untill [sic] they obey Christ himself, even the devil said *I am a savior and can save all,* he rose up in rebelion [sic] against God and was cast down." In Ehat and Cook, *Words,* 347; emphasis added. Richard C. Galbraith, in his *Scriptural Teachings of the Prophet Joseph Smith* (Salt Lake City: Deseret Book Co., 1993), 401, annotates the statement under discussion with a reference to Abraham 3:27. Abraham 3:27 reads: "And the Lord said: Whom shall I send? And one answered like unto the Son of Man: Here am I, send me. And another answered and said: Here am I, send me. And the Lord said: I will send the first."

13. See Moses 4:1–4; Abr. 3:24–28; *HC,* 5:388, 6:314; also *TPJS,* 297–98.

14. Orson F. Whitney, "Elect of Elohim," in *The Life and Teachings of Jesus and His Apostles* (Salt Lake City: The Church of Jesus Christ of Latter-day Saints, 1979), 16–17. Other versions of this poem have appeared, sometimes under different title, in other publications.

15. Marion G. Romney, *Ensign,* June 1971, 36.

16. The four recitals of Joseph Smith's First Vision may be found in the appendixes of Milton V. Backman, *Joseph Smith's First Vision* (Salt Lake City: Bookcraft 1980), and in Dean C. Jessee, comp. and ed., *The Personal Writings of Joseph Smith* (Salt Lake City: Deseret Book Co., 1984), 5–6, 75–76, 199–200, 213.

17. Neal A. Maxwell, *Ensign,* May 1984, 22.

18. Jessee, *Writings,* 75.

19. Ibid., 75–76.

20. Teaching by contrast is a powerful tool. Oliver Cowdery, relating a vision of Satan given to Joseph Smith by Moroni, reflected:

The heavens were opened and the glory of the Lord shone round about, and rested upon him. While thus he stood gazing and admiring, the angel said, "Look!" and as he thus spake Joseph beheld the "Prince of Darkness," surrounded by his innumerable train of associates. All this passed before him, and the heavenly messenger said: All this is shown, the good and the evil, the holy and the impure, the glory of God and the power of darkness, that you may know hereafter the two powers and never be influenced or overcome by that wicked one. (In B. H. Roberts, *A Comprehensive History of The Church of Jesus Christ of Latter-day Saints* [Salt Lake City: Deseret News Press, 1930], 1:78–79)

Moroni gave this vision to Joseph upon his first visit to Cumorah. The contrast was intended to illustrate the difference between God's glory and the condition of Satan. Elder Roberts later points out that this experience was part of "the instruction and intelligence" Joseph received "at the end of each year" from the angel at Cumorah (op. cit,. 1:80).

21. See *HC,* 1:20–23. See also Rhett James, *The Man Who Knew* (Cache Valley, Utah: Martin Harris Pageant Committee, 1983), 65–75, 150n., 150–56, 206.

22. Brigham Young, in *JD,* 13:4.

23. Ibid., 3:267.

24. See research regarding the Small and Large Plates of Nephi in John W. Welch, *ReExploring the Book of Mormon* (Salt Lake City: Deseret Book Co., 1992), 1–12. See also Cook, *Revelations,* 18–19.

25. Gordon B. Hinckley, in Conference Report, Oct. 4, 1986, 54–55.

26. *TPJS,* 373.

27. Ibid., 161.

28. Ibid.

29. Ibid., 212.

30. Ibid., 67.

31. Brigham Young, in *JD,* 8:279–80

32. Ibid., 3:157.

33. Ibid., 5:353.

34. Ibid., 11:141.

35. Wilford Woodruff, *Discourses of Wilford Woodruff,* sel. G. Homer Durham (Salt Lake City: Bookcraft, 1990), 237.

36. Ibid., 238.

37. Spencer W. Kimball, *The Teachings of Spencer W. Kimball,* ed. Edward L. Kimball (Salt Lake City: Bookcraft, 1982), 151.

38. Ibid.

39. Ibid., 35.

40. Ezra Taft Benson, *The Teachings of Ezra Taft Benson* (Salt Lake City: Bookcraft, 1988), 413.

41. Ezra Taft Benson, *Improvement Era,* 58 (December 1955): 952.

42. Benson, *Teachings,* 80.

43. Ibid., 399.

44. Ibid., 327.

THE PURPOSE OF MORTALITY

JOHN G. SCOTT

SINCE THE DAWN of time people have contemplated the purpose of their time in mortality. Even in our modern world, where seemingly every question has an answer, the query about our mortal purpose begs for an answer. In our contemporary lifestyles there are so many demands on our time, there is so much stress and confusion. The poet Chaucer summed up many feelings about life when he said: "The lyf so short, the craft so long to lerne."[1] Undoubtedly, the craft of life is a mystery to those who do not have the guidance of the oracles of God.

Thankfully, we have some definitive answers from the prophets as to why we have been sent here to this earthly existence. This chapter will be devoted to answering questions about our own mortality and why we are here. We will look to the words of the prophets coupled with scripture to find a clear answer.

President Ezra Taft Benson has commented extensively on the purpose of mortality throughout his ministry. In an address to the Saints in Tokyo, Japan, in 1957, Elder Benson said:

> Life has a fourfold purpose. *First* of all, we come to this mortal life to receive a physical, mortal body. Without a physical body man is limited in his progression and only with a spirit and a body united together permanently can man receive a fulness of joy; so we are living today part of eternity. We accepted that plan in the spirit world before we

came here, and we rejoiced at the opportunity of coming here.

Second, we came here to gain experience—experience with a physical, mortal world.

The third purpose of life is to give us an opportunity to prove ourselves (Abr. 3:25). To prove that even in the presence of evil and sin we can live a good life. To prove that in spite of temptation that we have the strength and the character to adhere to the principles of the gospel.

And fourth, this life is intended to provide an opportunity to help our Father in Heaven with His great plan, and we do that through honorable parenthood. We cooperate with our Heavenly Father in helping to prepare tabernacles to house spirits of His other children. So the matter of marriage, the home, and the family is a vital part of the plan of our Heavenly Father, and by keeping this fourfold purpose of life in mind constantly and carrying out these purposes faithfully we receive a fulness of joy here, insofar as it is possible to have a fulness of joy in mortal life, and we prepare ourselves for exaltation in the celestial kingdom where we will receive a fulness of joy. So the whole purpose of the Church is to help and assist us in carrying out these purposes in life.[2]

These four purposes of life, as outlined by the prophet, contain the seeds of true and enduring happiness in this life and forever. Let us examine in detail these four purposes of life: (1) gaining a physical, mortal body; (2) gaining experiences in a physical, mortal world; (3) having an opportunity to prove ourselves; and (4) helping Heavenly Father with his great plan—parenthood. In doing this we will be able to carefully consider the importance and direction of our own lives.

A Physical, Mortal Body

Before coming to this earth, we lived in the presence of our Heavenly Father as his spirit sons and daughters (see Abr. 3:23–24). As we gazed upon that being who gave us life, the differences between him and ourselves were very apparent. He had a wondrous, permanent, glorified body, and we did not. In his presence we were taught that without this type of permanent, physical body we could not "receive a fulness of joy" (D&C 93:33-34).

Our Father's desire for us was to experience the type of joy that he has. Only by allowing his spirit offspring to obtain bodies which could later be resurrected and glorified, as his is, would his children have that fullness of joy. Therefore, an earth was fashioned and humankind introduced upon it with physical, mortal bodies. Only through obedience to the plan of our Heavenly Father, which would bring about the sanctification of this mortal body, could we eventually gain a celestialized, resurrected body like our Father's (D&C 88:20).

Part of the test that comes to all mortals is whether or not they can master this mortal tabernacle. In a general conference address, Elder Russell M. Nelson stated this clearly:

> Your spirit acquired a body at birth and became a soul to live in mortality through periods of trial and testing. Part of each test is to determine *if* your body can become mastered by the spirit that dwells within it.[3]

The gospel plan preserves, as a fundamental principle, the testing of all mortals through a physical body (1 Cor. 9:27), with the goal of this earth life being the schooling of the spirit through experiences with the body (James 3:2). In the previously quoted address, Elder Russell M. Nelson specifies several gospel practices which help mortal beings to subject the flesh to the will of the spirit. Among some of those he outlines are keeping the Sabbath day holy, fasting, observing the Word of Wisdom, controlling our thoughts, and living the law of chastity. Let us now examine these five gospel practices in relation to President Benson's first purpose of mortality, obtaining a physical mortal body.

Keeping the Sabbath day holy

Thundering from Mount Sinai was the Lord's injunction to keep holy the Sabbath day (Ex. 20:8-11). In modern revelation the Lord once again gave this command to his young prophet Joseph Smith:

And that thou mayest *more fully* keep thyself *unspotted* from the world, thou shalt go to the house of prayer and offer up thy sacraments upon my holy day;

For verily this is a day appointed unto you to rest from your labors, and to pay thy devotions unto the Most High. (D&C 59:9–10; emphasis added)

Jesus knew that our bodies have a tendency to gravitate toward the worldly. To help keep our perspective in order and on the spiritual side, the Lord asks that we set aside one day in each seven, reserved for the remembrance of him.

This remembrance comes as we conscientiously keep this day holy. By "resting from our labors" we are able to devote time to prayer, contemplation of the word of God, renewing our sacramental covenants, and sharing testimony and the association of other Saints. By observing these aspects of devotion we merit the privilege of having the companionship of the Holy Ghost. With this influence of the Holy Ghost our spirit is in a position to throw off the bodily desires of our mortal condition and gravitate toward the spiritual in our lives (see Isa. 58:9–11). In this way we continually become more "unspotted from the world" as each Sabbath day passes. Elder Orson F. Whitney taught:

> The Lord's plan is perfect; his commandments have in view the salvation of the body as well as the spirit, for it is the soul that will be redeemed from the grave and glorified. God has commanded us to care for the spirit, as well as for the body, and give it food in due season, and He set aside the Sabbath day that man might rest from his temporal labors and go to the house of the Lord and be fed with holy influence which nourishes the spirit of man. That is why we meet together on the Sabbath day. Our spirits need their food, the same as do our bodies; and if we neglect them, they will starve and dwindle and die upon the same principle that the body will die when deprived of its proper nourishment.[4]

Clearly, observing the Sabbath day is of great advantage to our spiritual health.

Fasting

By fasting we learn to control bodily appetites. For a period of twenty-four hours our body is denied the food and water it requires to exist. If fasting is done for the proper reasons, for that same twenty-four hours our spirit receives that which it requires for health and vigor. While fasting with faith our spirit dominates our body and becomes an enhanced receiver for the promptings of the Holy Ghost. It is instructive to note how the Lord has linked our own fasting with joy in the Doctrine and Covenants:

> And on this day thou shalt do none other thing, only let thy food be prepared with singleness of heart that thy *fasting* may be perfect, or, in other words, that thy *joy* may be full.
>
> Verily, this is *fasting and prayer,* or in other words, *rejoicing and prayer.* (D&C 59:13-14; emphasis added)

Undoubtedly, this joy and rejoicing comes from the liberation of the spirit through the subjection of the flesh to the needs of the spirit. It is "through your spirit...[that] you develop personal power over your body's drives of hunger and thirst. Fasting gives you confidence to know that your spirit can master appetite."[5] Additionally, Elder Howard W. Hunter has taught:

> To discipline ourselves through fasting brings us in tune with God, and fast day provides an occasion to set aside the temporal so that we might enjoy the higher qualities of the spiritual. As we fast on that day we learn and better understand the needs of those who are less fortunate.[6]

The Word of Wisdom

The Lord is concerned about what we take into our bodies. In 1833 the Prophet Joseph Smith received a revelation known as the

Word of Wisdom. In these prophetic verses Jesus counsels the Saints to avoid substances which would prove harmful to the body and prescribes foods which are beneficial to our physical tabernacles (D&C 89:5-17). The revelation states that this counsel was given for "the temporal salvation of all saints in the last days" and that it was "given for a principle with promise" (D&C 89:2-3).

The principle associated with the Word of Wisdom is one of obedience. As we obey the commands of God he is bound to bless us (D&C 130:20-21). These blessings include freedom—including freedom from addicting drugs and chemicals and "evils and designs which do and will exist in the hearts of men in the last days" (D&C 89:4). In an address to students at Brigham Young University, Elder Boyd K. Packer commented that

> obedience—that which God will never take by force—he will accept when freely given. And he will then return to you freedom that you can hardly dream of—the freedom to feel and to know, the freedom to do, and the freedom to *be,* at least a thousandfold more than we offer him. Strangely enough, the key to freedom is obedience.[7]

As we obediently refrain from those substances the Lord has prohibited and partake of those he has recommended, we receive promised blessings of better health and greater spiritual knowledge. In his *Doctrine and Covenants Encyclopedia,* Hoyt W. Brewster quoted President Ezra Taft Benson as saying:

> Living the commandments of God is a condition of worthiness for entrance into the House of the Lord. There wisdom and "great treasures of knowledge" are given that relate to our happiness in this life and joy throughout eternity.
>
> The Lord will increase our knowledge, wisdom, and capacity to obey when we obey His fundamental laws. This is what the Prophet Joseph Smith meant when he said we could have "sudden strokes of ideas" which come into our minds as "pure intelligence" [*TPJS,* 151]. This is revelation.[8]

Through compliance to the Word of Wisdom the spirit is educated as to how to become master over the flesh, and as the spirit breaks the bondage of the flesh its capacity to commune with the heavenly is enhanced. Therefore, as we obey the Word of Wisdom we will, in part, fulfill the measure of our mortal existence, that being the training of our spirit. Elder Russell M. Nelson has said:

> If you yield to anything that can addict, and thus defy the Word of Wisdom, your spirit surrenders to the body. The *flesh* then enslaves the *spirit.* This is contrary to the purpose of your mortal existence. And in the process of such addiction, your life span is likely to be shortened, thereby reducing the time available for repentance by which your spirit might attain self-mastery over your body.[9]

The Word of Wisdom, then, becomes one of the greatest gifts we have been given to help us achieve self-control in this day of self-indulgence and abuse. By living this revelation we are protected spiritually and physically from the ill effects of alcohol, tobacco, coffee, tea, and other harmful drugs. Additionally, we draw closer to Jesus and our Heavenly Father through our obedience and obtaining the promised "great treasures of knowledge, even hidden treasures" (D&C 89:19).

Controlling our thoughts

Before we can act out anything with this mortal body we must first think it. The Lord has counseled his Saints by saying, "let virtue garnish thy thoughts unceasingly, then shall thy confidence wax strong in the presence of God" (D&C 121:45). It is interesting to note that Jesus teaches that virtuous thoughts will increase our confidence in God's presence. We are also taught that we should look to Jesus in all our thoughts (D&C 6:36) and that our unrighteous thoughts will condemn us (Mosiah 4:30). Thoughts are the motivating force which connects the body and spirit. In consequence of this we must ever be vigilant as to what we allow into the stream bed of our thought pattern. This applies not only to sin-filled thoughts but also to thoughts of hate, fear, greed, envy, jealousy, bitterness, anger, and pride. All of these evil thoughts must be controlled. President Spencer W. Kimball spoke of these as being some of the "Goliaths" that we might face in our lives. His admonition to us was

> whether your Goliath is a town bully or is the temptation to steal or to destroy or the temptation to rob or the desire to curse and swear; if your Goliath is the desire to wantonly destroy or the temptation to lust and to sin, or the urge to avoid activity, whatever is your Goliath, he can be slain. But remember, to be victor, one must follow the path that David followed:
>
> "David behaved himself wisely in all his ways; and the Lord was with him." (1 Sam. 18:14.)[10]

We learn to control our thoughts through practice and persistence. No greater man can be described than one who has learned to control what he thinks. President Heber J. Grant had a marvelous motto which he borrowed from Ralph Waldo Emerson that is relative to controlling our thoughts: "'That which we persist in doing becomes easier for us to do; not that the nature of the thing itself is changed, but that our power to do is increased.'"[11]

The law of chastity

Procreation is divinely instituted. We are taught early in the scriptures that it plays a significant role in the gospel plan, as God commands Adam and Eve to be "fruitful, and multiply, and replenish the earth" (Moses 2:28).

This power of procreation is sacred and is guarded by God through the law of chastity (Ex. 20:14; Mosiah 13:22; Alma 39:3-5; D&C 42:23-25). Instructions regarding this law are clear. We are to keep ourselves completely chaste before marriage, and we are to remain faithful to our spouse after marriage. The law of chastity is an eternal law. It will never be revoked. President Spencer W. Kimball taught:

That the Church's stand on morality may be understood, we declare firmly and unalterably, it is not an outworn garment, faded, old-fashioned, and threadbare. God is the same yesterday, today, and forever, and his covenants and doctrines are immutable; and when the sun grows cold and the stars no longer shine, the law of chastity will still be basic in God's world and in the Lord's church. Old values are upheld by the Church not because they are old, but rather because through the ages they have proved right. It will always be the rule.[12]

Today, the thought of abstinence before marriage and complete fidelity after marriage has been laughed at by the worldly. Many, however, stopped laughing when the plague of AIDS could be linked in part to the breaking of the law of chastity and indulgence in sexual perversion. The world's counsel in this area is one of ultimate freedom for pleasure's sake and a lack of moral responsibility to God. Jesus' counsel from the scriptures is very different:

And he that looketh upon a woman to lust after her shall deny the faith, and shall not have the Spirit; and if he repents not he shall be cast out.

Thou shalt not commit adultery; and he that committeth adultery, and repenteth not, shall be cast out.

But he that has committed adultery and repents with all his heart, and forsaketh it, and doeth it no more, thou shalt forgive. (D&C 42:23–25)

Take note what the Lord has said about this evil. He has equated it with a denial of the faith and a loss of the Spirit. Unless one extricates oneself from this sin he or she will be ever a slave to one of the most powerful bodily urges with which the spirit must deal. If a person will not take control of this part of the mortal being, that person is destined to become a serf of passion and desire.

Further consequences of breaking the law of chastity were given to Joseph Smith in his vision of the telestial kingdom. Here, the prophet saw that among those who inherit the telestial order are "adulterers, and whoremongers" (D&C 76:103). Webster defines a whoremonger as: "a man who fornicates or associates with whores."[13] Plainly, this law applies not only to married but to unmarried people as well.

Living a chaste life is one of the chief tests for all of the children of God. The control of the body while in mortality is paramount, and this control must extend to the expression of powerful sexual drives and desires, expressions which, when they take place within the bounds the Lord has set, can be some of the most spiritual experiences of mortality. In addressing this issue of temptation, President Brigham Young taught:

> When you are tempted, buffeted, and step out of the way inadvertently: when you are overtaken in a fault, or commit an overt act unthinkingly; when you are full of evil passion, and wish to yield to it, then stop and let the spirit, which God has put into your tabernacles, take the lead. If you do that, I will promise that you will overcome all evil, and obtain eternal lives. But many, very many, let the spirit yield to the body, and are overcome and destroyed.[14]

Intelligence dictates that we observe and implement this advice from President Young, allowing the spirit to take charge and not yielding to the temptations of the flesh (D&C 9:13).

These five gospel practices—keeping the Sabbath holy, fasting, obeying the Word of Wisdom, controlling our thoughts, and living the law of chastity—constitute some of the major testing arenas for the spirit's struggle for control over the body. Before we can return to live with God we must master these areas of gospel learning to the best of our ability. In doing so, we will gain a sense of self-mastery and sanctification that can come in no other way (see D&C 88:20-21).

Gaining Experiences in a Physical, Mortal World

The experiences we undergo in this mortal world and our responses to them shape our destiny. We come to know tragedy and triumph through life's tutorial lessons. In the classroom of mortal life we are to learn to endure the trials, resist the evil, and cherish the good in our physical world. And through submission to the will of God throughout these experiences, particularly in the midst of trial, we are brought to rely on Jesus.

The lessons taught to Joseph Smith when he was imprisoned in Liberty Jail are instructive. This was a most difficult time for the Prophet and his companions. They were jailed on trumped-up charges made by apostates and enemies of the Church.[15] The captives spent nearly four months in their prison, a description of which follows:

> In reality the two-story, twenty-two-foot square stone jail in Liberty was a dungeon. Small, barred windows opened into the upper level, and there was little heat. A hole in the floor was the only access to the lower level, where a man could not stand upright. For four winter months the Prophet and his companions suffered from cold, filthy conditions, smoke inhalation, loneliness, and filthy food.[16]

It was under these conditions of a very physical and mortal world that Joseph was instructed by the God of heaven. To the Prophet's yearning request, Jesus answered thusly:

> My son, peace be unto thy soul; thine adversity and thine afflictions shall be but a small moment;
>
> And then, if thou endure it well, God shall exalt thee on high; thou shalt triumph over all thy foes.
>
> Thy friends do stand by thee, and they shall hail thee again with warm hearts and friendly hands. (D&C 121:7-9)

Through this long ordeal the Prophet was instructed in a vital learning experience. The irony for him must have been vivid! Long were the days which he spent languishing in that pit, yet the Lord described his days there as being "but for a small moment." Could this then be one of the great lessons of life for all of us to learn—that no matter what we go through, our own experiences at "Liberty" are for but a short duration in the eternity which makes up our destiny?

Equally as vivid were Jesus' declarations to Joseph that even though all hell had combined against him, yet "all these things shall give thee experience, and shall be for thy good" (D&C 122:7). Joseph gained vital experiences through his deprivation at Liberty Jail, experiences that could come in no other way. The object lesson for Joseph was a dramatic one. Even though the conditions in that dungeon were reprehensible, Joseph rose above his physical, mortal circumstances and received three of the greatest revelations on the purpose of trials and testing during our mortal probation. This example begs the conclusion that we can do the same!

Elder Neal A. Maxwell reminds us that "our Father is full of pressing, tutorial love.... For we are to learn much by our own experience."[17] Truly, only through the experiences of this rough-and-tumble world of mortality can we be sincerely refined. Even Jesus Christ descended below all our earthy experiences that he might know how to comfort us (D&C 122:8). Undoubtedly we go through mortal afflictions in part that we might better know how to empathetically aid and comfort one another.

In dealing with tutorial opposition we may not recognize it for what it is. Fast is the pace of life, and rare are the occasions which we have to spend time in contemplating what is happening to us. Perhaps this is why Joseph's experience was so meaningful to him—he had time to think on the lessons that were affecting him. We, likewise, would be greatly blessed if we took time to think, ponder, and pray instead of merely reacting to life's present demands (2 Ne. 2:16). The end result of such introspection is often a realistic understanding of our ties with the infinite. Elder Neal A. Maxwell has taught that "faith is strongest when it is without illusions. Realistic faith alone provides allowances for the testing and proving dimensions of this mortal experience (D&C 98:12; Abr. 3:25)."[18]

The happenings at Liberty taught the Prophet to have greater faith in Jesus. During our own "Liberty" we can likewise learn to have increased faith. This is how the ancients were able to obtain their exaltation and develop the faith necessary to attain the presence of God. This aspect of the gospel was taught by Brigham Young:

All intelligent beings who are crowned with crowns of glory, immortality, and eternal lives must pass through every ordeal appointed for intelligent beings to pass through, to gain their glory and exaltation. Every calamity that can come upon mortal beings will be suffered to come upon the few, to prepare them to enjoy the presence of the Lord. If we obtain the glory that Abraham obtained, we must do so by the same means that he did.... [W]e must pass through the same experience, and gain the knowledge, intelligence, and endowments that will prepare us to enter into the celestial kingdom of our Father and God.... Every trial and experience you have passed through is necessary for your salvation.[19]

Only through the experiences of this mortal world can we develop the kind of faith that saves and exalts. The scriptures are replete with case studies of mortals who overcame the world (Gen. 39:5-23; 2 Tim. 4:7; Alma 45:19; D&C 135:3). All of us would do well to study these microcosms of life so that we can learn from the successful mortal experiences of others.

An Opportunity to Prove Ourselves

Because we are no longer in the presence of our Heavenly Parents we must learn to live by faith. Any effective proving ground necessitates that there be opposites. Through facing opposites we are placed in a position to choose what we will place our faith in: the power of God or the illusions of the devil (2 Ne. 2:11, 27). During this earth life fraught with temptations and opposite choices, we are under obligation to choose the better course. This method was outlined in the premortal councils of heaven when God said, "And we will prove them herewith, to see if they will do all things whatsoever the Lord their God shall command them" (Abr. 3:25).

An intrinsic part of this proving ground is the gospel element of agency. Without agency we would have no choices to make for there would be no opposites to choose from. However, part of the plan of our God is that we would face the forces of great opposites while living on this mortal sphere. Some of these opposites would be easy to unmask, for example, good versus evil. Others, however, would be more challenging and difficult to detect. In this way righteous mortals would be compelled to rely upon Jesus for their example.

All men and women are faced with sin. This is part of the "proving" the Lord speaks of when he states, "I will *try* you and *prove* you" (D&C 98:12; emphasis added). This testing is perhaps most acutely accomplished through the temptations we face throughout our mortal sojourn and how we react to these temptations. Under all circumstances we are to resist the temptations of the devil, as did Jesus, who has set the example for us in this regard. While in the Garden of Gethsemane, even Jesus was tempted to shrink from the cup of bitter gall, that he might not suffer. However, his words at the time are instructive: "Nevertheless, glory be to the Father, and I partook and finished my preparations unto the children of men" (D&C 19:19). President John Taylor taught:

> I have seen men tempted so sorely that finally they would say, "I'll be damned if I'll stand it any longer." Well, you will be damned if you do not. So you had better bear it, and go to the Lord and say, O God, I am sorely tempted; Satan is trying to destroy me, and things seem to be combined against me. O Lord, help me! Deliver me from the power and grasp of the devil. Let thy Spirit descend upon me that I may be enabled to surmount this temptation and to ride above the vanities of this world. This would be far better than giving way to sin, and proving yourself unworthy of the association of the good and pure.[20]

God will have a tried and proven people. This testing takes place for one reason: to see if we will remain true to the covenants which we have made and are thus worthy to abide in the presence of God. This is clearly outlined in the Doctrine and Covenants:

> Therefore, be not afraid of your enemies, for I have decreed in my heart, saith the Lord, that I will *prove* you in *all* things,

whether you will abide in my covenant, even unto death, that you may be found worthy. (D&C 98:14; emphasis added)

We stand proven as we repent and live the covenants of God. By our obedience, and ultimately by the Atonement, we are eventually made worthy to enter his presence.

As the vision of the celestial kingdom burst upon Joseph Smith and Sidney Rigdon as recorded in the 76th section of the Doctrine and Covenants, an understanding of the requirements necessary for entrance was given. Among other things, the revelation states that the celestial kingdom will be given to those "who overcome by faith" the trials and temptations of the world (D&C 76:53). In addition, Joseph learned that those entering this kingdom "shall overcome *all* things" (D&C 76:60; emphasis added).

Proving comes not only in the form of temptations but also in the form of commandments from a loving Jesus. An example of this came with the building of the Nauvoo Temple. The Lord asked the Saints, who in the midst of physical deprivation had just begun to rebuild their lives in Illinois, to stretch their souls when he said:

And again, verily I say unto you, I command you again to build a house to my name, even in this place, that you may *prove* yourselves unto me that ye are faithful in all things whatsoever I command you, that I may bless you, and crown you with honor, immortality, and eternal life. (D&C 124:55; emphasis added)

It is instructive to note how blessings from God come about—through our own willing obedience to his laws and commandments (D&C 130:20–21). Only by our faithful observance of his words can we learn the meaning of true happiness in this life. Our choices are governed by the value which we place on the commands of God. Jesus was not mocking us when he gave mortals commandments. Within the framework of his gospel plan is the notion that we can keep all of the commandments we have been given. This may take a considerable amount of time and practice, but it can be done either here or beyond the veil. The Apostle Paul concluded that

> there hath no temptation taken you but such as is common to man: but God is faithful, who will not suffer you to be tempted above that ye are able; but will with the temptation also make a way to escape, that ye may be able to bear it. (1 Cor. 10:13)

This revealed word teaches us that we can obey the laws of God. We can attain celestial glory by overcoming all things through action and faith in Jesus' atonement. By acting in accordance with the laws of God, not only is our faith exercised, but our determination to follow our Savior is also increased. This is why the Lord links the overcoming of the world with a valiant testimony of Jesus (D&C 76:51–60). By using our faith prompted agency we may prove ourselves worthy and obtain all that our Father has (D&C 76:95).

Helping Heavenly Father with His Great Plan—Parenthood

Parenthood is one of the greatest blessings that the Creator has shared with us. We have been given the power to clothe the spirit progeny of God with physical bodies. In this way we become copartners with God in fulfilling his purpose of bringing his spirit children into mortality with a body. Without our cooperation, the mortal testing of others would be thwarted, and billions of spirits would remain dormant in their premortal world. Parenthood, then, is one of the grand purposes which we have been sent here to experience. President Spencer W. Kimball counseled couples:

> You did not come on earth just to "eat, drink, and be merry." You came knowing full well your responsibilities. You came to get for yourself a mortal body which could become perfected and immortalized, and you understood that you were to act in partnership with God in providing bodies for other spirits equally anxious to come to the earth for righteous purposes.[21]

Parents who provide mortal bodies for the spirit sons and daughters of God are fundamental to the plan of God for our exaltation. Also, providing those souls a gospel-centered home is basic to the desires of Heavenly Father. The environment in the home is best when it is a positive one where love and trust are given the greatest consideration. These little ones are not ours to trifle with; they are the spirit offspring of God (Ps. 82:6). He has trusted them into our nurturing care in his stead.

With regard to what we are to teach these children Jesus has been very specific:

And again, inasmuch as parents have children in Zion, or in any of her stakes which are organized, that teach them not to understand the doctrine of repentance, faith in Christ the Son of the living God, and of baptism and the gift of the Holy Ghost by the laying on of the hands, when eight years old, the sin be upon the heads of the parents. (D&C 68:25)

In addition the Lord said:

And they shall also teach their children to pray, and to walk uprightly before the Lord. (D&C 68:28)

This teaching of children in the home is a solemn duty and responsibility which all parents have been given. Responsibility given by God cannot be ignored. It cannot be relegated to the Primary, Sunday School, Seminary, Institute, or the elementary, junior high or high schools. The prophets have spoken clearly on this matter, as illustrated by the following remarks made by President Ezra Taft Benson:

Parents, stay close to your children; you cannot delegate your responsibility to the educators, no matter how competent they may be. Parents have a duty to train their children, to talk over their problems with them, to discuss what they are learning at school.[22]

We share a unique partnership with God in this duty. It is a sobering fact to know just how we can influence the destiny of those spirits trusted to our care. The power that we have to lead them to righteousness is also the power to lead them into unrighteousness. Thus we must be constantly aware of the influences, positive or negative, that we bring into the lives of our children.

Our parenthood in this life is but a precursor to the parenthood which we will embrace in the celestial kingdom. In that light-filled future we will be given the opportunity to bring forth our own spirit children—this is what is meant in part when the revelations speak of "eternal lives" (D&C 132:24, 55). Elder Charles W. Penrose declared in a general conference address that the *eternal lives* means

> more than life, more than mere existence, it means perpetual increase of posterity, worlds without end, and these blessings shall be ours if we will prove faithful to that which we have received of the Lord, and this is what we are for in the Church.[23]

How we treat the spirit offspring of God here in mortality is one of the determining factors as to whether we will ever have the blessing of eternal lives in the life to come (D&C 121:19-22; Matt. 18:6).

Conclusion

We began this chapter with the question of the purpose of mortality. The scriptures and the words of the prophets conclude, as President Ezra Taft Benson has pointed out, that there are four grand purposes of mortality. These four purposes—obtaining a body, gaining experiences, proving ourselves worthy, and becoming parents—are calculated to bring about the ultimate freedom of the spirit. Our own willing obedience will lead us to "*the perfection of humanity through individual effort, under the guidance of God's inspiration.*"[24] Elder L. Tom Perry expressed this in another way:

> The main purpose of earth life is to allow our spirits, which existed before the world was, to be united with our bodies

for a time of great opportunity in mortality. The association of the two together has given us the privilege of growing, developing, and maturing as only we can with spirit and body united. With our bodies, we pass through a certain amount of trial in what is termed a probationary state of our existence. This is a time of learning and testing to prove ourselves worthy of eternal opportunities. It is all part of a divine plan our Father has for His children.[25]

By obtaining a physical body, gaining experiences with that body, demonstrating whether we will obey God, and assisting Heavenly Father in parenthood we may gain all that our Father has. These specified purposes of mortality are calculated to provide for us the richest soil for growth in this life. Likewise, these purposes are not easily accomplished. There are many pitfalls along the way. However, if we trust in God and are willing to have ourselves tested according to his purposes we can obtain the privilege of his glory. The scriptures and prophets testify that we can be successful, for this is the end to which our mortality was designed.

President Lorenzo Snow penned this poem which sums up the purpose of our Heavenly Father's plan in providing this mortal experience for us.

> Hast thou not been unwisely bold,
> Man's destiny to thus unfold?
> To raise, promote such high desire,
> Such vast ambition thus inspire?
>
> Still, 'tis no phantom that we trace
> Man's ultimatum in life's race;
> This royal path has long been trod
> By righteous men, each now a God:
>
> As Abra'm, Isaac, Jacob, too,
> First babes, then men—to gods they grew.
> As man now is, our God once was;

As now God is, so man may be,—
Which doth unfold man's destiny. . . .

The boy, like to his father grown,
Has but attained unto his own;
To grow to sire from state of son,
Is not 'gainst Nature's course to run.

A son of God, like God to be,
Would not be robbing Deity;
And he who has this hope within,
Will purify himself from sin. . . .[26]

Notes

Chapter Four

1. *The Oxford Dictionary of Quotations,* 2d ed. (London: Oxford University Press, 1941), 138.

2. Ezra Taft Benson, *The Teachings of Ezra Taft Benson* (Salt Lake City: Bookcraft, 1988), 27–28; emphasis added.

3. Russell M. Nelson, in Conference Report, October 1985, 39.

4. Orson F. Witney, "The Day of Rest," *Liahona: The Elder's Journal,* 7: 530.

5. Nelson, in Conference Report, 39.

6. Howard W. Hunter, *Ensign*, November 1985, 74.

7. Boyd K. Packer, *Obedience,* Brigham Young University Speeches of the Year, December 7, 1971 (Provo, Utah: Brigham Young Univesity, 1972), 4.

8. Hoyt W. Brewster, *Doctrine and Covenants Encyclopedia,* (Salt Lake City: Bookcraft, 1988), 242.

9. Nelson, Conference Report, 40.

10. Spencer W. Kimball, *The Teachings of Spencer W. Kimball*, ed. Edward L. Kimball (Salt Lake City: Bookcraft, 1982), 154.

11. Heber J. Grant, in Conference Report, April 1901, 63.

12. Spencer W. Kimball, *Ensign*, November 1980, 96.

13. *Webster's New World Dictionary*, 2d college ed. (New York: William Collins World Publishing Co., Inc., 1986), 1624.

14. Brigham Young, in *Journal of Discourses* (Liverpool, England: Latter-Day Saints' Book Depot, 1854–86), 2:256; hereafter cited as *JD.*

15. Joseph Smith, *Teachings of the Prophet Joseph Smith,* comp. Joseph Fielding Smith (Salt Lake City: Deseret Book Co., 1967), 122.

16. *Church History in the Fulness of Times* (Salt Lake City: The Church of Jesus Christ of Latter-day Saints, 1989), 208.

17. Neal A. Maxwell, *Not My Will, But Thine* (Salt Lake City: Bookcraft, 1988), 5.

18. Ibid., 4.

19. Brigham Young, *Discourses of Brigham Young,* comp. John A. Widtsoe (Salt Lake City: Deseret Book Co., 1954), 345.

20. John Taylor, in *JD,* 22:318.

21. Kimball, *Teachings,* 324–25.

23. Benson, *Teachings,* 500.

24. Charles W. Penrose, in Conference Report, October 1921, 22.

25. L. Tom Perry, *Ensign,* May 1989, 14.

26. Lorenzo Snow, as cited in the 1979–80 *Melchizedek Priesthood Personal Study Guide* (Salt Lake City: The Church of Jesus Christ of Latter-day Saints, 1978), 85.

THE NECESSITY FOR OBEDIENCE

ROBERT J. WOODFORD

THERE ARE SEVERAL maxims known to Latter-day Saints that urge us to obey the Lord and his commandments. Joseph Smith wrote, "I made this my rule: *When the Lord commands, do it.*"[1] The prophet Samuel instructed Saul: "To obey is better than sacrifice" (1 Sam. 15:22). And from Joseph F. Smith: "Obedience is the first law of heaven."[2]

Individually we entered into a covenant to obey the Lord's commandments when we were baptized (see Mosiah 18:10). We renew this covenant each Sabbath when we partake of the sacrament (see D&C 20:77). Additionally, all men who hold the Melchizedek Priesthood covenanted to obey the commandments when they accepted the oath and covenant of the priesthood (see D&C 84:43–44). Those who have been endowed in the temple have covenanted to live the law of obedience.[3] And the Lord has counseled us to obey the words of the prophet of the Church as though they were spoken by the Lord's own mouth (D&C 21:4–5). Yet willful, righteous obedience to the commandments of God seems to be one of our greatest challenges.

Obedience and Knowledge

Knowledge is essential to obedience. For this reason, "the devil delights in the benighted condition of mankind.... There is no salvation in believing false doctrines, and false doctrines are being promulgated on every front."[4] The Prophet Joseph Smith, in a sermon at Ramas, Illinois, revealed the important link between obedience and knowledge.

> Whatever principle of intelligence we attain unto in this life, it will rise with us in the resurrection.
>
> And if a person gains more knowledge and intelligence in this life through his diligence and obedience than another, he will have so much the advantage in the world to come.
>
> There is a law, irrevocably decreed in heaven before the foundations of this world, upon which all blessings are predicated—
>
> And when we obtain any blessing from God, it is by obedience to that law upon which it is predicated. (D&C 130:18–21)

We learn from this scripture the cyclical relationship of knowledge and obedience. We must obey the principles we already know in order to gain the blessings of the Lord, and one of those blessings is greater knowledge of the truth. This new knowledge then becomes the stimulus for greater obedience.

The Lord has revealed that "he that keepeth his commandments receiveth truth and light, until he is glorified in truth and knoweth all things" (D&C 93:28). We assume this light is the light of Christ by which we can judge the truth of all things (see Moro. 7:13–18). The truth spoken of is "knowledge of things as they are, and as they were, and as they are to come" (D&C 93:24).

The Holy Ghost gives to those who obey the truth feelings that what they are doing is correct, and this increases their desire to obey. The more obedience, the greater the desire. The plan of the Lord is for us to obey him in all things so that we can enjoy a fullness of light and truth and glory. Joseph Smith taught:

> We consider that God has created man with a mind capable of instruction, and a faculty which may be enlarged in proportion to the heed and diligence given to the light communicated from heaven to the intellect; and that the nearer man approaches perfection, the clearer are his views, and the greater his enjoyments, till he has overcome the evils of his

life and lost every desire for sin; and like the ancients, arrives at that point of faith where he is wrapped in the power and glory of his Maker, and is caught up to dwell with Him. But we consider that this is a station to which no man ever arrived in a moment: he must have been instructed in the government and laws of that kingdom by proper degrees, until his mind is capable in some measure of comprehending the propriety, justice, equality, and consistency of the same.[5]

The Lord further revealed that no one can receive a fullness of light, truth, and glory unless he or she keeps the commandments (see D&C 93:27). Then he added:

> The glory of God is intelligence, or, in other words, light and truth.
>
> Light and truth forsake that evil one.
>
> Every spirit of man was innocent in the beginning; and God having redeemed man from the fall, men became again, in their infant state, innocent before God.
>
> And that wicked one cometh and taketh away light and truth, through disobedience, from the children of men, and because of the tradition of their fathers. (D&C 93:36–39)

Thus, through disobedience a person can lose the knowledge that comes from the Spirit of the Lord concerning the truths of gospel principles. But those who obey can eventually receive light and truth until they have no desire to sin. They become of one heart and mind with the Savior: they see as he would see, feel as he would feel, do as he would do.

Elder Loren C. Dunn has given us an illustration of how obedience to gospel principles can bring us to this condition:

> Some think that our ultimate judgment and reward will be based on how many laws and commandments we keep and how many we do not keep. While in a sense this is true, it misses the broader and spiritual purpose for keeping the commandments. When I was younger, I lived to play basketball. It

was on my mind constantly. I spent countless hours practicing. Gradually I began to go through the moves automatically, without thinking about them. Physically and mentally I had become conditioned to do certain things by instinct. I had practiced them until they became natural to me.

In like manner, we keep the commandments and teachings of the gospel in order to condition us spiritually. It is not a matter of how many laws we keep and how many we do not keep. We keep the commandments because they are the laws that govern the Spirit. The Spirit in turn will sanctify us, condition us spiritually, and eventually prepare us to live in the kingdom where God is. Hence the scripture: "They who are not sanctified through the law which I have given unto you, even the law of Christ, must inherit another kingdom" (D&C 88:21). The laws that govern the Spirit are nothing more nor less than the laws that govern the Church. In addition, there is also an outpouring of the Spirit for those loyal to and willing to uphold the prophet and others who have been called to preside.[6]

Knowledge without obedience, however, does not have the power to save us. James Covill came to Joseph Smith and promised he would obey any commandment the Lord would reveal through Joseph Smith. The Prophet inquired of the Lord and received section 39 of the Doctrine and Covenants. In that revelation the Lord instructed James Covill to be baptized, receive the Holy Ghost and the priesthood, and then serve as a missionary in Ohio. This was more than James Covill wanted to do, and so he reneged on his promise. The Lord then told the Prophet in section 40 of the Doctrine and Covenants that James Covill had broken his covenant, and the Lord would deal with him as "seemeth me good" (D&C 40:3). James Covill could have had great blessings from the Lord and an honorable name among the Saints forever had he been able to obey. As it is, he is virtually an unknown person to the Latter-day Saints.

Elder William R. Bradford has shared with us another illustration of how knowledge alone will not save us:

I'm not a scientist, but this I have learned since those first totterings and falls as a babe that the law of gravity exists. I have never seen gravity, only its effects. Even so, it is obvious to me that it is in all things, that it is above all things, below all things, round about all things, and that all physical things are held in their positions and controlled in their spheres by this law.

The law of gravity has its limits and conditions. All of the inventions and movements of man take into account these conditions. If a man falls from a high place, he must descend; it matters not his motives. He may have jumped or it might have been an accident; it matters not. For the law of gravity cannot be frustrated, and so he must fall and suffer the destructive consequences.

Men who jump from airplanes have discovered a saving device. It is called the parachute. With proper study and application of this device, man, falling through space, can be saved.

If a man jumps from an airplane without a parachute, he must fall to his destruction. It matters not that he *knows* the saving power of the parachute. If he does not have one on and open it as he falls, he will not be saved, for the law of gravity cannot be defied. By this we can clearly see that not only is the knowledge of a saving law necessary for salvation but also the application of it in our lives.[7]

Obedience and Agency

Some people feel that if they yield obedience to the Lord they have somehow lost agency. Ordinances that bind them, prophets that counsel them, scriptures that command them are viewed as threats to the freedom of their own will. They feel that with every commandment or covenant their freedom is further restricted until they are like sheep walking lock step through life. Their own myopic view of the purpose of life stresses the freedom to do whatever they will.

With a little thought one can see that the freedom to choose that accompanies agency, as important as it is, has probably led more people to destruction than to salvation. The whole book of

Judges in the Old Testament is a series of shocking tales of man's inhumanity to man. It is a perfect example of what happens when selfish persons give unbridled expression to their own agency. The book ends with this insightful statement: "In those days there was no king in Israel: every man did that which was right in his own eyes" (Judges 21:25; see also Judges 17:6). This sounds very much like the saying of the 60s and 70s: "Do your own thing."

President Marion G. Romney has counseled:

> Free agency will always endure because it is an eternal principle. However, the free agency possessed by any one person is increased or diminished by the use to which he puts it. Every wrong decision one makes restricts the area in which he can thereafter exercise his agency. The further one goes in the making of wrong decisions in the exercise of free agency, the more difficult it is for him to recover the lost ground. One can, by persisting long enough, reach the point of no return. He then becomes an abject slave. By the exercise of his free agency, he has decreased the area in which he can act, almost to the vanishing point.[8]

Then President Romney said:

> Many years ago, while riding through Cleveland, Ohio, on a train, I saw on a building the inscription "Obedience to Law is Liberty." With the proper interpretation of the word *law,* we have in this inscription a statement of ultimate truth. By inserting three words, it is made to read, "Obedience to the law of Christ is liberty." (See D&C 88:21.) This is not only a statement of the perfect law of liberty, but also a statement of the way to perfect liberty.[9]

Thus, when we use our agency to obey God, we are giving direction to our lives and our freedom is enhanced. Conversely, freedom is severely limited in a society without law or without obedience to law. Suppose there were no law against taking whatever you want. Some might feel this would be a very enjoyable thing as they went from place to place gathering up what they wanted. But then they would have to spend their time closely guarding their new possessions because others would want to take them for themselves. We live in a society that punishes those who take things from others, and because enough of us obey the law, we can leave our home or our car with a reasonable expectation that our possessions will still be where we left them. Similarly, there are enough of us who obey traffic laws that we are all free to travel in relative safety. The reward for obedience by an individual is greater light and truth. Collective obedience by society brings peace and freedom.

In a talk entitled "Spiritual Crocodiles," Elder Boyd K. Packer addressed Primary-aged children at general conference. He told them of his decision to use his agency to increase his freedom. This is what he said:

> [When I was younger] I knew what agency was and knew how important it was to be individual and to be independent, to be free. I somehow knew there was one thing the Lord would never take from me, and that was my free agency. I would not surrender my agency to any being but to Him! I determined that I would give Him the one thing that He would never take—my agency. I decided, by myself, that from that time on I would do things His way.
>
> That was a great trial for me, for I thought I was giving away the most precious thing I possessed. I was not wise enough in my youth to know that because I exercised my agency and decided myself, I was not *losing* it. It was *strengthened!*[10]

There is also a higher expression of obedience in areas wherein the Lord has given no specific commandment. Joseph Smith received a revelation at the time the first Saints arrived in Jackson County, Missouri. In it some men were commanded to make that place their permanent residence (see D&C 57). Edward Partridge was one of those to stay. But he had a business in Ohio making hats, and his family was also there. He had many questions concerning how he was to close his business and move his family. The Lord responded:

> And now, as I spake concerning my servant Edward Partridge, this land is the land of his residence, and those whom he has appointed for his counselors; and also the land of the residence of him whom I have appointed to keep my storehouse;
>
> Wherefore, let them bring their families to this land, as they shall counsel between themselves and me.
>
> For behold, it is not meet that I should command in all things; for he that is compelled in all things, the same is a slothful and not a wise servant; wherefore he receiveth no reward.
>
> Verily I say, men should be anxiously engaged in a good cause, and do many things of their own free will, and bring to pass much righteousness;
>
> For the power is in them, wherein they are agents unto themselves. And inasmuch as men do good they shall in nowise lose their reward.
>
> But he that doeth not anything until he is commanded, and receiveth a commandment with doubtful heart, and keepeth it with slothfulness, the same is damned. (D&C 58:24–29)

We can assume from this revelation that there are great blessings for those who use their own initiative to do good things. Indeed, these seem to be the people on whom the Lord relies.

On the other hand, forced, begrudged, or halfhearted obedience does not secure for the individual the blessings promised to the faithful. Elder Dean L. Larson said that we may surrender ourselves to the commandments of the Lord, but unless we do this of our own free will and as the expression of our own desires, "the essential intrinsic development of personal qualities and values does not occur. The performance is sterile of any lasting benefit to the doer of the deed. The Lord has warned us against doing only those things we are commanded to do (D&C 58:29)."[11]

President John Taylor expressed a similar thought:

> I was not born a slave! I cannot, will not be a slave. I would
> not be a slave to God! I'd be His servant, friend, His son. I'd
> go at His behest; but would not be His slave. I'd rather be
> extinct than be a slave.... I'm God's free man: I will not,
> cannot be a slave![12]

Joshua exhibited willful obedience when he let the children of
Israel know that regardless of the direction they chose to go, he
would obey the Lord. It was his decision, independent of the
beliefs and actions of others. As Elder Howard W. Hunter said,
"Joshua was firmly in control of his actions and had his eyes fixed
on the commandments of the Lord. He was committed to obedience."[13]

Just as "there is no reward for half-hearted obedience,"[14]
obedience that is forced or controlled is likewise without merit.
Elder Boyd K. Packer had an experience that teaches this principle:

> Several weeks ago I had in my office a four-star general and
> his wife; they were very impressive people. They admire the
> Church because of the conduct of our youth. The general's
> wife mentioned her children, of whom she is justly proud.
> But she expressed a deep concern. "Tell me," she said, "how
> you are able to control your youth and build such character
> as we have seen in your young men?"
>
> I was interested in her use of the word "control." The
> answer, I told them, centered in the doctrines of the gospel.
> They were interested; so I spoke briefly of the doctrine of
> agency. I said we develop *control* by teaching *freedom.* Per-
> haps at first they thought we start at the wrong end of the
> subject. A four-star general is nothing if not a disciplinarian.
> But when one understands the gospel, it becomes very clear
> that the best control is self-control.
>
> It may seem unusual at first to foster *self-control* by cen-
> tering on *freedom of choice,* but it is a very sound doctrinal
> approach.

While either subject may be taught separately, and though they may appear at first to be opposites, they are in fact parts of the same subject.

Some who do not understand the doctrinal part do not readily see the relationship between obedience and agency. And they miss one vital connection and see obedience only as restraint. They then resist the very thing that will give them true freedom. There is no true freedom without responsibility, and there is no enduring freedom without a knowledge of the truth. The Lord said, "If ye continue in my word, then are ye my disciples indeed; and ye shall know the truth, and the truth shall make you free." (John 8:31–32.)

The general quickly understood a truth that is missed even by some in the Church. Latter-day Saints are not obedient because they are compelled to be obedient. They are obedient because they know certain spiritual truths and have decided, as an expression of their own individual agency, to obey the commandments of God.

We are the sons and daughters of God, willing followers, disciples of the Lord Jesus Christ, and "under this head are [we] made free." (Mosiah 5:8.)

Those who talk of blind obedience may appear to know many things, but they do not understand the doctrines of the gospel. There is an obedience that comes from a knowledge of the truth that transcends any external form of control. We are not obedient because we are blind, we are obedient because we can see. The best control, I repeat, is self-control.[15]

Society, in the past, has given support to many of the principles God commands us to obey. Unfortunately, as the world turns further away from the things of righteousness, that support is disappearing. Hence, it takes a lot more willpower to yield righteous obedience than ever before. Elder Neal A. Maxwell told the students at the LDS Business College:

You are, for instance, the first full generation of young members of the Church who have been asked to believe and to behave because the gospel is true and not because you are propped up with all sorts of aids and societal institutions. Those props are in the process, unfortunately, of being torn away in our American society and elsewhere. You've got to behave because you believe.[16]

Willful obedience is an exciting and challenging adventure in life. Like ascending to the top of a mountain peak, it takes great endurance. President Stephen L. Richards taught:

"In spite of the prosaic and commonplace aspect of this subject, I have long been convinced, my brothers and sisters, that the most challenging, dramatic, and vital thing in our lives is this: keeping the commandments. It tests every fiber of our beings. It is at once the demonstration of our intelligence, our knowledge, our character, and our wisdom."[17]

Disobedience

The Lord has told us: "I, the Lord, am bound when ye do what I say; but when ye do not what I say, ye have no promise" (D&C 82:10). He also said:

Who am I that made man, saith the Lord, that will hold him guiltless that obeys not my commandments?

Who am I, saith the Lord, that have promised and have not fulfilled?

I command and men obey not; I revoke and they receive not the blessing.

Then they say in their hearts: This is not the work of the Lord, for his promises are not fulfilled. But wo unto such, for their reward lurketh beneath, and not from above. (D&C 58:30–33)

Disobedience to the Lord's commandments usually does not result in an immediate, catastrophic punishment such as that which was meted to Uzzah who steadied the ark of the covenant (see 2 Sam. 6:6–7), but in the loss of opportunities. Quite often these opportunities are lost because the person squandered his or her time in less worthy endeavors. "Time," says Brigham Young, is "the property which we inherit from our Heavenly Father,"[18] and we are accountable for what we do with it. Time, like money, can be spent or invested. Time once spent is gone and we do not have the use of it again. Time wisely invested continues to give us a return on our investment. Time used in education can result in a better job, greater understanding of life, even satisfaction. Sinful, or even passive use of time, such as sitting for hours in front of a TV, gives us precious little that we can use elsewhere.

Even our use of leisure time can be an investment. Compare the person who uses some of that time in vigorous exercise (thus increasing personal well-being and health) with the proverbial "couch potato." The best used time is that which is spent in serving the Lord and our neighbor. Time used in the Lord's service is an investment in our future both here on earth and in the life hereafter and results in promised blessings.

President Ezra Taft Benson has commented on how we lose opportunities when we choose to use our time in less productive activities:

> Sometimes the Lord hopefully waits on his children to act on their own, and when they do not, they lose the greater prize, and the Lord will either drop the entire matter and let them suffer the consequences or else he will have to spell it out in greater detail. Usually, I fear, the more he has to spell it out, the smaller is our reward.[19]

Some may ask, how strict is the Lord in the obedience he commands of us? He has said that he "cannot look upon sin with the least degree of allowance" (D&C 1:31). Halfhearted obedience to the revelations can result in not acting wisely when temptations come. The Lord also said:

> And all they who receive the oracles of God [meaning the revelations received by Joseph Smith and the other prophets], let them beware how they hold them lest they are accounted as a

light thing, and are brought under condemnation thereby, and stumble and fall when the storms descend, and the winds blow, and the rains descend, and beat upon their house. (D&C 90:5)

The prophet Jacob counseled us to "seek not to counsel the Lord, but to take counsel from his hand" (Jacob 4:10). One way to take counsel from the Lord is to obey his commandments. But what constitutes counseling the Lord? President Marion G. Romney said:

In my view, seeking to counsel the Lord generally means disregarding the Lord's counsel, either knowingly or unknowingly, and in place thereof substituting our own counsel or the persuasions of men. Doing this is a very common human weakness. But until we are able to conquer it, real closeness to the Spirit of the Lord eludes us regardless of our other gifts and attainments.

On the other hand, when a person learns what the Lord's counsel is and follows it, he irresistibly draws close to the Spirit. From its very beginning, the history of God's dealings with his children on the earth testifies to the fact that those who disregard his counsel fail and come to grief.[20]

Thus, disobedience also results in a loss of the light and truth promised to the faithful.

Blessings for Obedience

The Lord has great blessings for those who choose to discipline themselves and obey him in all things, blessings that relate both to this earth and the life to come. The Lord said, "Learn that he who doeth the works of righteousness shall receive his reward, even peace in this world, and eternal life in the world to come" (D&C 59:23).

Those who live and are sanctified through the law of Christ receive a celestial kingdom (see D&C 88:21–22). They "shall overcome all things" and become gods (D&C 76:58–60), and they inherit all that God has. In contrast, those who inherit the terrestrial world are those who were "not valiant in the testimony of Jesus" (D&C 76:79), and those of the telestial world are the willfully disobedient (see D&C 76:82, 103).

One of the blessings for obedience that we realize while still living on earth is that of happiness; indeed, we believe that we came to earth to experience joy (see 2 Ne. 2:25). Joy, however, is not a free gift. It comes only as a result of righteous living. An important statement on this point comes from the Prophet Joseph Smith:

> Happiness is the object and design of our existence; and will be the end thereof, if we pursue the path that leads to it; and this path is virtue, uprightness, faithfulness, holiness, and keeping all the commandments of God.[21]

The Lord has also promised the gifts of the Spirit to those who love him and keep all his commandments and "[those who] seeketh so to do" (D&C 46:9). These gifts are given to help us correct any imperfections we might have. We are to pray for the gifts that will help us correct those imperfections.[22]

Another promised blessing for the obedient is "great treasures of knowledge, even hidden treasures" (D&C 89:19). These hidden treasures of knowledge are the mysteries of godliness. The Lord said:

> But unto him that keepeth my commandments I will give the mysteries of my kingdom, and the same shall be in him a well of living water, springing up unto everlasting life. (D&C 63:23)

He has also said:

> Behold, thou shalt observe all these things, and great shall be thy reward; for unto you it is given to know the mysteries of the kingdom, but unto the world it is not given to know them. (D&C 42:65)

And finally:

> For thus saith the Lord—I, the Lord, am merciful and gracious unto those who fear me, and delight to honor those who serve me in righteousness and in truth unto the end.
>
> Great shall be their reward and eternal shall be their glory.
>
> And to them will I reveal all mysteries, yea, all the hidden mysteries of my kingdom from days of old, and for ages to come, will I make known unto them the good pleasure of my will concerning all things pertaining to my kingdom.
>
> Yea, even the wonders of eternity shall they know, and things to come will I show them, even the things of many generations.
>
> And their wisdom shall be great, and their understanding reach to heaven; and before them the wisdom of the wise shall perish, and the understanding of the prudent shall come to naught.
>
> For by my Spirit will I enlighten them, and by my power will I make known unto them the secrets of my will—yea, even those things which eye has not seen, nor ear heard, nor yet entered into the heart of man. (D&C 76:5–10)

The word *mystery,* when used in scripture, comes from the Greek *musteerion,* which means "to shut the mouth." A *mystery,* therefore, is not something God is not willing to reveal; it is not something beyond our comprehension, nor is it something to be feared. A mystery is a sacred truth of which a person does not speak.[23] The mysteries taught in the temple immediately come to mind as an example. Mysteries are part of the light and truth promised those who obey the Lord. Brigham Young explained that God gives the mysteries only to those in whom he has confidence:

> There is one principle that I wish the people would understand and lay to heart. Just as fast as you will prove before your God that you are worthy to receive the mysteries, if you

please to call them so, of the kingdom of heaven—that you are full of confidence in God—that you will never betray a thing that God tells you—that you will never reveal to your neighbour that which ought not to be revealed, as quick as you prepare to be entrusted with the things of God, there is an eternity of them to bestow upon you. Instead of pleading with the Lord to bestow more upon you, plead with your-selves to have confidence in yourselves, to have integrity in yourselves, and know when to speak and what to speak, what to reveal, and how to carry yourselves and walk before the Lord. And just as fast as you prove to Him that you will pre-serve everything secret that ought to be—that you will deal out to your neighbours all which you ought, and no more, and learn how to dispense your knowledge to your families, friends, neighbours, and brethren, the Lord will bestow upon you, and give to you, and bestow upon you, until finally he will say to you, "You shall never fall; your salvation is sealed unto you; you are sealed up unto eternal life and salvation, through your integrity."[24]

Such confidence by God in man is exemplified by Nephi, the son of Helaman. He sought only to do the will of the Lord, and he did it with unwearingness. The Lord blessed him so that whatever he asked for in the name of the Lord, the Lord would do because the Lord knew Nephi would not ask for anything contrary to his will (see Hel. 10:4–5). The Lord has made similar promises in this day. He has said to the faithful and pure of this dispensation:

And if ye are purified and cleansed from all sin, ye shall ask whatsoever you will in the name of Jesus and it shall be done.
    But know this, it shall be given you what you shall ask. (D&C 50:29–30)

He also said:

He that asketh in the Spirit asketh according to the will of God; wherefore it is done even as he asketh. (D&C 46:30)

The crowning blessing in this life that is promised the obedient is to see the face of the Lord while yet alive:

> Verily, thus saith the Lord: It shall come to pass that every soul who forsaketh his sins and cometh unto me, and calleth on my name, and obeyeth my voice, and keepeth my commandments, shall see my face and know that I am;
>
> And that I am the true light that lighteth every man that cometh into the world;
>
> And that I am in the Father, and the Father in me, and the Father and I are one— (D&C 93:1-3)

He made this same promise on at least two other occasions:

> And again, verily I say unto you that it is your privilege, and a promise I give unto you that have been ordained unto this ministry, that inasmuch as you strip yourselves from jealousies and fears, and humble yourselves before me, for ye are not sufficiently humble, the veil shall be rent and you shall see me and know that I am—not with the carnal neither natural mind, but with the spiritual. (D&C 67:10)

And:

> And if your eye be single to my glory, your whole bodies shall be filled with light, and there shall be no darkness in you; and that body which is filled with light comprehendeth all things.
>
> Therefore, sanctify yourselves that your minds become single to God, and the days will come that you shall see him; for he will unveil his face unto you, and it shall be in his own time, and in his own way, and according to his own will. (D&C 68:67-68)

Beyond Obedience

As important as obedience may be, the Lord expects even greater things of us. Elder Bruce R. McConkie once pointed this out as he related the story of the rich young ruler. He said:

There came to Jesus, on a certain occasion, a rich young man who asked: "What good thing shall I do, that I may have eternal life?"

Our Lord's answer was the obvious one, the one given by all the prophets of all the ages. It was: "If thou wilt enter into life, keep the commandments."

The next question was: "Which commandments?"

Jesus listed them: "Thou shalt do no murder, Thou shalt not commit adultery, Thou shalt not steal, Thou shalt not. bear false witness, Honour thy father and thy mother: and, Thou shalt love thy neighbour as thyself."

Then came this response and query—for the young man was a good man, a faithful man, one who sought righteousness: "All these things have I kept from my youth up: what lack I yet?"

We might well ask, "Isn't it enough to keep the commandments? What more is expected of us than to be true and faithful to every trust? Is there more than the law of obedience?"

In the case of our rich young friend there was more. He was expected to live the law of consecration, to sacrifice his earthly possessions, for the answer of Jesus was: "If thou wilt be perfect, go and sell that thou hast, and give to the poor, and thou shalt have treasure in heaven: and come and follow me."

As you know, the young man went away sorrowful, "for he had great possessions." (Matt. 10:16–22.) And we are left to wonder what intimacies he might have shared with the Son of God, what fellowship he might have enjoyed with the apostles, what revelations and visions he might have received if he had been *able* to live the law of a celestial kingdom. As it is he remains nameless; as it might have been his name could have been had in honorable remembrance among the saints forever.

Now I think it is perfectly clear that the Lord expects far more of us than we sometimes render in response. We are not as other men. We are the saints of God and have the revelations of heaven. Where much is given much is expected. We are to put first in our lives the things of his kingdom.

We are commanded to live in harmony with the Lord's laws, to keep all his commandments, to sacrifice all things if need be for his name's sake, to conform to the terms and conditions of the law of consecration.

We have made covenants so to do—solemn, sacred, holy covenants, pledging ourselves before gods and angels.

We are under covenant to live the law of obedience.

We are under covenant to live the law of sacrifice.

We are under covenant to live the law of consecration.[25]

Obedience to law leads to the receiving of higher laws, eventually testing our willingness to give up all in this life for treasure laid up in the life to come. In the end, however, even the failure of the rich young man—or any one of us—to sacrifice all earthly things and consecrate his all to the kingdom of God is a failure to heed a commandment from the Lord. It is a failure to obey.

NOTES

CHAPTER FIVE

1. Joseph Smith, *History of The Church of Jesus Christ of Latter-day Saints,* 2d ed. rev., ed. B. H. Roberts (Salt Lake City: The Church of Jesus Christ of Latter-day Saints, 1932–51), 2:170; hereafter cited as *HC.*

2. Joseph F. Smith, in *Journal of Discourses* (Liverpool, England: Latter-Day Saints' Book Depot, 1854–86), 16:247–48; hereafter cited as *JD.*

3. James E. Talmage, *The House of the Lord* (Salt Lake City: Deseret Book Co., 1912), 84.

4. Jack H. Goaslind, Jr., "The Rewards for Obedience," *Brigham Young University 1982-83 Fireside and Devotional Speeches* (Provo, Utah: University Publications, 1983), 23.

5. *HC,* 2:8.

6. Loren C. Dunn, *Ensign,* May 1979, 70–71.

7. William R. Bradford, *Ensign,* November 1977, 64.

8. Marion G. Romney, *Ensign,* November 1981, 45.

9. Ibid.

10. Boyd K. Packer, *Ensign,* May 1976, 32.

11. Dean L. Larson, "Personal Accountability" (devotional address delivered at the Salt Lake Institute of Religion in Salt Lake City, 6 March, 1983), 4.

12. B. H. Roberts, *The Life of John Taylor* (Salt Lake City: Bookcraft, 1963), 424.

13. Howard W. Hunter, *Ensign,* November 1982, 58.

14. Mark E. Petersen, *Ensign,* May 1980, 70; and David B. Haight, *Ensign,* May 1988, 23.

15. Boyd K. Packer, *Ensign,* May 1983, 66.

16. Neal A. Maxwell (devotional address delivered at LDS Business College in Salt Lake City, 28 November, 1985), 2.

17. Stephen L. Richards, cited by Spencer W. Kimball, "The Savior: The Center of Our Lives," *New Era,* April 1980, 35.

18. Brigham Young, in *JD,* 18:354.

19. Ezra Taft Benson, in Conference Report, April 1965, 122.

20. Marion G. Romney, "Seek Not to Counsel the Lord," *Ensign,* August 1985, 2.

21. *HC,* 5:134–35.

22. George Q. Cannon, "Spiritual Gifts," *The Latter-day Saints' Millennial Star,* April 23, 1894, 260–61.

23. See Alma 12:9–10 and D&C 76:114–17.

24. Brigham Young, in *JD,* 4:371–72.

25. Bruce R. McConkie, *Ensign,* May 1975, 51.

THE NEED FOR REPENTANCE

PHILIP C. WIGHTMAN

WHEN JOSEPH SMITH went to the grove to ask God which church he should join, he also felt "to mourn for [his] own sins and for the sins of the world."[1] He wanted to repent. In response he was told that his sins were forgiven (D&C 20:5). He was also told to join none of the existing churches of his day because, as Jesus Christ explained, "'they draw near to me with their lips, but their hearts are far from me, they teach for doctrines the command-ments of men, having a form of godliness, but they deny the power thereof'" (JS–H 1:19). Over time Joseph would learn that the power of godliness must be available to men and women, or repentance would not be possible. As more revelations followed, the Prophet was taught the principles of true godliness, and he was given the power and keys necessary for us to obtain this blessed state. Repentance is the key to godliness, and as such is the means of becoming like our Father in Heaven.

Repentance, like any other aspect of the gospel, should not be seen as an end in itself; rather, it is the process by which we obtain the godliness that the Savior indicated to Joseph is missing in the world. The more common perception of repentance—ceasing to do bad things—leaves us short of the mark. When we see repentance as progression toward godliness, we can better understand that we must not rest until we have received a fullness of God's glory (D&C 93:19–20)—an end not achievable in this life. Perhaps this is why Joseph Smith taught that the first principle of the gospel is to know the true nature of God,[2] a being Elder Bruce R. McConkie has described in these terms:

> The simple, unadorned fact is that God is omnipotent and supreme. He has all power, all knowledge, all truth, and all wisdom, and is everywhere present by the power of his Spirit. In him every good and wholesome attribute dwells independently and in its eternal fullness and perfection. There is no charity, no love, no honesty, no integrity, no justice, mercy, or judgment, that he does not possess in the absolute and total and complete sense of the word.[3]

At first, given our Father in Heaven's greatness, this approach to repentance can be overwhelming. However, with the knowledge that God is our father and that he has great love for us, we can be confident that we may become as he is, given sufficient time and experience. Joseph Smith assures us that this is true:

> All the minds and spirits that God ever sent into the world are susceptible of enlargement. . . .
>
> God himself, finding he was in the midst of spirits and glory, because he was more intelligent, saw proper to institute laws whereby the rest could have a privilege to advance like himself. The relationship we have with God places us in a situation to advance in knowledge. He has power to institute laws to instruct the weaker intelligences, that they may be exalted with Himself, so that they might have one glory upon another, and all that knowledge, power, glory, and intelligence, which is requisite in order to save them in the world of spirits.[4]

God instituted laws that govern the advancement of his children to the celestial condition in which he lives. They are the laws which he followed to advance to his exalted station. They are the laws which he now lives. We know that if we are to become as God, we must learn to follow the laws he lives. As Joseph Smith said:

Here, then, is eternal life—to know the only wise and true God; and you have got to learn how to be gods yourselves, and to be kings and priests to God, the same as all gods have done before you, namely, by going from one small degree to another, and from a small capacity to a great one; from grace to grace, from exaltation to exaltation, until you attain to the resurrection of the dead, and are able to dwell in everlasting burnings, and to sit in glory, as do those who sit enthroned in everlasting power.[5]

We also know that there are laws that govern the terrestrial and telestial kingdoms (D&C 88:20-25). The kingdoms and the conditions in which we find ourselves in eternity depend upon the level of law to which our repentance brings us. We cannot expect to live in a celestial condition unless we abide a celestial law. If we cannot live a celestial law, then God will reward us with a glory suitable to the level of law we can live, but we must never forget that God intends to exalt us. Repentance is not intended to bring us merely to the lower kingdoms—it is a principle meant to perfect us.

Our Father in Heaven and his son Jesus Christ have brought their lives into conformance to celestial laws and thereby become omnipotent and supreme. They have been saved from all things which would affect their eternal perfection. Joseph Smith taught that

salvation is nothing more nor less than to triumph over all our enemies and put them under our feet. And when we have power to put all enemies under our feet in this world, and a knowledge to triumph over all evil spirits in the world to come, then we are saved, as in the case of Jesus, who was to reign until He had put all enemies under His feet, and the last enemy was death.[6]

The Father and the Son are saved because they have subdued all imperfections, or "enemies." Our personal salvation will depend on whether or not we use the principle of repentance to do the same.

An interesting footnote by Elder B. H. Roberts to the statement by Joseph concerning our enemies can help us understand that the things we must subdue are those things which inhibit our search for perfection:

> It is evident from this remark, "the last enemy was death," that the prophet in saying that "salvation is...to triumph over all our enemies," does not allude alone, or even chiefly, to personal "enemies;" but to evil inclinations, weaknesses, passions, sickness and death, as well.[7]

Our greatest enemies are hidden within us. Joseph F. Smith said they are things such as ignorance, "unrebuked sin," unsubdued passions, and hearts that are not right with God. He also said that such foes, if unchecked, "[cloud] our minds, [lead] our affections from God and his truth until they sap the very foundation of our faith" until all hope of redemption is lost.[8]

We are confronted by many of these enemies as a result of the Fall. Not only will we ultimately see our bodies in the grave because of the Fall, but we have also been separated from God as part of a probationary test (D&C 29:42–44). It was but a short time after Adam and Eve were cast out of the Garden that their children chose to follow Satan instead of God, and we have all followed him at some time, to one degree or another. In choosing to follow the devil we become subject to and led captive by him. We become "carnal, sensual, and devilish" (Moses 5:13), and thus the "natural man" pulls us and tempts us and becomes a great detriment to our eternal progression.

Many understand that this is all part of the test and that the Fall was a foreordained and necessary part of the plan essential to our overall development toward godhood. As the Lord told Joseph Smith, "all these things shall give thee experience, and shall be for thy good" (D&C 122:7).

However, though we know that the Fall was ultimately good, we also know that it brought about negative consequences, consequences that could only be resolved through the second part of God's plan, the atonement of Jesus Christ. This great act by the

Son of God overcame physical death, perhaps our greatest enemy (see 2 Ne. 9:8–9). More important to this discussion, it provided a way that we could overcome our fallen nature and inclinations to separate ourselves from God and godlike things. Through the Atonement, repentance—the means whereby we can be one with God again—is made possible and available to men and women:

> For, behold, the Lord your Redeemer suffered death in the flesh; wherefore he suffered the pain of all men, that all men might repent and come unto him.
>
> And he hath risen again from the dead, that he might bring all men unto him, on conditions of repentance.
>
> And how great is his joy in the soul that repenteth! (D&C 18:11–13)

Repentance thus becomes a positive principle of progress, not a dreadful chore. There is no need for it to carry the negative connotation we sometimes ascribe to it. As Neal A. Maxwell has said:

> Since we have been told clearly by Jesus what manner of men and women we ought to become—even as He is (see 3 Ne. 27:27)—how can we do so, except each of us employs repentance as the regular means of personal progression? Personal repentance is part of taking up the cross daily. (See Luke 9:23.) Without it, clearly there could be no "perfecting of the Saints." (Eph. 4:12.)....
>
> Repentance is a rescuing, not a dour doctrine. It is available to the gross sinner as well as to the already—good individual striving for incremental improvement.
>
> Repentance requires both turning away from evil and turning to God.[9]

Thus, repentance is not something we do once and are done with, but it is a principle we continually benefit from. We have need of it in overcoming the immediate evils of our lives, as well as in a lifetime search for godlike character.

We use repentance to conquer the enemies that hold us back from exaltation. First, we must be saved from the devil, who desires to "captivate" us while in the flesh (2 Ne. 2:29). The Lord would have us remain free as we choose light and truth (see John 8:32; D&C 131:6). However, the devil comes and takes away that light through our disobedience and traditions (D&C 93:39). If we are to combat the evil one's attempts to gain control in our lives, we must repent when disobedient to God's laws and overcome the false traditions in our lives. If we are to be saved we must follow the example of the Savior:

> I am Alpha and Omega, Christ the Lord, . . . the Redeemer of the world.
>
> I, having accomplished and finished the will of him whose I am, even the Father, concerning me—having done this that I might subdue all things unto myself—
>
> Retaining all power, even to the destroying of Satan and his works at the end of the world. (D&C 19:1-3)

By submitting to the will of the Father, as the Savior did, we become subject to him rather than the devil. As we become submissive "even as a little child," he can teach us through the Holy Spirit what aspects of our lives are contrary to celestial living. He can, as Elder Neal A. Maxwell has taught, become our personal tutor as we strive to gain godlike character.[10] This may require that we do things that, at the time, seem unreasonable. It may be that God will, as he did with the rich young ruler, ask us to sell all we have and give to the poor. It will more likely be that God asks a young man to give up a scholarship or an impending engagement to serve a mission. Perhaps it will be a young mother responding to the call to come home from the marketplace or a grandmother accepting a call to be over the nursery. As we respond to the calls that come, we will acquire attributes that enable us to overcome those enemies that lurk within us and retard our progress toward godliness.

Second, and tied closely to the devil's attempts to captivate us, are the damaging effects of sin. Whether we choose sin as a result of Satan's temptations or our own foolish desires, the results are the same—bad things happen. The Lord has advised, "Abide ye in the liberty wherewith ye are made free; entangle not yourselves in sin, but let your hands be clean, until the Lord comes" (D&C 88:86). When we choose to break eternal laws there are consequences that follow. Even when we repent and receive the Lord's forgiveness there are repercussions that may not be escaped. The smoker may repent but be left with poor health. A young woman may repent of fornication but still have an illegitimate child. We cannot escape some evil effects.

It is better to repent and avoid ever-increasing evil effects than to continue in sin, which further complicates matters. Joseph Smith and Martin Harris learned this lesson with the loss of the Book of Mormon manuscript. Even though they did not recover the manuscript, when they repented the Lord returned his spirit, the hell they experienced came to an end, and the work of translation continued.

There may be those who would procrastinate their repentance, thinking it will be easier to overcome their sins in the life to come. Things of the flesh, however, are easier to subdue while in mortality. Erastus Snow taught that the spirit is still responsible for those acts committed while in the flesh. We will suffer in the spirit world if we don't here.[11] Could it be that much of the weeping and wailing that the scriptures say the wicked will suffer after death comes from forced withdrawal from things their spirits still desire? As Amulek would say, "That same spirit which doth possess your bodies at the time that ye go out of this life, that same spirit will have power to possess your body in that eternal world" (Alma 34:34). All who obtain any degree of salvation will have to repent, whether in this life or in the next, and they will have to live in accordance with eternal laws.

There is a third aspect to being saved through repentance: escaping the accumulative effects of the sins of the world which will lead to its destruction. The world is ripening in iniquity, and many are rejecting the Lord's offer of repentance. He has indicated that the cup of his indignation is full, and he will soon come in judgment of the world to take vengeance upon the wicked. Through lightnings, thunderings, earthquakes, famines, and pestilence, he tries once more to bring about repentance. He has tried every other means with patience and long-suffering, but without success, and soon he will reprove with great sharpness (D&C 43:17-33).

From the Doctrine and Covenants we learn of an impending judgment that awaits the wicked (D&C 29:14-21). The wicked will suffer from the natural consequences of their chosen lifestyles; they will also suffer from the judgments of a just God who is coming to personally reign upon the earth. All that is corruptible will be removed. The only hope of being saved when the sword of justice falls will be to have repented and be living at least a terrestrial law. Is it any wonder that the revelations repeatedly tell us to declare nothing but repentance to this generation?

To this point we have shown that repentance saves us from a variety of different enemies and that there are at least two levels of repentance: telestial to terrestrial, terrestrial to celestial. These levels of repentance are more fully explained by Elder Neal A. Maxwell:

> When "a mighty change" is required, full repentance involves a *180-degree turn,* and without looking back! (Alma 5:12-13.) Initially, this turning reflects progress from telestial to terrestrial behavior, and later on to celestial behavior. As the sins of the telestial world are left behind, the focus falls ever more steadily upon the sins of omission, which often keep us from full consecration.[12]

The message of this quote for Latter-day Saints should be obvious: we cannot repent once and stop, but must consecrate our lives to the pursuit of godliness. The restoration through the Prophet Joseph Smith was not necessary if all we want to be is good, honorable, terrestrial people. If we fail to do no more than move out of the world, then we fail to take advantage of the principles and ordinances revealed to Joseph and found in the Doctrine and Covenants.

For Latter-day Saints, real repentance begins after we receive the ordinances of the gospel. The ordinances make us eligible for the power of godliness. The Lord explains that the purpose of the Melchizedek Priesthood is to administer these ordinances, so we can be taught the power of godliness.

> And this greater priesthood administereth the gospel and holdeth the key of the mysteries of the kingdom, even the key of the knowledge of God.
>
> Therefore, in the ordinances thereof, the power of godliness is manifest.
>
> And without the ordinances thereof, and the authority of the priesthood, the power of godliness is not manifest unto men in the flesh. (D&C 84:19–21; see also D&C 107:19–20)

The implications for repentance suggested by this revelation go far beyond anything that can come from a telestial to a terrestrial repentance. God expects Latter-day Saints to become like him. The result of the Fall which separated us from God can be overcome through the authority and ordinances revealed to Joseph Smith. When repentance leads to baptism, we are then entitled to a special gift. The Holy Ghost becomes available to lead us in a process of sanctification. The Holy Ghost will reveal to us what we need to become more godly. He will also prepare us for the ordinances of the temple so we can progress even further in our repentance. Elder Dallin Oaks has explained that our baptismal covenant to take upon us the name of Christ, which we renew each week at the sacrament table, presumes that we go on to receive the temple ordinances:

> It is significant that when we partake of the sacrament we do not witness that we *take upon* us the name of Jesus Christ. We witness that we are *willing* to do so. (See D&C 20:77.) The fact that we only witness to our willingness suggests that something else must happen before we actually take that sacred name upon us in the most important sense.
>
> What future event or events could this covenant contemplate? The scriptures suggest two sacred possibilities, one concerning the authority of God, especially as exercised in the

temples, and the other—closely related—concerning exaltation in the celestial kingdom.[13]

It seems evident from this quote that our repentance and obedience to the commandments must lead us to the temple if we want to do God's will and receive all the blessings available to us. There are covenants and responsibilities found in the temple that should take us far beyond just the normal repentance and goodness that most of the Christian world seeks.

The Lord revealed to the Prophet Joseph the glories of the eternities; he indicated that telestial to terrestrial repentance makes us good, but can only result in terrestrial glory. Speaking of terrestrial individuals the Lord said:

> These are they who are the honorable men of the earth, who were blinded by the craftiness of men.
>
> These are they who receive of his glory, but not of his fulness.
>
> These are they who receive of the presence of the Son, but not of the fulness of the Father. (D&C 76:75–77)

Exaltation requires more than just goodness. It requires that we receive the necessary ordinances, keep our covenants, and utilize the knowledge of godliness that God gives us as a result of our total commitment and consecration. Speaking of those who will be exalted, the Lord says:

> They are they who received the testimony of Jesus, and believed on his name and were baptized after the manner of his burial, being buried in the water in his name, and this according to the commandment which he has given—
>
> That by keeping the commandments they might be washed and cleansed from all their sins, and receive the Holy Spirit by the laying on of hands of him who is ordained and sealed unto this power;
>
> And who overcome by faith, and are sealed by the Holy Spirit of promise, which the Father sheds forth upon all those who are just and true....

They are they into whose hands the Father has given all things—

They are they who are priests and kings, who have received of his fulness, and of his glory;

And are priests of the Most High, after the order of Melchizedek, which was after the order of Enoch, which was after the order of the Only Begotten Son.

Wherefore, as it is written, they are gods, even the sons of God—

Wherefore, all things are theirs, whether life or death, or things present, or things to come, all are theirs and they are Christ's, and Christ is God's.

And they shall overcome all things.

Wherefore, let no man glory in man, but rather let him glory in God, who shall subdue all enemies under his feet.

These shall dwell in the presence of God and his Christ forever and ever. (D&C 76:51–53, 55–62)

The great blessings described result from great repentance, a type of repentance that requires great sacrifice and dedication. As Elder Maxwell has suggested, this type of repentance does not come about easily:

There is an attitudinal and behavioral bridge that we need to build in order for us to draw closer to Him, and then be ready to return Home—*cum laude* or *summa cum laude*—to receive of His loving fullness. We must want to do this more than we want to do anything else. Otherwise, even if we avoid wickedness, our journey will end in the suburbs, somewhere short of the City of God.[14]

Repentance, then, is the path to godliness. It is a blessing and a gift, not something to be feared.

We all need repentance, with few exceptions (D&C 29:49–50). Repentance at any level can benefit us. We will be saved to the degree that we exercise it in our lives. God desires that we use it to come to him. He gave us his Son to make it all possible. The Savior has done his work. The otherwise insurmountable enemies have been subdued. We are truly free to choose liberty and eternal life or captivity and death (2 Ne. 2:27). With the restoration of the gospel, with the understanding it gives us of its saving principles, we have the opportunity to see repentance in its true light and receive all that God wants to give us.

NOTES

CHAPTER SIX

1. Milton Backman, *Joseph Smith's First Vision* (Salt Lake City: Bookcraft, 1971), 156.

2. Joseph Smith, *History of The Church of Jesus Christ of Latter-day Saints,* 2d ed. (Salt Lake City: Deseret News, 1949), 6:305; hereafter cited as *HC.*

3. Bruce R. McConkie, *The Promised Messiah* (Salt Lake City: Deseret Book Co., 1978), 19–20.

4. *HC,* 6:311–12.

5. Ibid., 6:306.

6. Ibid., 5:387–88.

7. Ibid., 5:388n.

8. Joseph Fielding Smith, *Gospel Doctrine* (Salt Lake City: Deseret Book Co., 1919), 426.

9. Neal A. Maxwell, *Ensign,* November 1991, 30.

10. Neal A. Maxwell, *Ensign,* November 1982, 67.

11. Erastus Snow, in *Journal of Discourses* (Liverpool, England: Latter-Day Saints' Book Depot, 1854–86), 13:8.

12. Neal A. Maxwell, *Ensign,* May 1991, 91.

13. Dallin H. Oaks, *Ensign,* May 1985, 81.

14. Neal A. Maxwell, *All These Things Shall Give Thee Experience* (Salt Lake City: Deseret Book Co., 1980), 4.

THE WORKINGS OF THE HOLY SPIRIT

M. CATHERINE THOMAS

THE TERM *HOLY spirit* applies in scripture both to the divine substance that permeates the cosmos and to that divine personage who administers holy spirit under the direction of the Lord Jesus Christ. Since the substance holy spirit infuses all created things, to understand holy spirit is to understand not only God but also ourselves. To understand the office of the Holy Spirit is to comprehend the means by which God seeks access to fallen mankind in the telestial world to reconnect them consciously to their divine origins and to work an alteration on them leading to the divine nature. This process of salvation is totally dependent on a person's continuing, sensitive response to the Holy Spirit; therefore, one who intends to be exalted has no option but to discern, to obey, and to learn how to work by the Holy Spirit. We will consider here the nature of holy spirit, then the functions of the Holy Spirit as member of the Godhead, and finally how a person works by the Holy Spirit.

Holy Spirit as a Substance of Power

In the eternal heavens there is a godly power described as the *fullness*. This fullness consists of spirit, light, glory, intelligence, and truth, all of which are roughly equivalent (D&C 93). Those who obtain this fullness completely, obtain godhood. Several scriptures in the Doctrine and Covenants refer to this fullness; e.g., those in the celestial glory receive the *fullness* and glory of the Father (D&C 76:20) those in the terrestrial and telestial glories receive of the Lord's glory but not of his *fullness* (D&C 76:76–77, 86); the Father gave of his *fullness* to the Son (D&C 93:4); the Son "received not of the *fulness* at first, but continued from grace to grace until he received [it]" (93:13; emphasis added). Saints may receive the *fullness* and be glorified in Christ as he is in the Father, receiving "grace for grace" (D&C 93:20). This fullness consists of holy spirit (or light, truth, glory, and intelligence) over which the Father and the Son have complete control.

This substance referred to as holy spirit is the means by which the Father and Son are one and the means by which all the sons and daughters of God may become one in them (D&C 35:2). The *Lectures on Faith* (included with the Doctrine and Covenants beginning with the 1835 edition until the 1921 edition) teach how this at-one-ment is possible:

> The Only Begotten of the Father, full of grace and truth, and having overcome, received a *fulness* of the glory of the Father, *possessing the same mind* with the Father, which *mind is the Holy Spirit* that bears record of the Father and the Son, and these three are one; or, in other words, these three constitute the great, matchless, governing, and supreme power over all things.... The Father and the Son possessing the same mind, the same wisdom, glory, power, and fulness—filling all in all— the Son being filled with the fulness of the mind, glory, and power, or, in other words, the *spirit*, glory, and power of the Father...which spirit is shed forth upon all who believe on his name and keep his commandments; and all those who keep his commandments shall grow up from grace to grace and become heirs of the heavenly kingdom, and joint-heirs with Jesus Christ; possessing the same mind, being trans- formed into the same image or likeness, even the express image of him who fills all in all; being filled with the fulness of his glory; and become one in him, even as the Father, Son, and Holy Spirit are one. (Lecture 5; emphasis added)

The creation embraces at least two kinds of matter: spirit and element (D&C 93:33; 131:7–8). *Element* refers to the physical world as we perceive it with our senses. But *spirit* is matter which fallen man cannot see with his natural eyes: "All spirit is matter, but it is more fine or pure, and can only be discerned by purer eyes; We cannot see it; but when our bodies are purified we shall see that it is all matter" (D&C 131:7–8). Since matter and energy have a relationship to each other, that is, they are apparently variants of the same phenomenon, we could also describe spirit as having energy. Possessing fluid properties, it can be likened to electricity or to "living" water (John 7:38–39; and by implication D&C 63:23; 110:3; 121:45–46).

Holy spirit centers in God and from his presence "proceed[s] forth . . . to fill the immensity of space" (D&C 88:12). It is the principle of life because it is the "light which is in all things, which giveth life to all things" (D&C 88:13, 17; 33:16). God accomplished the creation by "the word of my power, which is the power of my Spirit. For by the power of my Spirit created I them; yea, all things both spiritual and temporal—First spiritual, secondly temporal" (D&C 29:30–32). God has full power over holy spirit, and because it permeates all things, he is able by and through it to maintain uninterrupted consciousness of (Moses 1:27) and communication with all his creations, as well as to sustain the life of all things. Through the power of this spirit, Christ is in all things as the light of truth,

> which truth shineth. This is the light of Christ. As also he is in the sun. . . . in the moon. . . . the light of the stars, and the power thereof by which they were made. . . . And the light which shineth, which giveth you light, is through him who enlighteneth your eyes, which is the same light that quickeneth your understandings; Which light proceedeth forth from the presence of God to fill the immensity of space—The light which is in all things, which giveth life to all things, which is the law by which all things are governed, even the power of God. (D&C 88:7–13)

Holy spirit, then, is the same as the light of Christ, which "light shineth in *darkness*, and the *darkness* comprehendeth it not" (e.g., D&C 88:49–50; emphasis added; compare 88:66 where "voice" and "wilderness" are used instead of "darkness"). We, the fallen inhabitants of the telestial world, constitute the "darkness" among which and into which Christ's light shines, from the sun, the moon, the stars; the earth itself is infused with this holy spirit. This light penetrates and infuses even the most minute systems in the human body and spirit, being also the principle of life and intelligence in these "kingdoms" of the body (D&C 88:37). But in general, the spiritually darkened world does not comprehend the nature of this light.

All light seems to exist on a continuum or in a spectrum which advances from very rudimentary forms of light, through light visible to humans, to the highly advanced forms of light and power visible to and used by higher beings. Joseph Fielding Smith explained:

> This Light of Christ . . . is the light by which the worlds are controlled, by which they are made. It is the light of the sun and all other bodies. It is the light which gives life to vegetation. It quickens the understanding of men, and has these various functions as set forth in these verses [D&C 88:7–11]. . . .
>
> Unless a man had the blessings that come from this Spirit, his mind would not be quickened; there would be no vegetation grow; the worlds would not stay in their orbits; because it is through this Spirit of Truth, this Light of Truth, according to this revelation [D&C 88], that all things are done.[1]

Parley P. Pratt wrote of the all-pervasive nature of this holy spirit:

> It penetrates the pores of the most solid substances, pierces the human system to its most inward recesses, and discerns the thoughts and intents of the heart. It has power to move through space with an inconceivable velocity, far exceeding the tardy motions of electricity, or of physical light. It comprehends the past, present, and future, in all their fulness. Its

inherent properties embrace all the attributes of intelligence and affection. It is endowed with knowledge, wisdom, truth, love, charity, justice, and mercy, in all their ramifications. In short, it is the attributes of the eternal power and Godhead.

Those beings who receive of its fulness are called sons of God, because they are perfected in all its attributes and powers, and being in communication with it, can, by its use, perform all things. Those beings who receive not a fulness, but a measure of it, can know and perform some things, but not all. This is the true light, which in some measure illuminates all men. It is, in its less refined particles, the physical light which reflects from the sun, moon, and stars, and other substances; and by reflection on the eye, makes visible the truths of the outward world.

It is, also, in his higher degrees, the intellectual light of our inward and spiritual organs, by which we reason, discern, judge, compare, comprehend, and remember the subjects within our reach. Its inspiration constitutes instinct in animal life, reason in man, vision in the Prophets, and is continually flowing from the Godhead throughout all His creatures.[2]

Human nature has as its essence this same holy spirit. The Lord refers to himself as the Father of Lights (D&C 67:9) and to us as the children of light (D&C 106:5). The Savior explains mankind's origins of light: "I am the true light that lighteth every man that cometh into the world" (D&C 93:2). "Ye were also in the beginning with the Father; that which is Spirit, even the Spirit of truth" (D&C 93:23). "Man was also in the beginning with God. Intelligence, or the light of truth, was not created or made, neither indeed can be" (D&C 93:29). "The glory of God is intelligence, or in other words, light and truth" (D&C 93:36). Therefore, the Lord's children were created in the beginning out of the same substance as the Father and the Son and have exactly the same nature and potential; that is, we were organized from spirit, light, truth, intelligence. Clearly, human beings are not basically evil, nor even neutral, but are fashioned out of the most supernal and pure and powerful elements of the universe. John Taylor wrote: "Knowest thou not that thou art a spark of Deity, struck from the fire of his eternal blaze, and brought forth in the midst of eternal burnings?"[3]

Our Heavenly Father did not wind up the universe like a great clock and set it aside to run on its own mechanical power; rather, after creation, he sent and does send a continual infusion of vitality into all his creations. The Lord says: "Nevertheless, the day shall come when you shall comprehend even God, being quickened in him and by him. Then shall ye know that ye have seen me, that I am, and that *I am the true light that is in you*, and that you are in me; *otherwise ye could not abound*" (D&C 88:49–50; emphasis added). We are in Christ and he is in us, and we do not with our natural eyes perceive that stunning reality. We can hardly fathom how utterly dependent we are on him and how much grace, or divine enabling power, has been given that we might experience our lives; nor do we fully realize how intimate our relationship with him already is.

Each of the Lord's children is designed to increase the light that forms the core of his or her being and to "grow up in [the Lord], and receive a *fulness* of the Holy Ghost" (D&C 109:15; emphasis added). "That which is of God is light; and he that receiveth light, and continueth in God, receiveth more light; and that light groweth brighter and brighter until the perfect day" (D&C 50:24). The Prophet Joseph said:

We consider that God has created man with a mind capable of instruction, and a faculty which may be enlarged in proportion to the heed and diligence given to the light communicated from heaven to the intellect; and that the nearer man approaches perfection, the clearer are his views, and the greater his enjoyments, till he has overcome the evils of his life and lost every desire for sin; and like the ancients, arrives at that point of faith where he is wrapped in the power and glory of his Maker and is caught up to dwell with Him. But we consider that this is a station to which no man ever arrived in a moment: he must have been instructed in the government and laws of that kingdom by proper degrees, until his mind is capable in some measure of comprehending the propriety, justice, equality, and consistency of the same.[4]

That degree of light or glory that we acquire in this life through diligence and obedience determines not only our "advantage in the world to come" (D&C 130:19), but even the degree of resurrection we obtain at the judgment: "Your glory shall be that glory by which your bodies are quickened. Ye who are quickened [now] by a portion of the celestial glory shall then receive of the same, even a fulness" (D&C 88:28–29; by inserting *now* I admittedly impose an interpretation, but perhaps a fair one, based on the idea that the portion of holy spirit that a person possesses in this life might be seen as a portion of celestial glory).

On the other hand, those who cease their obedience to the laws of light experience a darkening of their minds (D&C 10:2; see also Alma 12:9–11). The pressing insight here reveals how closely connected spiritual understanding and power are with one's own personal purity. While one can obtain a college degree no matter what his or her moral condition, one cannot progress in spiritual learning without increasing obedience to the laws of God. As a result, even in the eternal worlds, citizens of the telestial world will enjoy the least light that proceeds from God, namely "of the Holy Spirit through the ministration of the terrestrial world" (D&C 76:86), while those who have come up to the full measure of obedience and faith will enjoy a full intensity of light.

The Holy Spirit as a Personage

In addition to the holy spirit power that resides in both the Father and Son, the third member of the Godhead, the Holy Spirit (or Holy Ghost, Spirit of Truth, the Spirit of the Lord, or Spirit of God), administers to the children of God this holy spirit, according to the will of the Father and Son. Since the scriptures refer to the Holy Ghost both as a personage and as a power which can dwell in a person's heart (D&C 8:2), the context usually gives the clue as to which is meant. But that there is a personage in addition to the power is made clear in D&C 130:22–23:

The Father has a body of flesh and bones as tangible as man's; the Son also; but the Holy Ghost has not a body of flesh and bones, but is a *personage of Spirit*. Were it not so, the Holy Ghost could not dwell in us.

A man may receive the Holy Ghost, and it may descend upon him and not tarry with him.

The diary entry of William Clayton (2 April 1843) clarifies these verses:

The Holy Ghost is a personage, and a person cannot have the *personage* of the H. G. in his heart. A man receive the *gifts* of the H. G., and the H. G. may descend upon a man but not to tarry with him.[5]

The Prophet Joseph Smith also taught that the Holy Ghost "is now in a state of probation which if he should perform in righteousness he may pass through the same or similar course of things that the Son has."[6] George Laub reports a similar statement from another discourse of the Prophet Joseph: "But the Holy Ghost is yet a Spiritual body and waiting to take to himself a body as the Savior did or as God did, or the gods before them took bodies."[7]

The Holy Ghost has been commissioned by the Father and the Son to use holy spirit in performing a mission among and within the sons and daughters of men. In brief, his mission is to gain access to the spirits in men and women and teach them, spirit to spirit, how to reenter the presence of the Lord.

As subfunctions of this overall mission, the Holy Ghost performs a multitude of services as agent for the Lord. These are to speak to the mind and heart (D&C 8:2), be a "spirit of revelation" (D&C 8:3), give utterance (D&C 14:8), "[manifest] all things which are expedient" (D&C 18:18), provide convincing power to declare the gospel (D&C 18:32), "[bear] record of the Father and of the Son" (D&C 42:17); direct elders as to how to conduct meetings (D&C 20:45), give power in performing ordinances (D&C 20:60), act as a comforter (D&C 21:9), "[teach] peaceable things of the kingdom" (D&C 39:6), tell members of Christ's church what they should do (D&C 46:7), provide protection against deception (D&C 46:8), give gifts for the benefit of those who seek to keep all God's commandments (D&C 46:9), give a gift to every man for the profit of all (D&C 46:11–12), grant whatever one asks in Spirit (D&C 46:28–30), direct preaching (D&C 68:2–4), provide the gospel in every language (D&C 90:11), provide inspired reproof (D&C 121:43), and provide constant companionship for those who obey (D&C 121:46). The Holy Ghost's functions are so manifold that they finally exceed reduction into words; he performs an infinite number of functions based on our spiritual and temporal needs. Having access to a person's total system, to one's very most conscious and unconscious recesses, the Holy Ghost can magnify or rectify any part of that system.

Much of his influence upon a person is not even discerned in the early stages of spiritual development; but as one matures spiritually, one can sense an increasing presence. The Lord assures us that, "As often as thou hast inquired [of me] *thou hast received instruction of my Spirit*" (D&C 6:14; emphasis added). Through time and experience we learn to discern his presence and instruction.

The knowledge that the Holy Ghost imparts to man comes most commonly through the still small voice, Spirit seeking spirit. This voice is "the voice of one crying in the wilderness—in the wilderness, because you cannot see him—my voice, because my voice is Spirit; my Spirit is truth; truth abideth and hath no end; and if it be in you it shall abound" (D&C 88:66). A positive response to the Spirit causes him to "abound" in us, to proliferate light.

The truths, ideas, and assurances delivered by the Spirit to one's own spirit do not constitute *perfect* knowledge for the spiritual seeker. One must exercise faith in these revelations, which are designed ultimately to be *seen* or realized in some tangible way, either here or hereafter. Perhaps more accurately, the Holy Spirit imparts *pre*knowledge of spiritual truths. *Perfect* knowledge comes only when one actually *sees* for oneself what the Spirit has been teaching (D&C 50:45; 67:10, 14; 76:117; 88:67–68; 93:1; Alma 32:21, 26).

The Holy Ghost is involved as well in even greater manifestations, such as miracles, visions, the ministrations of angels, using divine instruments like the Urim and Thummim, the process of transfiguration in order for one to behold God without perishing (as in the case of the boy Joseph in the sacred grove, or in the case of the spiritually mature person who develops to the point that he could enjoy these manifestations while still in mortality) (D&C 67:10–12, Moses 1:11). Joseph was commanded not to write, while in the Spirit, the things which are not lawful for man to utter:

> Neither is man capable to make them [the mysteries of the kingdom] known, for they are only to be *seen* and *understood* by the power of the Holy Spirit, which God bestows on those who love him, and purify themselves before him;
>
>   To whom he grants this privilege of *seeing* and *knowing* for themselves;
>
>   That through the power and manifestation of the Spirit, while in the flesh, they may be able to bear his presence in the world of glory. (D&C 76:116–18; emphasis added)

Truly there is no communication that penetrates this telestial world from the celestial that is not facilitated by the Holy Spirit. Even after this telestial life, one's resurrection will be brought about through the agency of the Holy Ghost (2 Ne. 2:8).

The Holy Ghost seeks access even to a person's inner recesses to produce his divine regeneration. Elder Parley P. Pratt describes the renovating effects the receptive person can experience under the influence of the Holy Ghost:

> The gift of the Holy Ghost . . . quickens all the intellectual faculties, increases, enlarges, expands, and purifies all the natural passions and affections; and adapts them, by the gift of wisdom, to their lawful use. It inspires, develops, cultivates, and matures all the fine-toned sympathies, joys, tastes, kindred feelings, and affections of our nature. It inspires virtue, kindness, goodness, tenderness, gentleness, and charity. It develops beauty of person, form and features. It tends to health, vigor, animation, and social feeling. It invigorates all the faculties of the physical and intellectual

man. It strengthens, and gives tone to the nerves. In short, it is, as it were, marrow to the bone, joy to the heart, light to the eyes, music to the ears, and life to the whole being.[8]

The Holy Ghost functions only by virtue of the Lord Jesus Christ's atonement. The power that the Holy Ghost administers is the grace, or the divine enabling power, released to us through the sacrifice of the Lord Jesus Christ. Without the holy Atonement, this power would not be available to us. The Holy Ghost, referred to as the First Comforter (88:3, by implication), does not speak of or for himself; rather, he delivers the love, the mind, and the will of the Savior. Therefore, this Spirit connects us in the telestial world with our Savior in the celestial world; which is to say, that whenever we feel the workings of the Spirit, we are experiencing the conscious love and atoning power of the Savior. To have an experience with the First Comforter really amounts to interacting with the Lord Jesus Christ. In a sense, Jesus Christ is the First Comforter, facilitated inwardly by the Holy Ghost.

Joseph Smith taught that the Savior is also the Second Comforter. What is the difference between the two comforters? The First Comforter *develops the faculties of faith and revelation* within a person. Having perfected these, which is no small task, one can progress to the visual and physical presence of the Father and the Son. Were a person to receive the Second Comforter before the First, he would not be able to develop that inner mechanism which matures by faith, that is, by response to the Holy Spirit, rather than sight. Thus the Savior says to his apostles just before his departure: "It is expedient for you that I go away: for if I go not away, the Comforter [the first] will not come unto you; but if I depart, I will send him unto you" (John 16:7).

As there is an intimate relationship between the First Comforter and the Savior, so also there is an intimate relationship between the Second Comforter and the Holy Spirit of Promise:

Wherefore, I now send upon you another Comforter, even upon you my friends, that it may abide in your hearts, even the Holy Spirit of promise; which other Comforter is the same that I promised unto my disciples, as is recorded in the testimony of John. This Comforter is the promise which I give unto you of eternal life, even the glory of the celestial kingdom. (D&C 88:3-4)

D&C 130:3 clarifies John 14:23, where the two comforters are discussed:

The appearing of the Father and the Son, in that verse, is *a personal appearance*; and the idea that [the personages of] the Father and the Son dwell in a man's heart is an old sectarian notion, and is false. (emphasis added)

The Prophet Joseph Smith enlarged on the doctrine of the two comforters and the steps by which one could obtain the Second Comforter:

There are two Comforters spoken of. One is the Holy Ghost, the same as given on the day of Pentecost, and that all Saints receive after faith, repentance, and baptism. This first Comforter or Holy Ghost has no other effect than pure intelligence. It is more powerful in expanding the mind, enlightening the understanding, and storing the intellect with present knowledge....

The other comforter spoken of is a subject of great interest, and perhaps understood by few of this generation. After a person has faith in Christ, repents of his sins, and is baptized for the remission of his sins and receives the Holy Ghost, (by the laying on of hands), which is the first Comforter, then let him continue to humble himself before God, hungering and thirsting after righteousness, and living by every word of God, and the Lord will soon say unto him, Son, thou shalt be exalted. When the Lord has thoroughly proved him, and finds that the man is determined to serve Him at all hazards, then the man will find his calling and his election made sure, then it will be his privilege to receive the other Comforter, which the Lord hath promised the Saints....

Now what is this other Comforter? It is no more nor less than the Lord Jesus Christ Himself; and this is the sum and substance of the whole matter; that when any man obtains this last Comforter, he will have the personage of Jesus Christ to attend him, or appear unto him from time to time, and even He will manifest the Father unto him, and they will take up their abode with him, and the visions of the heavens will be opened unto him, and the Lord will teach him face to face, and he may have a perfect knowledge of the mysteries of the Kingdom of God; and this is the state and place the ancient Saints arrived at when they had such glorious visions.[9]

The Doctrine and Covenants gives further information on this Holy Spirit of Promise: "[Those] who shall come forth in the resurrection of the just...are sealed by the Holy Spirit of promise" (D&C 76:53). This sealing power is a function of the priesthood, as indicated in Doctrine and Covenants 124:124, where Hyrum Smith, as patriarch, holds the sealing blessings of the Holy Spirit of Promise, by which the Saints are sealed up unto the day of redemption. All covenants and performances must be sealed by the Holy Spirit of Promise to have force after this life (D&C 132:7, 18–19, 26).

The Holy Ghost performs several functions for repentant members that enable them to secure, through the process of time and obedience, the blessings necessary for exaltation. For example, a person can be born again of the water and of the Spirit when he or she receives the ordinances of baptism and the laying on of hands for the gift of the Holy Ghost, believing in the Lord Jesus Christ (D&C 5:16). In addition, the Spirit provides justification and sanctification through the grace of the Lord Jesus Christ (D&C 84:33; Alma 5:54; 13:11–12).

Divine law requires justification because of a problem which exists universally for fallen man, that is, that no unclean thing can enter the presence of God (D&C 67:12; 94:8; Moses 6:57). But fallen beings need a form of the presence and power of God to enable them to be sanctified and to reenter God's presence. What is to be done to help them in their fallen condition? The answer lies in justification, which is a gift of pure grace based on no merit in a person except repentance and sincere efforts at obedience. By virtue of the Savior's atonement, sincere baptism and the laying on of hands for the gift of the Holy Ghost *justify* a fallen person's receiving the Holy Ghost and pursuing sanctification. When a person is justified by the Spirit, he or she is still fallen, but through repentance and obedience, one fulfills the law of mercy that pays justice and grants one access to the sanctifying Holy Spirit.

After a probationary period of justification and conscious apprenticeship with the Holy Spirit, one may develop to the point where, having given diligent heed to the words of Christ, one has fulfilled the law that allows him or her to be sanctified, or redeemed from the Fall, so that one can then enter fully into the Lord's presence.

In other words, with respect to justification, the Holy Ghost is the *pro tem* presence of God, granted until one can be sanctified and enter the Lord's presence by virtue of spiritual development. When a person merits sanctification, the Holy Ghost produces the change in the person from a fallen to a redeemed state.

Indeed, how comprehensive are the powers of the Holy Ghost and his many benevolent and constant functions in our lives.

How the Saints Work by the Spirit

The laws that govern the workings of the Spirit are not magical or beyond comprehension or only for those who have extraordinary missions or gifts. The Lord invites all to learn and apply eternal laws the way he does (D&C 41:5, 88:35), and thus become as he is. The Spirit is not optional in doing the Lord's work, in working the Lord's way. In fact, he asks us to use his Spirit in all that we do as his covenant people (D&C 19:38; 46:7; 50:13–14; 2 Ne. 32:8–9; Alma 37:37; Moses 5:8). Those who take the Holy Spirit as their guide "shall abide the day," meaning the day of the Savior's second coming (D&C 45:57).

The Spirit works on very simple principles. That is, the comprehensive powers of the Spirit are worked by men and women through seemingly small means on earth: "You know, brethren, that a very large ship is benefited very much by a very small helm in the time of a storm, by being kept workways with the wind and the waves" (D&C 123:16).

But therein lies the problem: when the means are simple, the temptation to look beyond the mark for something more mysterious, more sophisticated, more complicated (cp. Jacob 4:14), may obscure the fact that "out of *small* things proceedeth that which is great" (D&C 64:33; emphasis added; cp. Alma 37). This section will focus on how the Spirit responds to the way we use our minds and our feelings, means which seem small to men, but are powerful influences with the Lord.

In one's own mind and feelings lies the foundation of all spiritual progress (D&C 20:31; 88:68). The Lord seeks access to our mind and feelings; desire for the Spirit opens the heart to the workings of the Spirit, for "the Lord requireth the *heart* and a *willing mind*" (D&C 64:34; emphasis added; cp. Alma 32:27). Under the influence of the Spirit, we can increase our agency over both mind and feelings. The Lord says, "Remain steadfast in your minds in solemnity and the spirit of prayer" (D&C 84:61; see also Moro. 7:30).

One simple mental adjustment that we have the agency to make, and that the Lord requires, is to see in the mind's eye (or the *eye of faith*: Alma 5:15, 32:40, Ether 12:19) that one's desire and belief actually begin to work the tumblers of the divine combination that unlocks the Spirit (D&C 5:16; 8:1; 11:10, 14; 14:8). The prayer of faith has great influence with heaven (D&C 42:14). Part of the reason that one has the divine power of imagination is so that he or she can carry mental images that enhance belief and faith. The power of the mind to imagine, to hold carefully chosen mental images, is the foundation of spiritual creation.

People who set out to work by the Spirit must cultivate, by their agency, positive emotional and mental energy. This energy is deliberately cultivated in the mind first and is then manifested in one's choice of words and actions. Prayer and immersion in the scriptures activate spiritual power. Without constant practice in prayer and frequent immersion in scripture, a person will never experience the full functioning of the Spirit. Through scripture study and prayer the Lord sensitizes the human spirit to what the Holy Spirit *feels* like, how to discern it, and the diverse ways in which the Holy Spirit operates (e.g. D&C 11:12–13). That is, one can only learn about spiritual things from the Spirit itself.

The Lord seeks to maintain a constant shaping influence on the human mind and heart, thereby teaching one through the unique moment-to-moment experiences of one's life and thought: "Pray *always* and I will pour out my Spirit upon you and great shall be your blessing" (D&C 19:38; emphasis added). To abandon a prayerful attitude is to cease to learn by the Spirit.

In addition, without the Spirit we have little protection against Satan who continually seeks access to our unguarded mental moments (D&C 10:5). Therefore, the Lord urges: "Look unto me in every thought, doubt not, fear not" (D&C 6:36). We covenant "always [to] remember him, that [we] may have his Spirit to be with [us]" (see D&C 20:77–79). Satan tries to convince people that their emotions exist outside their control—a dangerous deception. Our feelings are highly sensitive to the purifying power of the Holy Ghost. It is important to purify our feelings with meekness and love because the Holy Ghost works through them. Emotional purification clears the channel for revelation. We can come to the point where we can trust that what we feel in our hearts is influenced by the Spirit of the Lord:

> I will tell you in your mind and in your heart, by the Holy Ghost, which shall come upon you and which shall dwell *in your heart.* (D&C 8:2; emphasis added)

> You must study it out in your mind; then you must ask me if it be right, and if it is right I will cause that your bosom shall burn within you; therefore, you shall *feel* that it is right. But if it be not right you shall have no such *feelings,* but . . . a stupor of thought. (D&C 9:8–9; emphasis added)

The adversary's continual stalking of the Saints, combined with his readiness to counterfeit the things of God, requires that seekers of truth learn to discern: "Trust in that Spirit which leadeth to do good—yea, to do justly, to walk humbly, to judge righteously; and this is my Spirit" (D&C 11:12; see also 46:23; 50:15–35; 129). The Lord gives a further pattern for discernment: "He that prayeth, whose spirit is contrite.... whose language is meek and edifieth, the same is of God if he obey mine ordinances.... [H]e that trembleth under my power...shall bring forth fruits of praise and wisdom, according to the revelations and truths which I have given you.... Wherefore, by this pattern; ye shall know the spirits in all cases under the whole heavens" (D&C 52:15–17, 19).

Another reason to cultivate the Spirit is that emotional distress can plague us during those times in which we neglect the Spirit; on the other hand, meekly heeding the Spirit provides rest (D&C 19:20, 23).

The Lord invites men and women to ask, seek, knock for spiritual knowledge, the mysteries of the gospel, and the knowledge of God (D&C 42:61; 88:63–68; 93:1). These mysteries and knowledge are not offered to satisfy curiosity but to develop one's power to work as God works and to bring souls to him: "If thou wilt inquire, ... thou mayest find out mysteries, that thou mayest bring many to the knowledge of the truth, yea, [and] convince them of the error of their ways" (D&C 6:11; cp. Alma 26:22).

People who pursue spiritual knowledge through faith, study, prayer, and obedience for the purpose of obtaining greater serving power are promised a number of gifts: "If you shall ask the Father in my name, in faith believing, you shall receive the Holy Ghost, *which giveth utterance*, that you may stand as a witness" (D&C 14:8; emphasis added). Those who use their minds to "treasure up... continually the words of life... shall be given... in the very hour" the words they need for any situation (D&C 84:85). The Lord makes a similar promise later in the Doctrine and Covenants, adding some helpful directions:

Speak the thoughts that I shall put into your hearts, and you shall not be confounded before men;

For it shall be given you in the very hour, yea, in the very moment, what ye shall say.

But a commandment I give . . . that ye shall declare [it] in my name, in *solemnity of heart*, in the spirit of *meekness*, in all things.

And . . . inasmuch as ye do this the Holy Ghost shall be shed forth in bearing record unto all things whatsoever ye shall say. (D&C 100:5–8; emphasis added)

But, as the Lord is not able to work in a mental vacuum, he warns:

Seek not to declare my word, but *first seek to obtain my word*, and then shall your tongue be loosed; then, if you desire, you shall have my Spirit and my word, yea, the power of God unto the convincing of men. (D&C 11:21; emphasis added)

On the other hand, the Holy Ghost acts as a restraint when imparting certain knowledge might endanger either the cause of the Church or the spiritual growth of the receiver (D&C 19:21–22; 105:23; cp. Alma 12:9).

The Spirit of the Lord might also be called the Spirit of the at-one-ment, the reason being that a compelling power proceeds forth out of heaven to draw all people to the arms of the Lord Jesus Christ. This is the power of the at-one-ment, and it is one of the functions of this spirit and power to draw people together in love and to draw them to heaven. When the Church reaches out to gather Israel by missionary work, it cooperates with this spirit of the at-one-ment. When families seal their ancestors to themselves and their posterities, they practice the spirit of at-one-ment. When men and women marry in the temple they seal themselves to each other and to the Lord, responding to the power of the at-one-ment wrought by the Lord Jesus Christ. Thus the Lord is speaking primarily about people when he says:

I have committed the keys of my kingdom, and a dispensation of the gospel for the last times; and for the fulness of times, in the which I will *gather together in one all things*, both which are in heaven, are on earth;

And also with all those whom my Father hath given me out of the world.

Wherefore, lift up your hearts and rejoice. (D&C 27:13–15; emphasis added)

One of the most important characteristics of this holy at-one-ment spirit is that it is drawn to the positive energy and feeling generated by ordinary people. The Lord makes it clear that we have both the agency, the power, and indeed the command to generate positive energy in the form of gentleness, long-suffering, meekness, love unfeigned, kindness (D&C 121:41–42), faith, hope and charity. The opposites of these—pride, covering up sin, vain ambition, exercise of compulsion (D&C 121:37), contention (D&C 136:23), finding fault with one another (D&C 88:124), fears and jealousies (D&C 67:10)—cause an immediate interruption in the spiritual circuit. Until we manifest the positive energies of the loving divine nature in all our undertakings, our efforts will be inefficient and our spiritual power will be limited. Joseph Smith said:

Nothing is so much calculated to lead people to forsake sin as to take them by the hand, and watch over them with tenderness. When persons manifest the least kindness and love to me, O what power it has over my mind, while the opposite course has a tendency to harrow up all the harsh feelings and depress the human mind. . . .

[I]t is the doctrine of the devil to retard the human mind, and hinder our progress, by filling us with self-righteousness. The nearer we get to our heavenly Father, the more we are disposed to look with compassion on perishing souls; we feel that we want to take them upon our shoulders and cast their sins behind our backs. . . . [I]f you would have God have mercy on you, have mercy on one another.[10]

The Lord says: "Therefore, strengthen your brethren in *all* your conversation, in *all* your prayers, in *all* your exhortations, and in *all* your doings" (D&C 108:7; emphasis added). Another way to put that command would be: Let *all* your conversation, prayers, exhortations, and doings lead to the *strengthening* of those around you. Negative energy opposes godliness and faith and inhibits the workings of the Spirit.

Another principle the Lord stresses is the spiritual power people have in *uniting* in the spirit of at-one-ment to strengthen their prayers. The Prophet Joseph said, "It [is] by union of feeling [that] we obtain power with God."[11] The Lord has said:

> Whatsoever ye shall ask in faith, being *united* in prayer according to my command, ye shall receive. (D&C 29:6; emphasis added)

> Take the helmet of salvation, and the sword of my Spirit, which I will pour out upon you, and my word which I reveal unto you, and *be agreed as touching all things whatsoever ye ask of me*, and be faithful until I come, and ye shall be caught up, that where I am ye shall be also. Amen. (D&C 27:18; emphasis added)

> In your temporal things *you shall be equal*, and this not grudgingly, otherwise the abundance of the manifestations of the spirit shall be withheld. (D&C 70:14; emphasis added)

> Were it not for the transgressions of my people ... they might have been redeemed even now.
> But ... they have not learned to be obedient ... and are not united according to the union required by the law of the celestial kingdom;
> And Zion cannot be built up unless it is by the principles of the law of the celestial kingdom; otherwise I cannot receive her unto myself. (D&C 105:3–5; emphasis added)

When one seeks to work by the Spirit without cultivating the positive energies of the at-one-ment—humility, meekness, gentleness, patience, compassion, forgiveness, building up others, encouragement, praise, generosity, loving words—he spins his wheels. But when one diligently works away at multiplying these gentle virtues in one's thoughts and feelings, the Spirit always meshes with one's endeavors. God cannot practice for us, but by our practice and prayer we can become perfect in these personality attributes (cp. Moro. 10:32–33). Thus we practice to achieve the oneness of spirit that the Gods enjoy and draw into our midst the powers of the Spirit.

The mind and heart can be made very firm in godliness (D&C 4:2; 11:20; 43:34; 84:80; 88:68; 110:1; cp. Moro. 7:30). This mental firmness is one indispensable part that we play in obtaining spiritual power. Spiritual forces flow in and around us, like a great reservoir of living water. One may, if one will, draw joy in great drafts out of that living well.[12]

NOTES

CHAPTER SEVEN

1. Joseph Fielding Smith, *Doctrines of Salvation*, comp. Bruce R. McConkie (Salt Lake City: Bookcraft, 1955), 1:52.

2. Parley P. Pratt, *Key to Theology*, cited in *Discourses on the Holy Ghost*, ed. N. B. Lundwall (Salt Lake City: Bookcraft, 1964), 76.

3. John Taylor, "Origin, Object, and Destiny of Women," *The Mormon* 3 (29 Aug. 1857): 28.

4. Joseph Smith, *Teachings of the Prophet Joseph Smith*, comp. Joseph Fielding Smith (Salt Lake City: Deseret Book Co., 1977), 51; hereafter cited as *TPJS*.

5. Lyndon W. Cook, *The Revelations of the Prophet Joseph Smith* (Salt Lake City: Deseret Book Co.,1985), 289; emphasis added. See also *The Words of Joseph Smith*, comp. Andrew F. Ehat and Lyndon W. Cook (Provo, Utah: Religious Studies Center, 1980), 170; hereafter cited as *WJS*. See also *WJS*, 173. Compare also D&C 8:2, which this quote may also clarify.

6. Franklin D. Richards, "Scriptural Items," 27 Aug 1843, *WJS*, 245.

7. George Laub, 16 June 1844, *WJS*, 305, n. 26.

8. Parley P. Pratt, *Key to the Science of Theology* (Salt Lake City: Deseret Book Co., 1978), 61.

9. *TPJS*, 149–51.

10. Ibid., 240–41.

11. *WJS*, 123.

12. See, for example, D&C 11:13, 19:38, 42:61; 101:36; 136:29; Isaiah 12:3, John 7:38–39 for a treatment on spiritual forces and living water.

THE ORDINANCES AND PERFORMANCES THAT PERTAIN TO SALVATION

LINDA AUKSCHUN

> On April 6, 1830, under heavenly direction, the Prophet Joseph Smith organized the Church, and thus the true Church of Jesus Christ is once again operative as an institution among men, with authority to teach the gospel and administer the ordinances of salvation.
>
> —(Doctrine and Covenants, Explanatory Introduction)

Why was there a need for the restoration of the "only true Church"? The world had the commandment to love God and their neighbor. And baptism, the ordinance Christ taught in the Bible as being necessary for salvation, was available from a wide variety of religious congregations. What difference would the infant Church make in men and women's relationship to God? It's a question that has been asked by more than one student of the gospel.

The answer is stated in the historical notation opening this essay: Priesthood authority and the ordinances of salvation had long since been taken from the earth, and both are required if the children of God are to achieve their highest goal, that of becoming like God. Joseph Smith knew that there was more to the business of religion than just belief. "For how to *act* I did not know," he wrote of the dilemma he faced as he tried to decide which church to join, "and unless I could get more wisdom than I then had, I would never know" (JS—H 1:12; emphasis added). The revelations which were to come forth because of Joseph's seeking "how to act" for himself would include a restoration of the ordinances of the gospel of Jesus Christ that are necessary for the salvation of the entire human family.

What Are the Ordinances of Salvation?

The word *ordinance* can include the entire spectrum of "God's decrees, his laws and commandments, the statutes and judgments that issue from him.... The covenant of the saints, when they 'promise to keep all the commandments and statutes of the Lord' is: *'We will walk in all the ordinances of the Lord.* (D&C 136:2–4)'"[1]

However, the specific ordinances addressed in this paper will be the various rites and ceremonies pertaining to the kingdom of God conducted both outside the temple and within. Among these are baptism, confirmation (or the laying on of hands for the gift of the Holy Ghost), the conferring of the priesthood, and the temple ordinances of washings and anointings, the presentation of the endowment, and the sealing of a man and woman both to each other and to family. These are the "saving" ordinances, or the ordinances necessary for salvation.

The term *salvation* is a reference to a future state of being "saved." As Joseph Smith said:

> Salvation is nothing more nor less than to triumph over all our enemies and put them under our feet. And when we have power to put all enemies under our feet in this world, and a knowledge to triumph over all evil spirits in the world to come, then we are saved.[2]

The Lord spoke clearly about the ordinances required of those who obtain this state to and through his prophet Joseph Smith:

> All men who become heirs of God and joint heirs with Jesus Christ will have to receive the fulness of the ordinances of his kingdom; and those who will not receive all the ordinances

will come short of the fulness of that glory, if they do not lose the whole.[3]

The concept of salvation itself was one that was expanded upon and became more clear as the events of the Restoration unfolded. The Prophet Joseph realized that there must be much more to the prospect of being saved than the simple "either heaven or hell" the religious world of his day accepted:

From sundry revelations which had been received, it was apparent that many important points touching the salvation of man, had been taken from the Bible, or lost before it was compiled. It appeared self-evident from what truths were left, that if God rewarded every one according to the deeds done in the body the term "Heaven," as intended for the Saints' eternal home must include more kingdoms than one.[4]

On 16 February 1832, while translating the book of John in the New Testament, Joseph and Sidney Rigdon saw the "Vision of the Glories" as contained in Doctrine and Covenants 76. Through this vision they learned that the kingdom of God is made up of "many mansions," different levels of salvation which include the celestial, the terrestrial, and the telestial kingdoms. Additionally, there are three levels in the celestial kingdom, the highest of which is called *exaltation* (D&C 131:1). Participation in *all* of the saving ordinances as outlined by the Lord is key to the achievement of exaltation which is "a state that a person can attain in becoming like God—salvation in the ultimate sense."[5]

In our own day, Elder Vaughn J. Featherstone has made it clear that ordinances are fundamental to our claiming the promises of exaltation from the Lord:

To be exalted, a person must be baptized and confirmed in the Church of Jesus Christ. Every soul must receive his or her endowment. Every male must receive the Melchizedek Priesthood, and a man and a woman must be sealed in the new and everlasting covenant of temple marriage.... No

righteous member of the Church will be denied any of the
ordinances that exalt as long as he or she shall continue to
the end in worthiness. The ordinances may take place in this
life or in the life to come, but they will take place.[6]

An incident from Church history cited by S. Dilworth Young
indicates how saving ordinances such as the temple endowment
can be sustaining to us in this life, as well:

One day in the upper room of a house in Nauvoo the Prophet
Joseph gathered half a dozen men and their wives. After pre-
paring the proper clothing beforehand, he gave them the
covenant of the endowment. Each one there made his personal covenant with God. Then the commandment was given
that this should be done only in holy places. They now knew
why they were to build the Nauvoo Temple as commanded.
So they worked with all their might to build it. In my opinion, after the death of the Prophet, the thing that sustained
the Saints as they came West with all the hardships, terrible
hunger, thirst, sorrow and death was the covenant they had
made with the Lord. They were promised that if they kept it
they would attain the celestial kingdom. They knew that was
so. So they went forth to their bitter struggle with fairly light
hearts and assurances that they would be able to weather it
through.[7]

All of the ordinances of salvation should lead our thoughts
and hearts to the contemplation of eternal matters; they should
lift us from this fallen sphere to a greater understanding of and
desire for the things of God.

The Symbolism of the Ordinances

Each ordinance is based on gospel truths and teaches, through
symbolic representation, the plan of salvation:

And behold, all things have their likeness, and all things are
created and made to bear record of me, both things which

are temporal, and things which are spiritual; things which are in the heavens above, and things which are on the earth, and things which are in the earth, and things which are under the earth, both above and beneath: all things bear record of me. (Moses 6:63)

"'All the ordinances,' wrote Heber C. Kimball, 'are signs of things in the heavens. Everything we see here is typical of what will be hereafter.'"[8]

The ordinance of baptism is presented symbolically through different images which provide a foundation for, vary, and deepen our understanding. The Doctrine and Covenants teaches that baptism is performed for "the remission of sins" (D&C 19:31), being "a symbolic washing and cleansing of sins [that] is prerequisite to membership in the Church."[9] Elder Bruce R. McConkie notes that "[Baptism] is the gate to the celestial kingdom of heaven, that is, it starts a person out on the straight and narrow path which leads to eternal life."[10] Our return to Heavenly Father is often spoken of symbolically as being a journey. The journey takes place on a path which is "strait and narrow," or along a "way" which is Jesus Christ and his example, and the journey begins at a gate, which permits or denies entrance:

Wherefore, do the things which I have told you I have seen that your Lord and your Redeemer should do; for, for this cause have they been shown unto me, that ye might know the *gate by which ye should enter.* For the *gate by which ye should enter is repentance and baptism by water;* and then cometh a remission of your sins by fire and by the Holy Ghost.

And then are ye in the *strait and narrow path* which leads to eternal life; yea, ye have entered in by the *gate*; ye have done according to the commandments of the Father and the Son; and ye have received the Holy Ghost, which witnesses of the Father and the Son, unto the fulfilling of the promise which he hath made, that if ye *entered in by the way* ye should receive. (2 Ne. 31:17–18; emphasis added)

Baptism also symbolizes burial and resurrection, as recipients are immersed in water and thus "buried with him [Christ] by baptism into death.... For if we have been planted together in the likeness of his death, we shall be also in the likeness of his resurrection" (Rom. 6:3–5). According to the Doctrine and Covenants, it is those "who received the testimony of Jesus ... and were baptized after the manner of his *burial,* being *buried in the water* in his name" who become heirs to the celestial kingdom (D&C 76:51; emphasis added). The imagery of a grave and a resurrection (or of a birth and the coming forth out of a womb) is reflected by the symbolic destruction of our former sinful selves (Rom. 6:6) and our "rebirth" as we "walk in newness of life" (Rom. 6:4).

The imagery of the grave continues in the symbolism connected with fonts used in performing baptisms for the dead. In most temples, these fonts are "placed below the foundation, or the surface of the earth."[11] "The baptismal font was instituted as a similitude of the grave, and was commanded to be in the place *underneath* where the living are wont to assemble, to show forth the living and the dead, and that all things may have their likeness, and that they may accord one with another" (D&C 128:13; emphasis added).

The Holy Ghost is symbolized throughout the scriptures by fire. The gift of the Holy Ghost received by the laying on of hands is referred to as "the baptism of fire" (D&C 33:11; 39:6). This stems in part from the physical manifestation of ratification by the Spirit, which is often spoken of in terms of fire: "If it is right I will cause that your bosom shall *burn* within you" (D&C 9:8; emphasis added). This "fire" also serves another, sanctifying purpose by which "dross, iniquity, carnality, sensuality, and every evil thing is burned out of the repentant soul *as if* by fire."[12]

Through a lifetime of temple attendance, subtle yet important symbols are taught which provide reassurance, confidence, and strength to those who seek spiritual understanding. The endowment involves a symbolic journey through life, beginning with the pre-existence and passing through mortality into heavenly realms.[13] John A. Widtsoe made it clear that, in part because of the symbolic nature of the endowment, effort is part of the price the devoted patrons of the temples are asked to pay:

> The holy endowment is deeply symbolic. "Going through the temple" is not a very good phrase; for temple worship implies a great effort of mind and concentration if we are to understand the mighty symbols that pass in review before us. Everything must be arranged to attune our hearts, our minds, and our souls to the work. Everything about us must contribute to the peace of mind that enables us to study and to understand the mysteries, if you choose, that are unfolded before us....
>
> The endowment itself is symbolic; it is a series of symbols of vast realities, too vast for full understanding....
>
> We live in in a world of symbols. No man or woman can come out of the temple endowed as he should be, unless he has seen, beyond the symbol, the mighty realities for which the symbols stand.[14]

The temple itself,

> or House of the Lord, is also symbolic of the Lord's dwelling place, where one can go to learn godliness. For some, the temple symbolizes the conjunction of heaven and earth, where those who seek heaven come out of the world for instruction and receive symbolic reminders of God's plan for his children.[15]

Symbolism continues in the structure of rooms where temple ordinances take place. For example, the opposing mirrors in the sealing rooms present the new bride and groom with a moment to "look at eternity." As they view themselves together in endless reflections, they understand a little better the significance of kneeling together across the altar and are reminded of the sealing power which makes possible eternal marriages and families, as well as exaltation in the highest degree of glory in the celestial kingdom. Symbolically, those who enter the temple step from one kingdom to another and sense, for a short while, the things that lay in store for them there.

Prescribed Ordinances Existed in the Ancient Church as They Exist in the Church Today

The scriptures indicate that baptism is required of all. Jesus Christ was baptized "to fulfill all righteousness" (Matt. 3:13–17), and the baptism of Adam is recorded in scripture (Moses 6:64–65). The bestowal of the gift of the Holy Ghost, the next essential ordinance of the gospel, was so important that the resurrected Christ advised his apostles to wait in Jerusalem until such time as they would receive the Holy Ghost before taking their witness to the world (Acts 1:4, 5, 8). Thereafter, this saving ordinance was taught to all as a requirement for salvation in the kingdom of God.

Because of the sacred nature of temple ordinances and performances, they are not described in scripture to the modern-day Church. Similarly, references to them in ancient scripture are, at best, obscure, but they do exist.

A study of scripture, both ancient and modern, shows an awareness among the ancients of at least some of the ordinances:

> For, for this cause I commanded Moses that he should build a tabernacle, that they should bear it with them in the wilderness, and to build a house in the land of promise, that these ordinances might be revealed which had been hid from before the world was. (D&C 124:38)

Brigham Young, in an address given in St. George on January 1, 1877, at the completion of the St. George Temple, said:

> We that are here are enjoying a privilege that we have no knowledge of any other people enjoying since the days of Adam, that is, to have a Temple completed, wherein all the ordinance [*sic*] of the house of God can be bestowed upon his people.... It is true that Solomon built a Temple for the purpose of giving endowments, but from what we can learn of the history of that time they gave very few if any endowments,

and one of the high priests was murdered by wicked and corrupt men, who had already begun to apostatize, because he would not reveal those things appertaining to the Priesthood that were forbidden him to reveal until he came to the proper place.[16]

Receiving sacred ordinances has always been conditioned on worthiness. Today, recommends are required for entrance into the Lord's temples. This naturally keeps the details of temple ordinances from those who have not proved themselves worthy. The temple endowment is verbal scripture, to be learned by listening repeatedly while in the temple. Thus the temple ordinances themselves are not found in written scripture. However, the scriptures contain suggestions that appear to be veiled references to ordinances and covenant making, reminiscent of the temple. As we read the account of the wrestle that Abraham's grandson Jacob had with the angel, we readily see that there must be more to this incident than the Old Testament reveals (Gen. 32:24-30). Jacob's name is changed: "Thy name shall be called no more Jacob, but Israel" (v. 28). There is the mention of "the hollow of Jacob's thigh" (v. 25), and in Genesis 24:2, the thigh, it seems, is a part of an oath-taking situation. In Jacob's dream about a ladder upon which angels ascend and descend to heaven (Gen. 28:11-22), the Lord comes to Jacob and talks about the covenant that Jacob's grandfather has made and extends that covenant to Jacob, as well. As Jacob wakes, he comments, "Surely the Lord is in this place," and he calls the spot Beth-el, which means "House of God" (Gen. 28:16-19).

In a talk given in Salt Lake City on July 19, 1863, Heber C. Kimball intimated that Jesus presented his apostles with their endowments:

When the kingdom of God is organized upon the earth, it is done to protect the Church of Christ in its rights and privileges, so that you see the Church makes a government to protect itself, but who knows what that government is? All those to whom it has been revealed, and no others. Let the Saints reflect upon these matters which I am laying before them. Think of your holy endowments and what you have been anointed to become, and reflect upon the blessings which have been placed upon you, for they are the same in part that were placed upon Jesus; he was the one that inducted his Apostles into these ordinances; it was he who set up the kingdom of which we are subjects.[17]

Harold B. Lee added further insight into this experience:

"Ye have not chosen me, but I have chosen you, and ordained you ... that whatsoever ye should ask the Father in my name, he may give it you." (John 15:16.) Try to imagine, if you can, being "called" by the Master and "ordained" under His hands. That these ordinations resulted in an endowment of power from on high as well as giving authority to act officially as the Lord's representatives is well attested by the miraculous events that followed, which made of them "men different" because of that divine commission.

Not alone were these special apostolic witness [*sic*] to receive and enjoy these heavenly gifts. They were commissioned to transmit them by ordinations to others who had received the witness of the divine mission of the risen Lord. Acting by authority of their priestly office, it was as though the Lord were saying, as He did through a prophet in recent times, "And I will lay my hand upon you by the hand of my servant ... and you shall receive ... the Holy Ghost...." (D&C 36:2.)[18]

Elder John A. Widtsoe of the Quorum of the Twelve recognized that many cultures throughout the history of the world built and used temples, and these he saw as confirming that not only had temples existed with Adam but also that their importance from the beginning was undeniable:

All people of all ages have had temples in one form or another. When the history of human thought shall be written from the point of view of temple worship, it may well be found that temples and the work done in them have been the dominating influence in shaping human thought from the beginning of the race....

In every land and in every age temples have been built and used. In China, age old with four thousand years of written history; in India; on the islands of the sea; in South America; in North America; in Africa and in Australia; everywhere there are evidences of the existence and use of temples.

There is a fairly complete history of some of the temples of the priesthood, the temples built by the chosen people of God. There are evidences that even in patriarchal days, in the days of Adam, there was the equivalent of temples, for the priesthood was held in its fulness, as far as the people needed it; and there is every reason to believe that from Adam to Noah, temple worship was in operation. After the flood the Holy Priesthood was continued; and we have reason to believe, in sacred places, the ordinances of the temple were given to those entitled to receive them.

When Israel was in Egypt, the Priesthood was with them, and we may believe from certain sayings of the Scriptures that Israel had in Egypt a temple or its equivalent, the mysterious "testimony." When Israel was in the wilderness temple worship was provided for, for the Lord said to the Prophet Joseph (D. & C., 124:38):

"For, for this cause I commanded Moses that he should build a tabernacle, that they should bear it with them in the wilderness, and to build a house in the land of promise, that those ordinances might be revealed which had been hid from before the world was...."

Let me suggest that the reason why temple building and temple worship have been found in every age, on every hand, and among every people, is because the Gospel in its fullness was revealed to Adam, and that all religions and religious practices are therefore derived from the remnants of the truth given to Adam and transmitted by him to the patriarchs. The ordinances of the temple in so far as then necessary, were given, no doubt, in those early days, and very naturally corruptions of them have been handed down the ages.[19]

Hugh Nibley has shown, using accounts of ancient religious rites and practices, that the ancient Egyptians practiced rites and ordinances that may be familiar to many LDS Church members. Likely the relationship harkens back to an Egyptian relationship with Abraham and his people. Nibley cites Abraham 1:26–27, which says:

> Pharaoh, being a righteous man, established his kingdom and judged his people wisely and justly all his days, seeking earnestly to imitate that order established by the fathers in the first generations, in the days of the first patriarchal reign of Adam, and also of Noah, his father, who blessed him with the blessings of the earth, and with the blessings of wisdom, but cursed him as pertaining to the Priesthood.
>
> Now, Pharaoh being of that lineage by which he could not have the right of Priesthood, notwithstanding the Pharaohs would fain claim it from Noah, through Ham, therefore my father was led away by their idolatry.[20]

Likely, says Nibley, it was the Egyptian Pharaoh going through the motions of the priesthood without priesthood authority that was termed "idolatry" in scripture (Abr. 2:5). This eventually set in motion events that would cause Abraham to leave Ur (Abr. 1:11–12) and to travel to Canaan. Nibley continues:

> It was a procedure, a body of law and ordinance; for when imitated without authority, though with the best intention in the world, it merited the label of "idolatry." Abraham has described the nature of these idolatrous activities, which were impressive enough to convince his own father of their validity. He used the familiar motif of Facsimile I as an illustration of the rites; and this picture was found on the same roll of papyrus as our Book of Breathings, making it perfectly clear that the ordinances of the latter are among the

idolatrous rites to which he refers. Though unauthorized and corrupt (Abraham 1:5–14) they nonetheless began as an earnest and devout imitation of the order of "the first generations."[21]

Nibley goes on by pointing out that though the ancient Egyptians were the oldest civilization to use such rites, they are in no way unique.

Throughout the world we find such imitations and derivations, all corrupt and all unauthorized, but all quite instructive. Since the best and oldest of these are Egyptian, it is to them we turn for a check.[22]

And so, even with the limited information available in the scriptures, it becomes clear that the ordinances of salvation have existed from the beginning.

The Need for Priesthood Authority

The fifth article of faith reads:

We believe that a man must be called of God, by prophecy, and by the laying on of hands by those who are in authority, to preach the Gospel and administer in the ordinances thereof.

Why is there a need for priesthood and proper authority when the prayers of the faithful can summon the powers of heaven? As part of our progression toward godhood, we are permitted to act as God would act in the administration of the gospel. The ordination to the priesthood is a call to the Lord's work and the responsibility and power to act in his name to bless all nations. The bestowal of priesthood keys authorizes men to perform saving ordinances in the name of Jesus Christ that will be valid on earth and in heaven. As the ordinances of the gospel are essential to our progression in becoming like God, so priesthood authority is essential in the performance of those ordinances. Without the

power of the priesthood, exaltation, becoming like God, cannot
be achieved:

> And this greater priesthood administereth the gospel and
> holdeth the key of the mysteries of the kingdom, even the
> key of the knowledge of God.
>
> Therefore, in the ordinances thereof, the power of godli-
> ness is manifest.
>
> And without the ordinances thereof, and the authority of
> the priesthood, the power of godliness is not manifest unto
> men in the flesh;
>
> For without this no man can see the face of God, even the
> Father, and live. (D&C 84:19–22)

President Ezra Taft Benson has said:

> Priesthood transcends this mortal life. Its power and great-
> ness have been referred to by prophets—modern and ancient.
> We may have the priesthood without the Church, but never
> the Church without the priesthood.[23]

Joseph Smith and Oliver Cowdery could be baptized only
after the restoration of the Aaronic Priesthood through John the
Baptist, which priesthood holds the keys of baptism for the remission of sins, as is recorded in Doctrine and Covenants section 13:

> Upon you my fellow servants, in the name of Messiah I confer
> the Priesthood of Aaron, which holds they keys of the minis-
> tering of angels, and of the gospel of repentance, and of bap-
> tism by immersion for the remission of sins; and this shall
> never be taken again from the earth, until the sons of Levi do
> offer again an offering unto the Lord in righteousness.

Baptisms can be performed by priests bearing the Aaronic
Priesthood (D&C 20:46). The laying on of hands for the gift of the
Holy Ghost must be done by one holding the Melchizedek Priest-
hood (D&C 20:41, 43). The mysteries of the gospel, specifically

those revealed in the temple, are also administered through proper priesthood authority:

> The power and authority of the higher, or Melchizedek Priesthood, is to hold the keys of all the spiritual blessings of the church—
>
> To have the privilege of receiving the mysteries of the kingdom of heaven, to have the heavens opened unto them, to commune with the general assembly and church of the Firstborn, and to enjoy the communion and presence of God the Father, and Jesus the mediator of the new covenant. (D&C 107:18–19)

The restoration of all things necessarily included a restoration of the saving ordinances and the priesthood which has always been required to perform these holy rites. Amidst all the work surrounding the translation of the Book of Mormon and the organization of the Church, Joseph, Oliver Cowdery, and others did not lose sight of the importance of priesthood authority in bringing about God's purposes:

> We now became anxious to have that promise realized to us, which the angel that conferred upon us the Aaronic Priesthood had given us, viz., that provided we continued faithful, we should also have the Melchizedek Priesthood which holds the authority of the laying on of hands for the gift of the Holy Ghost.[24]

In a letter written 6 September 1842, and contained in D&C 128:19–22, Joseph recalled in terms of exhilaration and celebration those days thirteen years earlier:

> [T]he voice of Michael, the archangel; the voice of Gabriel, and of Raphael, and of divers angels, from Michael or Adam down to the present time, all declaring their dispensation, their rights, their keys, their honors, their majesty and glory, and the power of their priesthood...!

Brethren, shall we not go on in so great a cause: Go forward and not backward. Courage, brethren; and on, on to the victory! Let your hearts rejoice, and be exceedingly glad. Let the earth break forth into singing. (vv. 21–22)

This rejoicing was in part for priesthood authority and ordinances which would make possible the redemption of both the living and the dead.

Our Need for Temples

Some of the most profound doctrines revealed in the Doctrine and Covenants are those surrounding vicarious ordinance work for the dead. The Lord has said, concerning the necessity of various saving ordinances:

Verily, verily, I say unto thee, Except a man be born of water and of the Spirit, he cannot enter into the kingdom of God. (John 3:5)

In the celestial glory there are three heavens or degrees;
And in order to obtain the highest, a man must enter into this order of the priesthood [meaning the new and everlasting covenant of marriage];
And if he does not, he cannot obtain it. (D&C 131:1–3)

For whoso is faithful unto the obtaining these two priesthoods of which I have spoken, and the magnifying their calling....
They become...the elect of God.
And also all they who receive this priesthood receive me, saith the Lord;...And he that receiveth me receiveth my Father;
And he that receiveth my Father receiveth my Father's kingdom; therefore all that my Father hath shall be given unto him. (D&C 84:33–38)

Elder James E. Talmage noted that death does not excuse one from the responsibility for receiving these ordinances: "It follows as a necessary consequence that if any soul has failed, either through ignorance or neglect, to render obedience to these requirements, the obligation is not removed by death."[25]

In this, the dispensation of the fullness of times, all necessary ordinances have been made available in the temples.

The Bible makes passing reference to one vicarious ordinance, baptism for the dead, being performed in the early Christian church:

> Else what shall they do which are baptized for the dead, if the dead rise not at all? why are they then baptized for the dead? (1 Cor. 15:29)

This doctrine was expounded upon by the Prophet Joseph Smith in a letter which became, in part, section 128 of the Doctrine and Covenants, wherein the Prophet explains:

> You may think this order of things to be very particular; but let me tell you that it is only to answer the will of God, by conforming to the ordinance and preparation that the Lord ordained and prepared before the foundation of the world, for the salvation of the dead who should die without a knowledge of the gospel. . . .
>
> Now the great and grand secret of the whole matter, and the *summum bonum* of the whole subject that is lying before us, consists in obtaining the powers of the Holy Priesthood. For him to whom these keys are given there is no difficulty in obtaining a knowledge of facts in relation to the salvation of the children of men, both as well for the dead as for the living. . . .
>
> An now my dearly beloved brethren and sisters, let me assure you that these are principles in relation to the dead and the living that cannot be lightly passed over, as pertaining to our salvation. For their salvation is necessary and essential to our salvation, as Paul says concerning the fathers—that they without us cannot be made perfect—neither can we without our dead be made perfect. . . .

> ...It is sufficient to know, in this case, that the earth will
> be smitten with a curse unless there is a welding link of some
> kind or other between the fathers and the children, upon
> some subject or other—and behold what is that subject? It is
> the baptism for the dead.... (vv. 5, 11, 15, 18)

As baptism can be performed by proxy for the dead in temples set
apart and dedicated to that purpose, so can all other ordinances
required for the salvation of the living and the dead, including the
laying on of hands for the gift of the Holy Ghost, ordination to
the priesthood, the temple endowment, and the sealing of husbands, wives, and families for eternity.

Once we have completed our own temple work, our responsibilities for temple work continue as we return to stand as proxies
for the dead. As with all service to God and to our fellow beings,
there are attendant blessings. Franklin D. Richards of the First
Quorum of the Seventy spoke to the 156th Semiannual Conference about the importance of service in the temple: "Temple worship provides an opportunity to do ordinance work for our
kindred dead and for others, an opportunity for us to serve the
dead. This service is the source of eternal satisfaction."[26]

The importance of temples and the work performed in them is
also reflected in how the prophets have viewed them. Gordon B.
Hinckley reported Brigham Young's view of temples in a statement
showing affection and feeling:

> Temple building and the dedication of temples have gone on
> at such a pace in the last few years that some pay little atten-
> tion and feel it is of small significance.
>
>   But the adversary has not been unmindful of it. The
> building and dedication of these sacred edifices have been
> accompanied by a surge of opposition from a few enemies of
> the Church as well as criticism from a few within. This has
> brought to mind a statement of Brigham Young in 1861
> while the Salt Lake Temple was under construction. Evidently
> when someone with previous experience was asked to work
> on the Salt Lake Temple, he responded, "I do not like to do it,

for we never begin to build a Temple without the bells of hell beginning to ring."

To which Brigham Young replied, "I want to hear them ring again."[27]

John A. Widtsoe noted that "when Joseph Smith was commissioned to restore the Gospel and to re-establish the Church of Jesus Christ, the building of temples and temple worship became almost the first and the last issue of his life."[28] He continued: "A temple is a place where God will come; a place where the pure in heart shall see God."[29]

Conclusion

Covenants between ourselves and God can never be taken lightly. The scriptures speak in various terms about the deep and abiding regret that follows for those who make, then break, sacred commitments at the waters of baptism or within the walls of the temples. References to a "never-ending torment" or a drink "out of the cup of the wrath of God" (Mosiah 5:5) refer to the deep sorrow to come to those who cannot "abide in my covenant" and who are not "worthy of me" (D&C 98:15).

But scripture also reminds us of the great blessings to come to those who are mindful of God and his plan for his children:

But blessed are they who have kept the covenant and observed the commandment, for they shall obtain mercy. (D&C 54:6)

Verily I say unto you, blessed are you for receiving mine everlasting covenant, even the fulness of my gospel, sent forth unto the children of men, that they might have life and be made partakers of the glories which are to be revealed in the last days, as it was written by the prophets and apostles in days of old. (D&C 66:2)

Verily I say unto you, all among them who know their hearts are honest, and are broken, and their spirits contrite, and are willing to observe their covenants by sacrifice—yea, every

sacrifice which I, the Lord, shall command—they are accepted
of me. (D&C 97:8)

Each member of the Church of Jesus Christ of Latter-day
Saints should be taught to be mindful of the sacred nature of the
covenants he or she has made with God and to seek understanding of the ordinances that have been performed in his or her
behalf. Taking the sacrament each week should bring to mind the
broken body and the atoning blood of the Savior. The prayer over
the tokens of Christ's sacrifice reminds those who listen of the
covenants made at baptism: (1) a willingness to take upon them
the name of Christ, (2) a willingness to always remember him,
and (3) a willingness to keep his commandments. For honoring
these commitments, partakers are promised that "they may *always*
have his Spirit to be with them" (D&C 20:77; emphasis added). A
stabilizing and reassuring part of temple worship is to return
often to the temple to act as proxy for those who have died without receiving their own endowments while hearing again for
themselves the covenants they have made along with attendant
promises and giving ear to the many sweet utterings of the Spirit.

With the complexities of life and the designs of the adversary,
it is sometimes difficult to maintain a lively and heartening appreciation of the significance of the sacred and symbolic covenants
and ordinances that are to be an important part of our lives. We
become discouraged to find ourselves, even in the midst of performing our sacred duties, unable sometimes to muster enough
gratitude and appreciation for the great blessings they offer. But as
is always the case with God, he fills the gap between what is and
what should be if we are willing to call upon him. As was the case
with Joseph Smith in the Sacred Grove, so might it be with us as
we seek truths that will also be life altering for us: "If any of you
lack wisdom, let him ask of God, that giveth to all men liberally,
and upbraideth not; and it shall be given him" (James 1:5).

Some years ago, I was driving the Interstate to attend the sealing of a family in our ward that was taking place in the Salt Lake
Temple. My two sons and my husband, Carl, were driving on
ahead of me on their way to the Utah State Fairgrounds so that

my son Ben might sing with his children's choir as part of the entertainment for the fair. I was feeling stressed and torn, wishing Carl could be with me at the temple and that I could attend the fair to be with my family and watch my son perform.

As I was driving along, I began to pray silently that I might feel the significance of what was about to happen at the temple. Suddenly in my mind I could see my husband's car off to the side of the road, on its top, with smoke and fire all around it. I truly thought that I was seeing in my mind an actual event, and I was horrified to think that my little family was gone and that I had been left alone. I followed the side of the road ahead with my eyes, searching for signs of what I feared had actually happened. As I came to my exit, I realized that nothing had happened to my family. But something had happened to me. That day, as never before, I understood with my heart as well as with my mind the importance of the true Church and my membership in it, as well as the eternal nature of the ordinances performed therein.

Elder Boyd K. Packer said in a training meeting for members of the First Quorum of the Seventy:

> "If we have our ordinances performed, and if we have made the higher covenants, what other things we might have missed in this life here on earth really do not matter. We can even be sick and we can be afflicted and we can be poor and we can be ignorant of many things, but if we have received our ordinances and covenants and keep them, we have truly lived. If we do not have these sacred things anchored in our lives, whatever else we may have achieved in mortality will be of very little value in eternity."[30]

This is so because, as Jacob de Jager said at a BYU devotional:

> The ultimate purpose of these ordinances is *perfection,* because we have to learn how to reach and live in the presence of our Heavenly Father. We also have to learn the laws of heaven and how to obey them so we may learn how to become exalted.[31]

NOTES

CHAPTER EIGHT

1. Bruce R. McConkie, *Mormon Doctrine*, 2d ed. (Salt Lake City: Bookcraft, 1966), 548.

2. *Teachings of the Prophet Joseph Smith*, comp. Joseph Fielding Smith (Salt Lake City: Deseret Book Co., 1976), 297.

3. Ibid., 309.

4. Joseph Smith, *History of The Church of Jesus Christ of Latter-day Saints* (Salt Lake City: Deseret Book Co., 1974), 1:245; hereafter cited as *HC*.

5. Margaret McConkie Pope, "Exaltation," *Encyclopedia of Mormonism*, ed. Daniel H. Ludlow (New York: Macmillan, 1992), 1:479.

6. Vaughn J. Featherstone, in *Priesthood* (Salt Lake City: Deseret Book Co., 1981), 112.

7. S. Dilworth Young, in Brigham Young University Speeches of the Year, August 3, 1971 (Provo, Utah: University Publications, 1972), 6.

8. Heber C. Kimball, in "Temple Ordinances," *Encyclopedia of Mormonism*, 4:1444.

9. Marie Kartchner Hafen, "First Principles of the Gospel," *Encyclopedia of Mormonism*, 2:514.

10. McConkie, *Mormon Doctrine*, 70.

11. Hoyt W. Brewster, *Doctrine and Covenants Encyclopedia* (Salt Lake City: Bookcraft, Inc., 1988), 37.

12. McConkie, *Mormon Doctrine*, 73; emphasis added.

13. Allen Claire Rozsa, "Temple Ordinances," *Encyclopedia of Mormonism*, 4:1444.

14. John A. Widtsoe, "Temple Worship," *Utah Genealogical and Historical Magazine* 12 (April, 1921): 60–61, 62.

15. Rex E. Copper, "Symbols, Cultural and Artistic," *Encyclopedia of Mormonism*, 3:1431.

16. Brigham Young, in *Journal of Discourses* (Liverpool, England: Latter-Day Saints' Book Depot 1855–86), 18:303; hereafter cited as *JD*.

17. Heber C. Kimball, in *JD,* 10:240–41. In a footnote in *The Mortal Messiah* (Salt Lake City: Deseret Book Co., 1979), 1:492, Bruce R. McConkie writes: "President Joseph Fielding Smith suggests that Peter, James, and John received their endowments from Jesus on the Mount of Transfiguration. (*Doctrines of Salvation* 2:165.)"

18. Harold B. Lee, *Stand Ye in Holy Places,* (Salt Lake City: Deseret Book Co., 1976), 42.

19. John A. Widtsoe, "Temple Worship," 52–54.

20. Hugh Nibley, *The Message of the Joseph Smith Papyri* (Salt Lake City: Deseret Book Co., 1975), 14.

21. Ibid.

22. Ibid.

23. Ezra Taft Benson, *The Teachings of Ezra Taft Benson* (Salt Lake City: Bookcraft, 1988), 215.

24. *HC,* 1:60, including footnote.

25. James E. Talmage, *The House of the Lord* (Salt Lake City: Deseret Book Co., 1968), 64.

26. Franklin D. Richards, *Ensign,* November 1986, 71.

27. Gordon B. Hinckley, *Ensign,* November, 1985, 54.

28. Widtsoe, "Temple Worship," 53.

29. Ibid., 55.

30. Boyd K. Packer, in Jacob de Jager, "Perfecting the Saints," *Brigham Young University 1988–89 Devotional and Fireside Speeches* (Provo, Utah: University Publications, 1989), 89.

31. de Jager, "Perfecting the Saints," 93.

THE DESTINY OF THE EARTH

JAMES A. CARVER

IN OUR HIGHLY mobile world, many families will move several times during their lifetime. Without question most humans are concerned about where they are going to live. There always seems to be an air of excitement about new surroundings. As we contemplate a move, we take out the maps and study the location of our new home. We look at the geographical and geological setting, the neighboring communities, the schools, businesses, industry, etc., picturing in our minds what our new home will look like. If the move involves a different culture or environment, we may even read a few books to better prepare ourselves.

Our feelings must have been similar when as premortal spirits we learned we were going to be sent to planet Earth, located in the Milky Way Galaxy, the third planet from the sun. Did we know then that there were millions, even billions of earths like our earth? Did we realize that of these billions of worlds, our world would be different? This world would be special in a very unique way.

In his book *Extraterrestrial Civilizations,* Isaac Asimov, the late, famous science and science fiction writer, tries to determine the number of inhabitable planets that could exist in our galaxy where a "technological civilization" like our own might have developed. Starting with the figure of 300 billion stars in the Milky Way, he gradually works up to the necessary conditions for life like ours, limiting in each step those stars that do not qualify, until he arrives at the figure of 390 million planets in our galaxy on which a "technological civilization" could have developed.[1]

Asimov also suggests that there are a "billion trillion" stars in the observable universe, and "up to a billion galaxies can be detected by modern telescopes stretching out to distances of a billion light years."[2]

With greater certainty, the Lord proclaimed to Moses, "Worlds without number have I created; and I also created them for mine own purpose; and by the Son I created them, which is mine Only Begotten" (Moses 1:33).

Moses then learned an even more startling truth when the Lord said:

> For behold, there are many worlds that have passed away by the word of my power. And there are many that now stand, and innumerable are they unto man; but all things are numbered unto me, for they are mine and I know them. (Moses 1:35)

In a prior verse (v. 32) the Lord makes it clear that the "word of my power" is his "Only Begotten Son."

Section 76 of the Doctrine and Covenants teaches this same concept in verses 22–24. However, the poetic version of this great revelation, written by Joseph Smith at the request of W. W. Phelps, is even more emphatic:

> And I heard a great voice bearing
>   record from heaven,
> He's the Saviour and Only Begotten
>   of God;
> By him, of him, and through him,
>   the worlds were all made,
> Even all that careen in the heavens
>   so broad.
> Whose inhabitants, too, from the first
>   to the last,
> Are sav'd by the very same Saviour
>   of ours;

And, of course, are begotten God's
daughters and sons
By the very same truths and the
very same powers.[3]

How marvelous and exciting it must have been to us to know that the infinite Atonement for these "worlds without number" would take place on our earth. But why was this earth selected for this wondrous destiny? A possible answer is found in the scriptures.

The antediluvian prophet Enoch saw in vision the wickedness of this earth. He was told by the Lord that "among all the workmanship of mine hands there has not been so great wickedness as among thy brethren" (Moses 7:36). Jacob, the son of Lehi, told his people that "Christ... should come among the Jews, among those who are the more wicked part of the world;... and there is none other nation on earth that would crucify their God" (2 Ne. 10:3).

Brigham Young's view on this matter was in harmony with these scriptures:

I suppose that God never organized an earth and peopled it that was ever reduced to a lower state of darkness, sin and ignorance than this. I suppose this is one of lowest kingdoms that ever the Lord Almighty created, and on that account is capable of becoming exalted to be one of the highest kingdoms that has ever had an exaltation in all the eternities. In proportion as it has been reduced so it will be exalted, with that proportion of its inhabitants who in their humiliation have cleaved to righteousness and acknowledged God in all things. In proportion to our fall through sin, so shall we be exalted in the presence of our Father and God through Jesus Christ and by living the righteousness of his Gospel.[4]

Since this earth was selected as the site for the Atonement, it was necessary that this world become wicked enough to put their Messiah to death. In the Book of Acts, Paul said that God "hath made of one blood all nations of men for to dwell on all the face of the earth, and hath determined the times before appointed, and the bounds of their habitation" (17:26). God has controlled the balance of wickedness and righteousness on the earth through this principle of foreordination, allowing secret combinations, Master Mahans, and Gadianton robbers to organize their insidious groups to attack God's kingdom whenever it has been upon the earth. Thus, he has prepared this earth for the events that would need to transpire in order to bring about the infinite Atonement and the redemption of the earth.

All worlds are special and important in God's plan of salvation. But the "morning stars" who shouted for joy concerning this world had an extra reason for their joy. Their world would be a hazard, but what a privilege! The infinite Atonement would take place here.

The Earth before the Fall

Very little has been written in scripture or spoken by modern-day prophets about the creation of the earth as a spirit entity. Bruce R. McConkie has said, "There is no revealed account of the spirit creation."[6] He wrote:

> We may suppose, as is the case with all other forms of life, that this earth was created first as a spirit, and that it was thereafter clothed upon with tangible, physical element. We know that the Creators planned all things incident to the creation in advance; and that all things were created "spiritually, before they were naturally upon the face of the earth."
>
> Following its physical creation, the earth was pronounced good.[7]

Brigham Young instructed the Saints that "when the earth was framed and brought into existence and man was placed upon it, it was near the throne of our Father in heaven.... [B]ut when man fell, the earth fell into space, and took up its abode in this planetary system, and the sun became our light."[8] Moreover, Brigham Young indicated that "when it [the earth] is celestialized it will go back into the presence of God, where it was first framed."[9]

President John Taylor likewise proposed that the earth "had fled and fallen from where it was organized near the planet Kolob."[10] And when Abraham spoke of the earth's reckoning of time, he indicated that the earth's time "was after the Lord's time, which was after the time of Kolob; for as yet the Gods had not appointed unto Adam his reckoning" (Abr. 5:13).

This seems to indicate that the premortal earth must have been associated with the great Kolob, which was "the first creation, nearest to the celestial, or residence of God,"[11] and reckoned its time after God's time.

The Mortal Earth

After its creation, the physical earth became mortal through the fall of Adam and Eve. Elder Bruce R. McConkie stated, "This earth was created as a living thing, and the Lord ordained that it should live a celestial law."[12] Hence, like all humankind, the earth must become a mortal sphere, be born of the water and of the spirit, die as we must die, and be resurrected to abide by a celestial law.

As a mortal earth, it became subjected to death and sin. It was baptized by water in the days of Noah and it will be confirmed by fire and the Holy Ghost at the Millennium, when it receives its paradisiacal glory. At the conclusion of the Millennium the earth will be resurrected and glorified to become a celestial kingdom for its inhabitants.

The Lord told the Prophet Joseph Smith that

> the earth abideth the law of a celestial kingdom, for it filleth the measure of its creation, and transgresseth not the law—
>
> Wherefore, it shall be sanctified; yea, notwithstanding it shall die, it shall be quickened again, and shall abide the power by which it is quickened, and the righteous shall inherit it. (D&C 88:25–26)

Mortality shall then take on immortality, and the fallen earth shall prove itself worthy of exaltation and eventual celestial glory. But first it must receive its paradisiacal glory.

The Paradisiacal Earth

The tenth article of faith states:

> We believe in the literal gathering of Israel and in the restoration of the Ten Tribes; that Zion (the New Jerusalem) will be built upon the American continent; that Christ will reign personally upon the earth; and, that the earth will be renewed and receive its paradisiacal glory.

When Jesus took Peter, James, and John up on the Mount of Transfiguration, apparently he showed these apostles the future transfiguration of the earth. Referring to this event, modern revelation tells us:

> Nevertheless, he that endureth in faith and doeth my will, the same shall overcome, and shall receive an inheritance upon the earth when the day of transfiguration shall come;
> When the earth shall be transfigured, even according to the pattern which was shown unto mine apostles upon the mount; of which account the fulness ye have not yet received. (D&C 63:20-21)

Doctrine and Covenants section 101 follows closely the events found in chapter 15 of the book of Revelation, but describes them in greater and clearer detail. The events detailed are those leading to the battle of Armageddon and the cleansing of the earth of its wickedness. The Doctrine and Covenants states:

> And prepare for the revelation which is to come, when the veil of the covering of my temple, in my tabernacle, which hideth the earth, shall be taken off, and all flesh shall see me together.
> And every corruptible thing, both of man, or of the beasts of the field, or of the fowls of the heavens, or of the fish of the sea, that dwells upon all the face of the earth, shall be consumed;

And also that of element shall melt with fervent heat; and all things shall become new, that my knowledge and glory may dwell upon all the earth. (101:23–25)

Some of the Brethren have taught that this paradisiacal glory will come at the end of the Millennium,[13] while others have indicated that it would take place at the beginning of the Millennium, after the wicked have been destroyed.[14] Section 101 of the Doctrine and Covenants suggests that this latter interpretation is correct. On the other hand, section 29 might favor the former interpretation:

And again, verily, verily, I say unto you that when the thousand years are ended, and men again begin to deny their God, then will I spare the earth but for a little season;

And the end shall come, and the heaven and the earth shall be consumed and pass away, and there shall be a new heaven and a new earth.

For all old things shall pass away, and all things shall become new, even the heaven and the earth, and all the fulness thereof. (vv. 22–24)

It seems to me that both interpretations could be generally acceptable, seeing as how a metamorphosis of the earth is to take place both at the beginning and at the end of the Millennium. However, the first change will be to the paradisiacal, or terrestrial, order; the second change will be to the highest, or celestial, order.

Whichever interpretation one chooses, the Doctrine and Covenants is very clear concerning the transfiguration of the earth at the beginning of the Millennium:

Wherefore, be not deceived, but continue in steadfastness, looking forth for the heavens to be shaken, and the earth to tremble and to reel to and fro as a drunken man, and for the valleys to be exalted, and for the mountains to be made low, and for the rough places to become smooth—and all this when the angel shall sound his trumpet. (49:23)

And again:

That thy church may come forth out of the wilderness of darkness, and shine forth fair as the moon, clear as the sun, and terrible as an army with banners;

And be adorned as a bride for that day when thou shalt unveil the heavens, and cause the mountains to flow down at thy presence, and the valleys to be exalted, the rough places made smooth; that thy glory may fill the earth. (109:73-74)

One of the more fascinating accounts of the earth's transfiguration is found in section 133.

For behold, the Lord God hath sent forth the angel crying through the midst of heaven, saying: Prepare ye the way of the Lord, and make his paths straight, for the hour of his coming is nigh—

When the Lamb shall stand upon Mount Zion, and with him a hundred and forty-four thousand, having his Father's name written on their foreheads.

Wherefore, prepare ye for the coming of the Bridegroom; go ye, go ye out to meet him.

For behold, he shall stand upon the mount of Olivet, and upon the mighty ocean, even the great deep, and upon the islands of the sea, and upon the land of Zion.

And he shall utter his voice out of Zion, and he shall speak from Jerusalem, and his voice shall be heard among all people;

And it shall be a voice as the voice of many waters, and as the voice of a great thunder, which shall break down the mountains, and the valleys shall not be found.

He shall command the great deep, and it shall be driven back into the north countries, and the islands shall become one land;

And the land of Jerusalem and the land of Zion shall be turned back into their own place, and the earth shall be like as it was in the days before it was divided.

And the Lord, even the Savior, shall stand in the midst of his people, and shall reign over all flesh.

And they who are in the north countries shall come in remembrance before the Lord; and their prophets shall hear his voice, and shall no longer stay themselves; and they shall smite the rocks, and the ice shall flow down at their presence.

And an highway shall be cast up in the midst of the great deep.

Their enemies shall become a prey unto them,

And in the barren deserts there shall come forth pools of living water; and the parched ground shall no longer be a thirsty land.

And they shall bring forth their rich treasures unto the children of Ephraim, my servants.

And the boundaries of the everlasting hills shall tremble at their presence. (vv. 17–31)

Verse 24 above shows that the Zion of Jerusalem and the Zion of America will return to their former places. Joseph Smith noted this returning of the two Zions and indicated that they would become contiguous:

There shall be famine and pestilence, and earthquake in divers places; and the prophets have declared that the valleys should rise; that the mountains should be laid low; that a great earthquake should be, in which the sun should become black as sackcloth of hair, and the moon turn into blood; yea, the Eternal God hath declared that the great deep shall roll back into the north countries and that the land of Zion and the land of Jerusalem shall be joined together, as they were before they were divided in the days of Peleg. No wonder the mind starts at the sound of the last days.[15]

If one considers the dimensions of the New Jerusalem as recorded in Revelation 26(which indicates the city as being approximately 1380 miles in length and breadth), one can see how the "land of Jerusalem" might be "joined together" with the Zion of

America (see Rev. 21:16). Independence, Missouri, is approximately 1300 miles from the Atlantic coast. Thus, if the land of Israel became contiguous, or "joined together," with the Atlantic seaboard, the two centers of Zion, Jerusalem and Independence, would be approximately 1380 miles apart.

Some have questioned whether or not the New Jerusalem is the same as the Old Jerusalem. Joseph Smith felt it necessary to clarify to the Saints the difference between the two Jerusalems and to identify the New Jerusalem as the city of Zion that was to be established in America. In a letter to the Saints, Joseph taught:

> Now many will feel disposed to say, that this New Jerusalem spoken of is the Jerusalem that was built by the Jews on the eastern continent. But you will see, from Revelation XXI: 2, there was a New Jerusalem coming down from God out of heaven, adorned as a bride for her husband; that after this, the Revelator was caught away in the Spirit, to a great and high mountain, and saw the great and holy city descending out of heaven from God. Now there are two cities spoken of here. As everything cannot be had in so narrow a compass as a letter, I shall say with brevity, that there is a New Jerusalem to be established on this continent, and also Jerusalem shall be rebuilt on the eastern continent.[16]

Orson Pratt taught that the two Jerusalems would be caught up into heaven at the end of the Millennium:

> As the earth passes through its great last change, two of its principal cities—the Old Jerusalem of the eastern continent, and the New Jerusalem of the western continent, will be preserved from the general conflagration, being caught up into heaven. These two cities, with all their glorified throng, will descend upon the redeemed earth, being the grand capitals of the new creation.[17]

The question is often asked, will the resurrected Saints live upon the earth during the Millennium? Won't it be too crowded to have all of the resurrected Saints and the millions of mortal Saints living on the earth? In addition, there will be the great numbers of terrestrial beings; and since death and the resurrection will take but a moment, the numbers will multiply rapidly.

Joseph stated that it was his opinion that the resurrected Saints "will not probably dwell upon the earth, but will visit it when they please, or when it is necessary to govern it."[18]

The Celestial Earth

John the Revelator saw that at the end of the Millennium Satan and his angels would be loosed from their prison to try to deceive the world one last time:

> And when the thousand years are expired, Satan shall be loosed out of his prison,
> And shall go out to deceive the nations which are in the four quarters of the earth, Gog and Magog, to gather them together to battle: the number of whom is as the sand of the sea. (Rev. 20:7–8)

President Joseph Fielding Smith commented that those mortals who are tested in this last effort of Satan to deceive will become sons of perdition if they follow Satan, because of the great knowledge they will have acquired during the Millennium.[19]

President Smith also submitted that at the end of the world, the terrestrial inhabitants will be taken away from this earth and assigned to their terrestrial world. The earth will then be celestialized and become like unto the sun. He then quoted Brigham Young as saying "that this earth when it is celestialized will shine like the sun, and why not."[20] President Smith believed that "the great stars that we see, including our sun, are celestial worlds."[21]

The apostle John saw the glorified earth as needing no sun or moon to give it light. Its source of light would be the Lamb of God: "And the city had no need of the sun, neither of the moon, to shine in it: for the glory of God did lighten it, and the Lamb is the light thereof" (Rev. 21:23). In addition, there would be "no night," nor any need for a closed gate (Rev. 21:25). In the next chapter, to reinforce this concept, John again says: "And there shall be no night there; and they need no candle, neither light of the sun; for the Lord God giveth them light: and they shall reign for ever and ever" (22:5).

Orson Hyde interpreted the scriptures and words of the prophets as indicating that this earth, when celestialized, would be

> removed out of its present orbit. Where will it go to? God says He will gather all things into one; then He will gather the earth likewise, and all that is in it, in one. The gathering will be upon a larger scale in time to come; for by and by the stars of Heaven will fall. Which way will they go? They will rally to a grand centre, and there will be one grand constellation of worlds.
>
> The earth will have to be removed from its place, and reel to and fro like a drunkard. The fact is, it has got to leave the old track in which it has roamed in time passed, and beat a new track... the earth... will come in contact with the rays of other suns that illuminate other spheres; their rays will dazzle our earth, and make the glory of God rest upon it, so that there will be no more night there.[22]

Brigham Young said that "when all this is done, and the Savior has presented the earth to his Father," then it will be "placed in the cluster of the celestial kingdoms."[23] Joseph Smith prophesied that "this earth will be rolled back into the presence of God, and crowned with celestial glory."[24] All this seems to indicate that perhaps this earth will return to the orbit it maintained before it fell, in the proximity of Kolob, where its revolutions will be in synchronization with God's time, or where, as the scriptures say, "time will be no longer."[25]

It is possible that this reckoning of time will change at the beginning of the Millennium, as section 88 verse 110 of the Doctrine and Covenants clearly states that this event precedes Satan being bound for a thousand years.

However, regardless of just when these things take place, the Lord is very clear in stating that

> this earth, in its sanctified and immortal state, will be made like unto crystal and will be a Urim and Thummim to the inhabitants who dwell thereon, whereby all things pertaining to an inferior kingdom, or all kingdoms of a lower order, will be manifest to those who dwell on it; and this earth will be Christ's. (D&C 130:9)

God's works are eternal. Through his plan of salvation we become a part of God's works. Those who are worthy and become perfect as he is perfect[26] will continue his works. Orson Pratt put this in simple terms for all to understand:

> [T]he fact is, man will continue to multiply and fill up this creation, inasmuch as it is not filled up by the resurrected Saints after it is made new.
>
> And what will we do when this is filled up? Why, we will make more worlds, and swarm out like bees from the old hive, and prepare new locations. And when a farmer has culti-vated his farm, and raised numerous children, so that the space is beginning to be too strait for them he will say, "My sons, yonder is plenty of matter, go and organize a world, and people it; and you shall have laws to govern you, and you shall understand and comprehend through your experience the same things that we knew."[27]

Conclusion

In this chapter I have attempted to trace the destiny of this earth as it has been revealed in the sacred scriptures and to modern-day prophets. Still, there may be more questions than answers. How-ever, the essentials are clear, and we can be certain about the earth's ultimate destiny and what we must do as individuals to share in this destiny.

As we become ready, and it is appropriate, more knowledge and answers to questions will come. But without any apology, we know this earth to be sacred and special, perhaps above all others. When we have fulfilled our mortal probation we can look forward to obtaining a comprehensive understanding of this earth and the heavens. When we are each given a white stone, if we are worthy, we will be able to discern those things "pertaining to a higher order of kingdoms."[28]

While we await that great day we can contemplate the Lord's promise, that when he shall come he shall reveal all things—

> Things which have passed, and hidden things which no man knew, things of the earth, by which it was made, and the purpose and the end thereof—
>
> Things most precious, things that are above, and things that are beneath, things that are in the earth, and upon the earth, and in heaven." (D&C 101 32–34)

In addition, the Lord has said that the time will come when

> nothing shall be withheld, whether there be one God or many gods, they shall be manifest.
>
> All thrones and dominions, principalities and powers, shall be revealed and set forth upon all who have endured valiantly for the gospel of Jesus Christ.
>
> And also, if there be bounds set to the heavens or to the seas, or to the dry land, or to the sun, moon, or stars—
>
> All the times of their revolutions, all the appointed days, months, and years, and all the days of their days, months, and years, and all their glories, laws, and set times, shall be revealed in the days of the dispensation of the fulness of times—
>
> According to that which was ordained in the midst of the Council of the Eternal God of all other gods before this world was, that should be reserved unto the finishing and the end thereof, when every man shall enter into his eternal presence and into his immortal rest. (D&C 121:28–32)

To a Latter-day Saint, this earth should be sacred. As a result, Latter-day Saints should want to take good care of it. It is their immediate home, and it can be their eternal home. The earth is not just matter, but living matter. It has an interminable destiny, a destiny that is set and certain. And our individual destiny and future residency on this earth will depend upon our personal obedience to Jesus Christ, its creator.

NOTES

CHAPTER NINE

1. Isaac Asimov, *Extraterrestrial Civilizations* (New York: Crown Publishers, 1979), 92–174.

2. Ibid., 91.

3. *Millennial Star* 4:49–55, 1843. Also in Bruce R. McConkie, *Mormon Doctrine* (Salt Lake City: Bookcraft, 1958), 63.

4. Brigham Young, in *Journal of Discourses* (Liverpool, England: Latter-Day Saints' Book Depot, 1855–85), 10:175; hereafter cited as *JD*.

5. Ibid., 19:293.

6. McConkie, *Mormon Doctrine,* 158.

7. Ibid., 195.

8. Brigham Young, in *JD,* 17:143

9. Ibid., 9:317

10. N. B. Lundwall, comp., *The Vision* (Salt Lake City: Bookcraft, n.d.), 146.

11. Abraham, Explanation to Facsimile No. 2, Fig. 1.

12. McConkie, *Mormon Doctrine,* 195.

13. George Q. Cannon, *Gospel Truth* (Salt Lake City: Deseret Book Co., 1974), 1:91.

14. Joseph Fielding Smith, *Doctrines of Salvation* (Salt Lake City: Bookcraft, 1954), 1:84–85.

15. Ibid., 1:85

16. Joseph Smith, *Teachings of the Prophet Joseph Smith,* comp. Joseph Fielding Smith (Salt Lake City: Deseret Book Co., 1976), 86; hereafter cited as *TPJS.*

17. Orson Pratt, in *JD,* 1:332.

18. *TPJS,* 268.

19. Smith, *Doctrines of Salvation,* 1:87.

20. Ibid., 1:88–89.

21. Ibid., 1:87.

22. Orson Hyde, in *JD,* 1:130.

23. Brigham Young, in *JD*, 17:117

24. *TPJS*, 181.

25. Rev. 10:6; D&C 84:100; 88:110.

26. Matt. 5:48; 3 Ne. 12:48.

27. Orson Pratt, in *JD*, 1:294.

28. Rev. 2:17; D&C 130:10–11. The celestial kingdom itself is a Urim and Thummim which will manifest "all things pertaining to an inferior kingdom, or all kingdoms of a lower order" (D&C 130:9).

The Future Conditions of Man

After the

Resurrection and the Judgment

Richard H. Berrett

In old testament times, Job asked a profound and universal question: "If a man die, shall he live again?" (Job 14:14). Without doubt, there has been no subject in history that has caused more concern and interest to each and every person than death and what would follow. Virtually all world religions attempt to answer this query, and, though they have varying opinions, all reflect the basic desire of humankind for a better world after this life is past.

In the Christian world the affirmation of the continuing existence of humankind resounds in the startling announcement of the angel that first Easter morning, "He is not here, but is risen" (Luke 24:6). Through the shedding of the precious blood of Christ in Gethsemane and on the cross of Calvary, the promised resurrection of all the children of God became an undeniable reality, and each person may have his or her sins remitted by obedience to the principles and ordinances of the gospel of Jesus Christ, enabling all who become worthy to enter into the presence of God. The Lord has stated: "For behold, this is my work and my glory—to bring to pass the immortality and eternal life of man" (Moses 1:39).

The prophet Alma was given to know that the spirits of all people, upon death in the flesh, pass into a world of departed spirits. The righteous are received into a state of rest and peace called paradise, while the unrighteous are received into a spirit prison. The Savior, during the period between his death on the cross and his resurrection, visited the spirits shut up in prison and opened the way for his gospel to be taught to them. President Joseph F. Smith, in a remarkable vision, was shown that Jesus organized the spirits of the righteous and opened the way for his gospel to be preached (D&C 138). The great latter-day work going on in the temples allows for the earthly ordinances of baptism, the endowment, and celestial marriage to be performed for those who are dead. This work is ongoing at the present and will continue through the great Millenium to come.

Once all of God's children have had the opportunity to hear the gospel of Christ and receive the saving ordinances, then will come the great day of resurrection and judgment. At this time, those who are worthy will inherit the promised blessings of eternal life. Those who have rejected the gospel or who are not worthy of exaltation will receive a lesser reward. In this chapter, we will examine the state of all the children of God following the day of resurrection and judgment.

Most of the various Christian denominations affirm that Jesus offers the blessings of heaven to the righteous and punishment to the wicked. Beyond this, however, much misunderstanding remains among the various denominations of Christianity. The simple doctrine of the passage of all who have lived from this life into a place of departed spirits—a "state of rest and peace" for the righteous and a place of remorse and sorrow, called "hell" or "spirit prison"—was mistaken as the *final* abode of humankind. What the Christian world views as "heaven" is a conglomerate of statements about both the spirit world and eternal life in the celestial kingdom, while "hell" is a composite of spirit prison and the final sufferings of those called "sons of perdition."

By adding pagan superstition and Greek philosophy with uninspired speculation and tradition, Christianity after the apostles built a fearful picture of judgments, hellfire, and eternal torment.

The optimistic anticipation of death by the early Christians was replaced with fear and dread, and, lacking revelation and a firm testimony of the joys hereafter, the formulators of Christian thought sought answers in the empty reasonings of philosophy. As Hugh Nibley put it:

One of the most striking features of primitive Christianity was its constant and hardheaded insistence on the nearness and reality of the other side. A pagan critic of the early Christians remarked with wonder and annoyance that "they think nothing of present torments, but worry about what is to happen hereafter; and while they dread perishing *after* death, they don't fear dying here at all, so completely taken in are they by the false hope of living hereafter." In *Androcles and the Lion,* George Bernard Shaw attempted to depict the odd and intriguing phenomenon of people who did not fear death; he saw that the contrast of this point of view with the normal one is so great as to create in itself hilarious situations; he saw that without any irreverence, there was something perfectly delightful in a religion which could view the life to come without any of the somber Mumbo Jumbo of cult practices; and he also realized that in the primitive Christian church he found a view of death unlike that of the later Christian churches.

Now there is nothing unusual in a belief in an afterlife—as St. Augustine observed, it was a view quite commonly held by pagan philosophers. What set the early Christians apart was that they were not at all vague about the business. Just as for them the charismatic gifts—prophecy, tongues, healings, etc.—were real, literal, and concrete, so the life to come was not an abstraction or a rational necessity, but a thing to be experienced. As long as we find living prophets in the church, these things cannot be thought of as anything but real; they are all part of the same picture and have the same explanation—a living bond with the heavens, a continuous intercourse between this world and the other. And when the gift of prophecy departs, we witness at the same time the cessation of the other heavenly gifts, and with that the church changes its views of the other world, becoming perplexed and uncertain about things which it once knew so well.[1]

The long night of spiritual darkness was shattered in 1820 by the appearance of the Father and the Son to the boy prophet, Joseph Smith. Their very presence bore witness to the reality of the world beyond and the promises of the gospel of Jesus Christ. The call given to young Joseph began a long process of visions, revelations, and other divine manifestations that led to the restoration of the Church of Jesus Christ and an unfolding of the mysteries of God. Those who joined the Church in the beginning had little of what might be thought of today as "Mormon" doctrine, since the distinctive teachings of the gospel were unfolded "line upon line" over a period of several years (and indeed, this is an ongoing process today, as there continue to be living prophets and seers within the Church). Those early converts were convinced that Joseph had seen the Father and the Son, that he was in reality the Lord's prophet, that heavenly messengers had restored the doctrines and ordinances of the original Church of Jesus Christ established in the meridian of time, and that the priesthood of God with all its empowering keys was once again upon the earth so that the saving ordinances of baptism and receiving the gift of the Holy Ghost were theirs. The Spirit bore witness to this simple message of the early missionaries, and the converts began to join in greater and greater numbers.

However, God was only beginning the great flood of knowledge that was to be poured out on the heads of the Latter-day Saints. Within two months after the organization of the Church, God commanded his young prophet to begin a new "translation" of the Bible, an endeavor that would occupy Joseph off and on to the day of his martyrdom. Joseph's inquisitive mind, his interest in the original languages of the Bible, his experience in translation, and his love of the scriptures all combined with his ability to learn the mind and will of the Lord to assist him in his effort to restore the original thought and intent of the biblical writers. In retrospect, however, it appears that the reason God gave the command was not so much that the world needed a new translation, but that the inquiry and search would lead Joseph to seek revelation on many topics and scriptural problems that would arise through the process. A perusal of the Doctrine and Covenants illustrates that many of the most important and definitive revelations were given as a result of questions that arose during the Prophet's work on the translation.

Persecution pushed the fledgling church from western New York to the Kirtland area in northern Ohio. In the winter of 1832, Joseph and Emma were living with the John Johnson family in Hiram, while Joseph and his scribe, Sidney Rigdon, worked on the translation of the Bible. Joseph says during this period of intense Bible study:

> Upon my return from the Amherst conference, I resumed the translation of the scriptures. From sundry revelations which had been received, it was apparent that many important points touching the salvation of man had been taken from the Bible, or lost before it was compiled. It appeared self-evident from what truths were left, that if God rewarded every one according to the deeds done in the body, the term "Heaven," as intended for the Saints' eternal home, must include more kingdoms than one.[2]

On February 16, Joseph and Sidney were working on the fifth chapter of the Gospel of John and were pondering on the twenty-eighth and twenty-ninth verses. They felt impressed that the twenty-ninth verse should read "resurrection of the just" and "resurrection of the unjust" instead of "resurrection of life" and "resurrection of damnation" as recorded in the King James Version. Joseph states: "Now this caused us to marvel, for it was given unto us of the Spirit. And while we meditated upon these things, the Lord touched the eyes of our understandings and they were opened, and the glory of the Lord shone round about" (D&C 76:18–19). The resulting vision bestowed upon them was perhaps the most transcendent and beautiful of all the great and marvelous manifestations of the latter days and is recorded as section 76 of the Doctrine and Covenants.

This great vision of the glories of the eternal realms burst the shackles of centuries of misunderstanding, fear, and dread about God's great plan of salvation and the final state of his children. The revelation was given in several parts: (1) a glorious vision of the Father and Son on their eternal thrones, surrounded by numberless hosts of angels worshipping them; (2) the rebellion and fall of Lucifer and his angels from the presence of God in the beginning of the world, and the sufferings of those who become sons of perdition; (3) the glory of the celestial kingdom of God—compared to the brightness of the sun—and those who chose to obey the gospel of Jesus Christ; (4) the terrestrial kingdom, composed of the honorable and good; and (5) the telestial kingdom, made up of those who lived unworthily and never accepted the truths of the gospel. Thus, in this one great vision, the Lord gave to his prophet and scribe a view extending from the premortal existence to the realms of eternal glory, unveiling truths that had eluded the Christian thinkers for centuries. Of this revelation the Prophet stated, "Nothing could be more pleasing to the Saints upon the order of the kingdom of the Lord than the light which burst upon the world through the foregoing vision."[3]

The Sons of Perdition

Considering the state of each person who has lived on the earth in ascending order as they are discussed in 76th section, the first are a group who are made up of the Saints of God who, having received a fullness of understanding and partaking of God's power, deliberately choose to deny the truth and to war against the Lamb.

And we saw a vision of the sufferings of those with whom he [Satan] made war and overcame, for thus came the voice of the Lord unto us:

Thus saith the Lord concerning all those who know my power, and have been made partakers thereof, and suffered themselves through the power of the devil to be overcome, and to deny the truth and defy my power—

They are they who are the sons of perdition, of whom I say that it had been better for them never to have been born;

For they are vessels of wrath, doomed to suffer the wrath of God, with the devil and his angels in eternity;

Concerning whom I have said there is no forgiveness in this world nor in the world to come—

Having denied the Holy Spirit after having received it, and having denied the Only Begotten Son of the Father, having crucified him unto themselves and put him to an open shame.

These are they who shall go away into the lake of fire and brimstone, with the devil and his angels—

And . . . the only ones who shall not be redeemed in the due time of the Lord, after the sufferings of his wrath. (D&C 76:30–38)

The Prophet Joseph Smith further explained the nature of the sin against the Holy Ghost and those who would become sons of perdition:

All sins shall be forgiven, except the sin against the Holy Ghost; for Jesus will save all except the sons of perdition. What must a man do to commit the unpardonable sin? He must receive the Holy Ghost, have the heavens opened unto him, and know God, and then sin against him. After a man has sinned against the Holy Ghost, there is no repentance for him. He has got to say that the sun does not shine while he sees it; he has got to deny Jesus Christ when the heavens have been opened unto him, and to deny the plan of salvation with his eyes open to the truth of it; and from that time he begins to be an enemy. This is the case with many apostates of the Church of Jesus Christ of Latter-day Saints.

When a man begins to be an enemy to this work, he hunts me, he seeks to kill me, and never ceases to thirst for my blood. He gets the spirit of the devil—the same spirit that

they had who crucified the Lord of Life—the same spirit that
sins against the Holy Ghost. You cannot save such persons;
you cannot bring them to repentance; they make open war,
like the devil, and awful is the consequence.[4]

The Lord added additional understanding in a revelation
given in 1843:

The blasphemy against the Holy Ghost, which shall not be
forgiven in the world nor out of the world, is in that ye commit murder wherein ye shed innocent blood, and assent unto
my death, after ye have received my new and everlasting
covenant, saith the Lord God; and he that abideth not this
law can in nowise enter into my glory, but shall be damned,
saith the Lord. (D&C 132:27)

The phrase "the shedding of innocent blood" was explained
by President Joseph Fielding Smith as follows:

Shedding innocent blood is spoken of in the scriptures as
consenting to the death of Jesus Christ and putting him to
shame. For those who have had the witness of the Holy Ghost,
fighting with wicked hate against his authorized servants is
the same, for if this is done to them, it is also done against
him. For men who have had the light of the Holy Ghost to
turn away and fight the truth with murderous hate, and those
who are authorized to proclaim it, there is no forgiveness in
this world neither in the world to come.[5]

From the previous references, some assumptions can be
made: Most likely, relatively few of God's children will qualify to
be included in this group because so few have received a fullness
of the gospel through the Holy Ghost; also, the conditions generally described as *hell* in sectarian Christianity, to which many
would condemn the majority of humankind, refer only to this
relatively small group. In addition, these make up the group who
suffer the "second death" referred to in the scriptures, that is, the

banishment from the presence of God that will come to those who are unworthy to abide his glory. As Alma put it:

> And now behold, I say unto you then cometh a death, even a second death, which is a spiritual death; then is a time that whosoever dieth in his sins, as to a temporal death, shall also die a spiritual death; yea, he shall die as to things pertaining unto righteousness. (Alma 12:16)

The Lord reveals little of what will be the final state of the sons of perdition, saying that only those who become such will know the full extent of the judgment:

> Wherefore, he saves all except them—they shall go away into everlasting punishment, which is endless punishment, which is eternal punishment, to reign with the devil and his angels in eternity, where their worm dieth not, and the fire is not quenched, which is their torment—
>
> And the end thereof, neither the place thereof, nor their torment, no man knows;
>
> Neither was it revealed, neither is, neither will be revealed unto man, except to them who are made partakers thereof;
>
> Nevertheless, I, the Lord, show it by vision unto many, but straightway shut it up again;
>
> Wherefore, the end, the width, the height, the depth, and the misery thereof, they understand not, neither any man except those who are ordained unto this condemnation. (D&C 76:44–48)

Although much of Christianity would describe the torments of hell in very physical terms, the everlasting punishment of the sons of perdition appears to refer more to their mental and spiritual state as they reside forever with the devil and his angels. Alma stated that

> their torments shall be *as* a lake of fire and brimstone, whose flame ascendeth up forever and ever; and then is the time that

they shall be chained down to an everlasting destruction, according to the power and captivity of Satan, he having subjected them according to his will. (Alma 12:17; emphasis added)

The Prophet Joseph Smith said:

A man is his own tormentor and his own condemner. Hence the saying, They shall go into the lake that burns with fire and brimstone. The torment of disappointment in the mind of man is as exquisite as a lake burning with fire and brimstone. I say, so is the torment of man.[6]

Even though it is impossible for us to fully comprehend the magnitude of the misery and suffering of those condemned to this fate, the picture given should be an adequate deterrent to every person.

Kingdoms of Joy

One of the most remarkable insights coming from the revelation of the three degrees of glory (D&C 76) is that for the great majority of God's children there will be a kingdom of glory in which they will be *happy*. Although those who are able to abide only the telestial or terrestrial glories may regret that they did not live in such a way that they could merit the greater blessings of the celestial world, they will receive all that they can abide and will have the joy commensurate with that glory. The suffering for sin will have been completed in the spirit world prior to judgment and resurrection—the Lord makes it plain that suffering for sins, though it may be called "eternal punishment," does not go on forever:

And surely every man must repent or suffer, for I, God am endless.

Wherefore, I revoke not the judgments which I shall pass, but woes shall go forth, weeping, wailing and gnashing of teeth, yea, to those who are found on my left hand.

Nevertheless, it is not written that there shall be no end to this torment, but it is written *endless torment*.

Again, it is written *eternal damnation;* wherefore it is more express than other scriptures, that it might work upon the hearts of the children of men, altogether for my name's glory.

Wherefore, I will explain unto you this mystery, for it is meet unto you to know even as mine apostles.

I speak unto you that are chosen in this thing, even as one, that you may enter into my rest.

For, behold, the mystery of godliness, how great is it! For, behold, I am endless, and the punishment which is given from my hand is endless punishment, for Endless is my name. Wherefore—

Eternal punishment is God's punishment.

Endless punishment is God's punishment. (D&C 19:4–12)

The celestial, the terrestrial, and the telestial kingdoms are *all* kingdoms of glory. Wilford Woodruff once quoted Joseph Smith as saying

that if the people knew what was behind the veil they would try by every means to commit suicide that they might get there, but the Lord in his wisdom had implanted the fear of death in every person that they might cling to life and thus accomplish the designs of their creator.[7]

No wonder the early Christians looked forward to life after death—they knew by revelation that God's eternal plan included provisions for the eternal happiness of *all* but a very few of his children, and that for those who lived the principles of the gospel of Jesus Christ and received the saving ordinances by his authorized servants, the promises of the celestial world would be greater than their most fervent expectations.

The telestial kingdom

The vision related in Doctrine and Covenants 76 describes the lowest of the three degrees of glory, the telestial, as a kingdom designed for the wicked of the earth—the liars, sorcerers, adulterers, and whoremongers. These are the ones who received not the gospel of Christ nor a testimony of Jesus. These are the ones who come forth in the last resurrection, the resurrection of the unjust, and are thrust down to hell until that time. They will live in a kingdom of glory which is compared to the brightness of the stars (as being less than the light of the sun and the moon), one that will have the ministration of the Holy Ghost alone of the Godhead. There will be innumerable gradations or degrees within this kingdom (D&C 76:98; 1 Cor. 15:41) and in the glorified bodies of its inhabitants.

Although they have suffered the wrath of God on earth and the vengeance of eternal fire in the spirit world and are now consigned to the lowest degree of glory, those who reside in the telestial kingdom will have been cleansed in the spirit world, resurrected with a glorified body, and will enjoy a glory "which surpasses all understanding" (D&C 76:89).

The terrestrial kingdom

The glory of the terrestrial kingdom is likened unto the glory of the moon, relative to the light of the sun (celestial) and the light of the stars (telestial). The comparative level of glory in this kingdom is much greater than the telestial, but still much less than the celestial. Those who are of this kingdom are the "honorable" men and women of this earth who lived the law they received but were "blinded by the craftiness of men" and never received the fullness of the gospel either on earth or in the spirit world (D&C 76:71–75). They are described as "not valiant in the testimony of Jesus; wherefore, they obtain not the crown over the kingdom of our God" (D&C 76:79). Although not stated, it is reasonable to assume that there are innumerable degrees of glory within this kingdom also and that advancement within the kingdom is possible.[8]

Little description of the terrestrial kingdom is given aside from its relative glory. The inhabitants of this kingdom will receive the ministration and presence of Jesus but not of the Father (D&C 76:77) and will themselves minister to those of the telestial kingdom (D&C 76:86–88).

The celestial kingdom

Joseph Smith and Sidney Rigdon were also permitted a view of the greatest of the kingdoms of glory, the celestial, and given a summary of the qualifications and the promised blessings of those worthy to inherit this realm. Since all of the commandments of God are given with the intent of bringing his children to this kingdom, then obtaining it must be the quest of every man and woman who desires to do the will of God. This glorious blessing is not restricted from anyone, but is open to all of the children of God who have lived, now live, or ever shall live upon the earth. God makes it plain in a later revelation that each person will obtain that glory he or she is able to abide (D&C 88:22–24). The object of our existence is not just to avoid sin but also to live such a life that God can endow us with spiritual blessings and power to the point that we become celestial persons, capable of dwelling in the presence of glorified beings.

Those who are worthy to enter are those who (1) have received the testimony of Jesus, (2) have believed on his name, (3) have been baptized by immersion for the remission of their sins, (4) have received the gift of the Holy Ghost by the laying on of hands by those authorized to do so, (5) have overcome by faith, (6) are sealed by the Holy Spirit of Promise, and (7) are just and true (D&C 76:51–53). Joseph Smith elaborated as follows:

I will proceed to tell you what the Lord requires of all people, high and low, rich and poor, male and female, ministers and people, professors of religion and non-professors, in order that they might enjoy the Holy Spirit of God to a fulness and escape the judgments of God, which are almost ready to burst upon the nations of the earth. Repent of all your sins, and be baptized in water for the remission of them, in the name of the Father, and of the Son, and of the Holy Ghost, and receive the ordinance of the laying on of the hands of him who is ordained and sealed unto this power, that ye may receive the Holy Spirit of God; and this is according to the Holy Scriptures, and the Book of Mormon; and the only way that man can enter into the celestial kingdom. These are the requirements of the new covenant, or first principles of the Gospel of Christ; then "Add to your faith, virtue; and to virtue, knowledge; and to knowledge, temperance; and to temperance, patience; and to patience, godliness; and to godliness, brotherly kindness; and to brotherly kindness, charity [or love]; for if these things be in you, and abound, they make you that ye shall neither be barren nor unfruitful, in the knowledge of our Lord Jesus Christ" [2 Pet. 1:5–8]. (first brackets in original)[9]

The telestial and terrestrial kingdoms undoubtedly have many levels or gradations, but the Lord explained in a later revelation that there are three divisions within the celestial kingdom, and in order to obtain the highest, men and women must enter into marriage for time and eternity, called "celestial marriage," in order to qualify:

> In the celestial glory there are three heavens or degrees;
> And in order to obtain the highest, a man must enter into this order of the priesthood [meaning the new and everlasting covenant of marriage];
> And if he does not, he cannot obtain it.
> He may enter into the other, but that is the end of his kingdom; he cannot have an increase. (D&C 131:1–4; brackets in original)

The covenant of celestial marriage is made only in the temples of the Lord and is administered by his authorized servants and through the power of the priesthood. The qualifications for the other two degrees of the celestial kingdom are not differentiated.

To those who qualify for the celestial glory, the promised blessings are marvelous and almost inconceivable to contemplate. The Lord enumerated them as follows (D&C 76:54–70):

(1) *They are the Church of the Firstborn.* According to Elder Bruce R. McConkie, "baptism is the gate of the Church itself, but celestial marriage is the gate to membership in the Church of the Firstborn, the inner circle of faithful saints who are heirs of

exaltation and the fullness of the Father's kingdom (D&C 76:54, 67, 71, 94, 102; 77:11; 78:21; 88:1-5; Heb. 12:23)."[10]

The Lord said, "If you keep my commandments you shall receive of his fulness, and be glorified in me as I am in the Father; therefore, I say unto you, you shall receive grace for grace.... I was in the beginning with the Father, and am the Firstborn; [a]nd all those who are begotten through me are partakers of the glory of the same, and are the church of the Firstborn" (D&C 93:20-22).

(2) *They are gods, even the sons of God.* In the resurrection they will come forth with glorified celestial bodies like the Father and the Son. The potential of all offspring is to become as their parents—since we are literal children of divine parents, those of us who prove themselves worthy will be exalted to the ultimate perfection of godhood.

In the King Follett discourse, Joseph Smith taught this marvelous doctrine:

Here, then, is eternal life—to know the only wise and true God; and you have got to learn how to be Gods yourselves, and to be kings and priests to God, the same as all Gods have done before you, namely, by going from one small degree to another, and from a small capacity to a great one; from grace to grace, from exaltation to exaltation, until you attain to the resurrection of the dead, and are able to dwell in everlasting burnings, and to sit in glory, as do those who sit enthroned in everlasting power....

What is it? To inherit the same power, the same glory and the same exaltation, until you arrive at the station of a God, and ascend the throne of eternal power, the same as those who have gone before.[11]

(3) *They are Christ's, and Christ is God's.*
(4) *They shall overcome all things.* This includes all the conditions of mortality: the temptations, power, and influence of Satan; sin and its effects; ignorance, death, and all other things that limit our ability to dwell with God and be like him.

(5) *They shall dwell in the presence of God and Christ forever and ever.* Not only will they enjoy the glorious presence of both the Father and the Son, but they will reign with Christ during the great Millenium since they are promised to come forth at the beginning of the first resurrection and to be with Christ at his second coming.

(6) *They will come to Mount Zion, the New Jerusalem, the heavenly city of the Living God.* In the revelation received by John on the Isle of Patmos, the Lord unfolded a vision of the celestialized earth, the heavenly New Jerusalem. John was shown the walls of the celestial city, the twelve gates of pearl with each containing a name of one of the twelve tribes of Israel, the foundations of precious stones and the whole city of gold. It was of immense size, a cube nearly 1400 miles in breadth, width, and height (which may be symbolic, rather than a precise measurement). It had no temple since God and Christ dwell therein, making the city itself a temple of God, and did not need the light of the sun since the light of God illuminated the whole of it. Only those who are saved would walk therein, those whose names were written in the Lamb's Book of Life (Rev. 21). Each person entering has the name of God engraven in his or her forehead (Rev. 21:4) and is given a white stone upon which is written a new name (Rev. 2:17). Of this the Lord revealed to Joseph Smith:

This earth, in its sanctified and immortal state, will be made like unto crystal and will be a Urim and Thummin to the inhabitants who dwell thereon, ... and this earth will be Christ's.

Then the white stone mentioned in Revelation 2:17, will become a Urim and Thummin to each individual who receives one, whereby things pertaining to a higher order of kingdoms will be made known;

And a white stone is given to each of those who come into the celestial kingdom, whereon is a new name written, which no man knoweth save he that receiveth it. The new name is the key word. (D&C 130:9–11)

Not only will those worthy of celestial glory be a part of the holy city forever, but they will also dwell in the presence of the Father and the Son. The receipt of a personal Urim and Thummin suggests that they begin a great process of learning the great truths of the universe, the great mysteries of the kingdom of God. Thus, obtaining the celestial kingdom is not an end, but a great beginning.

(7) *They will have company with the hosts of heaven,* the innumerable angels, the general assembly and church of Enoch and of the Firstborn.

(8) *They are they whose names are written in heaven.*

(9) *They are just men and women made perfect through Jesus Christ,* the mediator of the new covenant and Savior of the world.

In addition, those who enter into the new and everlasting covenant of celestial marriage have the promise of their eternal companions and of eternal increase:

> And again, verily I say unto you, if a man marry a wife by my word, which is my law, and by the new and everlasting covenant, and it is sealed unto them by the Holy Spirit of promise, by him who is anointed, unto whom I have appointed this power and the keys of this priesthood; and it shall be said unto them—Ye shall come forth in the first resurrection ... and shall inherit thrones, kingdoms, principalities, and powers, dominions, all heights and depths—then shall it be written in the Lamb's Book of Life, that he shall commit no murder whereby to shed innocent blood, and if ye abide in my covenant ... it shall be done unto them in all things whatsoever my servant hath put upon them, in time, and through all eternity; and shall be of full force when they are out of the world; and they shall pass by the angels, and the gods, which are set there, to their exaltation and glory in all things, as hath been sealed upon their heads, which glory shall be a fulness and continuation of the seeds forever and ever.
>
> Then shall they be gods, because they have no end; therefore shall they be from everlasting to everlasting, because

they continue; then shall they be above all, because all things are subject unto them. Then shall they be gods, because they have all power, and the angels are subject unto them. (D&C 132:19-20)

This lofty objective is the highest in God's eternal plan. It is nothing less than becoming like God himself, to be exalted with all the power and glory and dominion and joy that God can bestow on his children. The priesthood of God is the key, the atonement of Jesus Christ is the means, and the righteousness of women and men is the necessary condition to reach the ultimate destiny of celestial exaltation. Brigham Young bore witness to this ultimate destiny of the righteous:

Having fought the good fight we then shall be prepared to lay our bodies down to rest to await the morning of the resurrection when they will come forth and be reunited with the spirits, the faithful, as it is said, receiving crowns, glory, immortality and eternal lives, even a fullness with the Father, when Jesus shall present his work to the Father, saying, "Father, here is the work thou gavest me to do." Then will they become gods, even the sons of God; then will they become eternal fathers, eternal mothers, eternal sons and eternal daughters; being eternal in their organization, they go from glory to glory, from power to power; they will never cease to increase and to multiply worlds without end. When they receive their crowns, their dominions, they then will be prepared to frame earths like unto ours and to people them in the same manner as we have been brought forth by our parents, by our Father and God.[12]

It is obvious that many will obtain the celestial glory, but not the highest kingdom within it, since many will keep the laws required to enter into the kingdom, but not having entered into celestial marriage, they will not be eligible for the highest degree of glory. The Lord has said of these:

Therefore, if a man marry him a wife in the world, and he marry her not by me nor my word, and he covenant with her so long as he is in the world and she with him, their covenant and marriage are not of force when they are dead...; therefore, they are not bound by any law when they are out of the world.

Therefore, when they are out of the world they neither marry nor are given in marriage; but are appointed angels in heaven, which angels are ministering servants, to minister for those who are worthy of a far more, and an exceeding, and an eternal weight of glory. (D&C 132:15–16)

President Joseph Fielding Smith made the following statement concerning those who are not in the highest kingdom: "Those who receive a lesser degree in the celestial kingdom will not be made equal in power, might, and dominion, and many blessings of the exaltation will be denied them."[13] To be an "administering servant" in the celestial kingdom may be a marvelous and glorious destiny, but is obviously a lesser crown than that obtained by those who enter the new and everlasting covenant of marriage.

Some have wondered, considering the law of eternal progression, whether it is possible to advance within a kingdom or even to advance eventually from one kingdom to another. Elder James E. Talmage made the following observation:

It is reasonable to believe, in the absence of direct revelation by which absolute knowledge of the matter could be acquired, that, in accordance with God's plan of eternal progression, advancement within each of the three specified kingdoms will be provided for; though as to possible progress from one kingdom to another the scriptures make no positive affirmation. Eternal advancement along difficult lines is conceivable. We may conclude that degrees and grades will ever characterize the kingdoms of our God.[14]

For many, the contemplation of eternities in one kingdom while loved ones are assigned to another does not describe a condition of heaven, for happiness and fulfillment would not be a part of separate existence even if the person were in the celestial kingdom. Elder Melvin J. Ballard addressed this concern:

> I have several times been asked, how is it possible for those who attain celestial glory ever to feel fully happy and satisfied to know that their children are in the telestial world, and never would have the privilege of coming up with their parents in the celestial kingdom.
>
> We must not overlook the fact that those who attain to the higher glories may minister unto and visit and associate with those of the lesser kingdoms (D&C 76:86–88). While the lesser may not come up (D&C 76:112), they may still enjoy the companionship of their loved ones who are in higher stations. Also we must not forget that even the least degree of glory, as the Lord has expressed it, is beyond all our present understanding. So that they are in the presence of glorious conditions, even though they obtain into the least place, and we must not forget either that these, our sons, are our Father's sons and daughters.[15]

Much speculation exists concerning the kingdoms of glory and that of the sons of perdition, and many of the questions await further revelation—probably most will not be answered until we arrive there. But the glorious revelations received by Joseph Smith and succeeding prophets have made it clear that there are many, many degrees of glory and that truly magnificent blessings await those who are worthy of exaltation in the highest level of the celestial kingdom. The promise is real and the promise is sure—centuries of darkness and confusion are laid to rest by the light of the restored gospel and the sons and daughters of God can look up on passage from mortality to the life beyond with faith, with hope, and with the knowledge of the love of our Father in Heaven.

NOTES

CHAPTER TEN

1. Hugh Nibley, *The World and the Prophets,* 3d ed. (Salt Lake City: Deseret Book Co., 1987), 164–65.

2. Joseph Smith, *History of the Church of Jesus Christ of Latter-day Saints,* 2d ed. rev., ed. B. H. Roberts (Salt Lake City: The Church of Jesus Christ of Latter-day Saints, 1932–51)1:245; hereafter cited as *HC.*

3. Ibid., 1:252.

4. Ibid., 6:314–15.

5. Joseph Fielding Smith, "The Sin against the Holy Ghost," *Improvement Era* 58 (July 1955): 494.

6. *HC,* 6:314.

7. *Charles Walker Diary, 1855–1902,* entry dated August 19, 1877.

8. James E. Talmage, *The Articles of Faith* (Salt Lake City: Deseret Book Co., 1977), 409.

9. *HC,* 1:314–15.

10. Bruce R. McConkie, *Mormon Doctrine,* 2d ed. (Salt Lake City: Bookcraft, 1966), 139.

11. Joseph Smith, *Teachings of the Prophet Joseph Smith,* comp. Joseph Fielding Smith (Salt Lake City: Deseret Book Co., 1976), 347–48.

12. Brigham Young, in *Journal of Discourses* (Liverpool, England: Latter-day Saints' Book Depot, 1855–86), 18:259.

13. Joseph Fielding Smith, *Church History and Modern Revelation* (Salt Lake City: The Council of the Twelve Apostles of The Church of Jesus Christ of Latter-day Saints, 1953), 2:58.

14. Talmage, *Articles of Faith,* 409.

15. Bryant S. Hinckley, *Sermons and Missionary Services of Melvin J. Ballard* (Salt Lake City: Deseret Book Co., 1949), 257.

The Eternity of
the Marriage Relationship

Danel W. Bachman

Introduction

Marriage has always been an important part of the Judeo-Christian tradition, but Latter-day Saints bring a unique perspective to the theology of marriage when compared with modern Christian doctrine. The Prophet Joseph Smith taught that the relationship of a man and a woman in marriage was intended to be eternal. Vestiges of this idea linger in the Bible—both the Old and the New Testaments—but they are only vestiges, and other Christian leaders have not found in them justification for a doctrine of marriage for eternity. In light of the revelations given to Joseph Smith, however, Latter-day Saints can see with the clarity of hindsight that eternal marriage has been an integral part of the gospel plan from the beginning.

Marriage is at the center of the creation story in Genesis, with God creating woman because "it is not good that the man should be alone" (Gen. 2:18). The law given to Moses, including the Ten Commandments, had several provisions that served to protect the sanctity of marriage and the family. The Hebrew tradition had a vestige of the idea of eternal marriage embedded in its "Levirate law," which stipulated that the brothers or other close male relatives of a deceased man had at least the right, if not the obligation, to marry his widow, care for her, and raise up children to the name and honor of the deceased father (see Deut. 25:5–10). Most Jewish interpreters of this law see immortality preserved in this system only in the perpetuation of the deceased father's name through the children born to his wife, but the doctrine is much more meaningful if it is seen as part of the Latter-day Saint theology of marriage, which perpetuates the family in eternity.

The record of the teachings of Jesus contains several passages which also suggest the eternal nature of marriage. One came when the Pharisees tempted Jesus with the question, "Is it lawful for a man to put away his wife for every cause?" (Matt. 19:3). Jesus replied by referring them to the creation story wherein God said men and women were to leave their parents and become "one flesh" (Gen. 2:24). He then affirmed that "what therefore God hath joined together, let not man put asunder." They asked why, then, had Moses allowed the Israelites to give a bill of divorcement? Jesus answered, "Moses because of the hardness of your hearts suffered you to put away your wives: *but from the beginning it was not so*" (Matt. 19:3–8; emphasis added).

More evidence is found in Jesus' answer to a question about the Levirate law. The Sadducees posed a problem to Jesus in which a woman had a succession of seven husbands, all brothers, and all of whom died without leaving any posterity. They wanted to know to which of the brothers the woman would be married in the resurrection. Jesus told the Sadducees that "in the resurrection they neither marry, nor are given in marriage," but were "as the angels" (Matt. 22:23–30). Jesus' reply was perhaps a veiled reference to eternal marriage.

Finally, one modern apostle sees in Peter's comment that husbands and wives would be "heirs together of the grace of life" (1 Peter 3:7) another indication that the ancients knew of eternal marriage.[1]

Latter-day Saint theology does not depend upon these "hints" for its doctrine of eternal marriage; rather, it looks to the revelations of the Prophet Joseph Smith. Mormon doctrine developed as Joseph Smith received numerous revelations "line upon line," with new additions dovetailing nicely with those that preceded them. Indeed, to observe this development, to see how harmoniously each new revelation and doctrine meshed with its predecessors to make up the intricate and unified whole of Mormon theology, is to begin to recognize the Omnipotent Intellect that inspired Joseph Smith and to reinforce the conviction that he was God's prophet.

Mormon doctrines on marriage were no different. Like other aspects of Latter-day Saint theology, they were revealed piecemeal, yet each fit into the larger pattern like the latest thread of a Persian rug on the loom. This essay is an attempt to place some of the pieces of this phenomenal puzzle together in chronological sequence. It is an introductory probe rather than a comprehensive review, and we can only suggest some relationships—space will not allow us to explore them all.

The doctrines of the Mormon theological rug woven together produce the beauty of the whole. The family is at the core of every stage of existence: the premortal realm, mortality, and life in the celestial kingdom. Yet this would not have been clear without revelations on many subjects. For example, eternal marriage would have little meaning without knowing of the premortal existence, the necessity of the priesthood and its keys and powers, the degrees of glory, or the concept of temples and eternal covenants.

When we examine the question of how the Latter-day Saint doctrine of eternal marriage developed we observe a number of threads converging to produce the final picture. Factors such as the positive influence of Joseph's experiences with marriage, the religious environment around Kirtland, the Prophet's work on the "translation" of the Bible (particularly the Old Testament), and the relationship of other doctrines to marriage and family all contributed at least indirectly. Revelation was the vehicle, but often these other things were the stimulus that led to receiving the revelations.

Joseph grew up in a stable, loving family, one which doubtless left him with a positive outlook on the relationship between men and women in general and marriage in particular. Kenneth Godfrey's examination of the marriage of Joseph's parents concludes that their relationship was democratic, tolerant, unified, marked by open communication, and genuinely affectionate. The children were nurtured in a family that saw them as something far more important than mere economic necessities in an agrarian culture. Indeed, according to Godfrey, some scholars—proffering naturalistic explanations for Joseph's doctrines—believe that Joseph's home life was so good that his belief in the eternal family arose naturally from the feelings he cherished for his own family.[2]

Joseph's marriage, while marked by typical problems of family life which on occasion were exacerbated by his position as leader of the Church, seems to have been a reflection of that of his parents. Moreover, negative ideas sometimes attributed to Mormon doctrine such as anti-feminist bias and the subjugation of women or relegating them to second class status were not significant factors in the Prophet's seventeen-year marriage.[3] His attitude about how men should treat their wives demonstrated itself long before his own marriage. In Nauvoo he recalled that as a boy he once fought a man who beat his wife. Even though the man was older and larger, Joseph fought with determination on behalf of the beleaguered woman.[4] It is, therefore, not surprising that both his children and his wife affirm that Joseph was not abusive and harsh. Joseph Smith III was probably incorrect when he said he could only remember his parents quarreling once, but his statement, along with the overwhelming evidence of Church history, suggests that Joseph did not verbally or physically abuse or even domineer Emma.[5] She also acknowledged that Joseph was respectful of her: "[W]e did not disagree. He usually gave some heed to what I had to say. It was quite a grievous thing to many that I had any influence with him."[6]

Perhaps even during the translation of the Book of Mormon Joseph began to get glimpses of the eternal nature of marriage. Charles Walker reported hearing Brigham Young say that it was then that Joseph "had a revelation that the order of Patriarchal marriag [sic] *and the Sealing* was right" (emphasis added).[7] Also, while Joseph was translating the Bible, it became customary for him to take questions about the content of what he was working on to the Lord. He learned many principles and doctrines in the process, and some of these revelations pertained to eternal marriage.[8]

The Lord often revealed concepts to Joseph which he sometimes taught before the written revelations were given to the

Church. This was the case as the doctrines of marriage emerged. Therefore, we must study closely the history of Joseph's teachings as well as the Doctrine and Covenants to understand the development of our doctrines on marriage.

The Cosmic Context of Marriage

One of the most important revelations on marriage was given in March of 1831 in Kirtland. It came in response to doctrines taught by a nearby Shaker communal society established at North Union, Ohio (near Cleveland), as early as 1822. A number of Latter-day Saint converts from the Kirtland area were once to one degree or another associated with the Shaker people, either as members, friends, or through family members who were Shakers.

Shakerism was brought into existence in the mid-1700s in England by James Wardley as a protest against Quakerism. In about 1757, Ann Lee, imprisoned because of rebellion against marriage and deserting her husband and family, joined the Shakers. She led a colony to America in 1774 and proclaimed herself the "female principle" of God. Shakerism was known for its unique worship and unusual spiritual manifestations. Shakers believed God was both male and female and that Christ was the male principle and Ann Lee the female principle. They taught the possibility of attaining a higher, or angelic, order of existence, and virginity was requisite to achieving this status. Thus marriage and connubial relations were not practiced in Shaker colonies. Married couples who joined the Shakers were divorced and not allowed to associate together again except in public dances and worship.

In the spring of 1831, Parley P. Pratt, Sidney Rigdon, and former Shaker Leman Copley were sent to preach to the colony at North Union. They carried with them a copy of what is now section 49 of the Doctrine and Covenants, a revelation for the Shaker people. A passage on marriage in the revelation read:

> And again, verily I say unto you, that whoso forbiddeth to marry is not ordained of God, for marriage is ordained of God unto man.

Wherefore, it is lawful that he should have one wife, and they twain shall be one flesh, and all this that the earth might answer the end of its creation;

And that it might be filled with the measure of man, according to his creation before the world was made. (49:15–17)

The unique contribution of this revelation is found in the latter part of the passage, which places marriage in a new cosmic context. The logic proceeds from one idea to the next as follows:

1. Marriage is ordained of God, and it is lawful for a man to have one wife.
2. Marriage and sexual union are directly related to the "end" or purpose of the creation of the earth.
3. There was apparently a finite number of spirits created for this world, as suggested by the word *measure*, which means number or amount.
4. In having children, couples become partners with God by helping the earth "answer the end" or fulfill the purpose of its creation. Thus marriage is the mechanism through which pre-existent beings were to be brought into mortality.
5. All of this is according to the plan and design of God.

Suddenly and dramatically, in one brief passage, the concepts of a premortal existence, the creation of the earth, marriage, and procreation were woven together. The pattern lets us begin to see the design of God. Marriage is the thread that links together the first two of the three stages of our existence. It only remained for the Lord to show Joseph Smith how marriage pertained to life after death. Moreover, the fundamental philosophy of sex and marriage was outlined, and every doctrine relating to marriage revealed subsequently built upon this foundation. It is not insignificant that Benjamin F. Johnson remembered that in Kirtland Joseph Smith taught:

The First Command was to "Multiply" and the Prophet taught us that Dominion & power in the great Future would be Comensurate with the no [number] of "Wives Children & Friends" that we inherit here and that our great mission to earth was to organize a Neculi of Heaven to take with us. To the increase of which there would be no end.[9]

It was apparently in this period, while laboring on the Joseph Smith Translation of the Bible (JST), that Joseph began to receive revelations regarding plural marriage.[10] Revelations were also given in the fall of 1831 and in January of 1832,[11] but February 1832 was a watershed in Mormon theology.

While Joseph was working on the fifth chapter of John, the Lord inspired a significant change in verse 29.[12] The alterations caused Joseph and Sidney Rigdon to marvel and meditate. This environment was conducive to the Spirit, and the eyes of their understandings were touched, as they experienced a series of successive visions in which they learned that there are "degrees of glory" in the eternal rewards given to God's children. The revelation specified some of the conditions required to obtain the various rewards, but it was not until the publication of sections 131 and 132 of the Doctrine and Covenants that the role marriage played in these qualifications was announced.

One insight regarding marriage is embedded in section 76. Verse 29, speaking of Christ, says that "by him, and through him, and of him, the worlds are and were created, and the inhabitants thereof are begotten sons and daughters unto God." Again we get a glimpse of the cosmic context of Mormon theology, especially as it relates to the family of God. The verse affirms that there are other worlds, inhabited by God's children.[13] This is a companion doctrine to an important concept revealed later to the effect that we are destined to become gods and through the same processes will enjoy "eternal increase." What God has been doing, we can someday be privileged to do.

Importance of the Authority of the Priesthood

During the Kirtland era, events transpired which underscored the necessity of priesthood authority, especially as it pertained to performing marriages. The idea that priesthood authority was necessary to perform sacred religious ordinances was first made clear in April of 1830 when the Lord revealed to Joseph that baptisms performed in other faiths were unacceptable (see D&C 22).[14] In Kirtland, Joseph taught that marriage was also a religious ordinance and began to teach that it should be solemnized by the power of the priesthood. Amid hostile discrimination against the Latter-day Saints he also maintained the right of Church officers to perform marriages. In doing so he demonstrated his view that priesthood authority transcended civil authority in performing marriages and divorces.

Beginning in 1835, the authority of officers of the Church to perform marriages in Ohio became an issue and remained a source of contention between Mormons and non-Mormons throughout the last half of the Kirtland period. About 1835 Sidney Rigdon was indicted for "solemnizing marriages without a license." He was acquitted of this charge, however, when it was learned that his license as a Campbellite minister had never been revoked.[15] In another example, a Kirtland justice of the peace said that during this same period he married couples who were later remarried by the Prophet in church rites.[16] We know that Joseph asserted his prophetic authority over the civil authority on several occasions.[17]

In the fall of 1835 Joseph married Lydia Goldthwaite Baily to Newell Knight. It was the first marriage Joseph ever performed, and the circumstances were important. At the age of seventeen Lydia had married Calvin Baily and later bore him two children, both of whom died in infancy. According to Knight, Baily turned out to be a drunkard who let Lydia "suffer and pine in sorrow, while he was carousing and spending even the aviles [sic.] of the last cow."[18] Consequently, Lydia left Baily and joined some friends in Canada where she accepted Mormonism in the fall of 1833. From Canada she moved to Kirtland in May of 1835 where she met and fell in love with Knight, who eventually proposed marriage. The couple wanted Joseph to perform the wedding but had said nothing about their wish except in prayer to the Lord. Newell asked Hyrum Smith, who was going to invite the guests to the wedding, to ask Seymour Brunson to officiate because his authority to perform marriages had been recognized in southern Ohio.[19] Knight explained that he didn't expect that Joseph would perform the ordinance because he had no license from the state, which "refused to give such licence [sic] to the Elders of this Church on the ground that they were not considered by the State to be preachers of the gospel, & if any attempted to marry with out such licence they would & did cause them to pay a penalty."[20] When Joseph said he would perform the wedding himself Hyrum feared this would endanger his brother, but Joseph used the occasion to assert his authority and solemnized the marriage anyway.

Newell Knight wrote that on the evening of the wedding Joseph Smith said "many things relative to marriages anciently, which were yet to be revealed."[21] Knight also recorded Joseph's remarks at a Sabbath service five days after the marriage. Relative to his action at the wedding, the Prophet said:

I have done it by the authority of the holy Priesthood, and the Gentile law has no power to call me to an account for it. It is my religious privilege, and even the Congress of the United States has no power to make a law that would abridge the rights of my religion. I have done as I was commanded.[22]

Lydia remembered it similarly. She added that Joseph said:

Our Elders have been wronged and prosecuted for marrying without a license. The Lord God of Israel has given me authority to unite the people in the holy bonds of matrimony. And from this time forth I shall use that privilege and marry whomsoever I see fit.[23]

But the issue was more than a conflict with the authorities of Ohio over whether Mormons had authority to perform marriages. In his account, Joseph stressed not only his *right* as a prophet to perform marriages, but he also taught that "marriage was an institution of heaven, instituted in the garden of Eden; it was *necessary* it should be solemnized by the authority of the everlasting Priesthood." He went on to say the ceremony was "original" with him.

"I ... also pronounced upon them the blessings that the Lord conferred upon Adam and Eve in the garden of Eden, that is, to multiply and replenish the earth, with the addition of long life and prosperity" (emphasis added).[24]

These teachings are important for two additional reasons. First, the Latter-day Saint notion that the first marriage was performed by God in the Garden of Eden comes from the Prophet himself. And the argument has been made subsequently that since it was done before the Fall it was intended to be eternal. Second, Joseph's reference to the commandment given to Adam and Eve to multiply and replenish the earth is significant because the Lord's law of chastity forbids sexual relations except with one's legal spouse. Humans gain the power to procreate at the time of puberty, but the authority to use those powers is given when the couple is married. The blessings bestowed upon newly married couples contain the injunction "multiply and replenish the earth," which is in effect God's authorization, even a commandment, to engage in sexual union to bring to pass his eternal purposes.

The action of the Prophet in performing the Knight-Baily wedding takes on even more significance when it is known that Lydia Goldthwaite Baily was never granted a legal divorce from her first husband. In reference to this Knight remarked, "But, I prayed to the Lord and then took President Smith's Council [sic] [and] was married to her."[25] Indeed, Joseph viewed civil marriages in the same way he did sectarian baptisms.[26] The ethical rightness of his actions was perhaps best expressed in a statement he made later in Nauvoo to the effect that "whatever God requires is right, no matter what it is...."[27]

In January of 1836 Joseph also married Apostle John F. Boynton to Susan Lowell. After a hymn and prayer Joseph read a license granting ministers of the gospel the "privilege of solemnizing the rights of matrimony." He spoke again of the "ancient" order of marriage and said, "I pronounced upon them the blessings of Abraham, Isaac and Jacob, and such other blessings as the Lord put into my heart."[28] Reminiscing about the pleasantries of the celebration that followed, Joseph commented that the wedding "was conducted after the order of heaven."[29] It is noteworthy that the promises the Lord gave to the ancient patriarchs were part of Joseph's inspired blessing upon the Boyntons because one of the most prominent of those promises to the ancients was that they would have a posterity more numerous than the stars in the heavens or the sands of the seashore. Latter-day Saints have come to understand that this has meaning particularly in the context of eternal marriage and the continuation of procreative powers in eternity.[30]

The doctrines of marriage developed rapidly and became an integral part of the doctrines of the gospel revealed in the Kirtland era but they were not all canonized at the time. Some did not appear in the revelations now in the Doctrine and Covenants until the Nauvoo period. During these years the Saints must have frequently heard instructions relative to the duties that "are incumbent on husbands and wives, in particular the great importance there is in cultivating the pure principles of the institution, in all its bearings and connexions [sic] with each other."[31] Gradually they began to understand, and though they perhaps comprehended it imperfectly, glimpses of the doctrine of the eternal nature of marriage enlivened their minds and gladdened their hearts. In May of 1835 W. W. Phelps spoke of a "new idea" in a letter to his wife, Sally. "If you and I continue faithful to the end," he wrote, "we are certain to be one in the Lord throughout eternity; this is one of the most glorious consolations we can have in the flesh."[32] The following month, addressing a similar theme, he expressed his gratitude for "new light" which "is occasionally bursting in to our minds":

> We shall by and bye learn that we were with God in another world, before the foundation of the world, and had our agency: that we came into this world and have our agency, in order that we may prepare ourselves for a kingdom of glory; become archangels, even the sons of God *where the man is neither without the woman, nor the woman without the man in the Lord:* A consummation of glory, and happiness, and perfection so greatly to be wished, that I would not miss of it for the fame of ten worlds. (emphasis added)[33]

Phelps's reference to archangels in a heavenly state where men and women are not without each other hints at a similar distinction between being an angel and being married made by Joseph Smith in Section 132.

The Temple and Eternal Marriage

Doctrines about the temple that were important to the development of the Latter-day Saint concept of marriage were also revealed in Kirtland. In January of 1836 Joseph received what is now known as section 137 of the Doctrine and Covenants. This important revelation teaches that those who die without a knowledge of the gospel who would have received it with all their hearts will be heirs of celestial glory (see D&C 137:7). Through indicating the possibility of accepting the gospel in the spirit world, this revelation makes sensible passages in scripture which speak of preaching to the "spirits in prison" and alludes to vicarious ordinance work for the dead. Three months later the Lord and three ancient prophets appeared in the newly completed Kirtland temple to accept it as the "house of the Lord" and reveal additional information regarding the keys of the priesthood.

Moses restored the keys of the gathering of Israel. Later Joseph said that the *purpose* of gathering people in every dispensation was to

> build unto the Lord a house whereby He could reveal unto His people the ordinances of His house and the glories of His kingdom, and teach the people the way of salvation; for there are certain ordinances and principles that, when they are taught and practiced, must be done in a place or house built for that purpose.[34]

By gathering people the Lord also gathers the spiritual and financial resources necessary to build the temple. This is perhaps what Joseph meant when he said that "the greatest temporal and spiritual blessings" come "from faithfulness and *concerted effort*" rather than through "individual exertion or enterprise" (emphasis added).[35]

Elias restored the keys of the dispensation of the gospel of Abraham. God gave to Abraham great and precious promises, pre-eminent among them being that the Savior would be born through his lineage. But he was also promised that his heirs would have the rights to the priesthood and that he would have a numberless posterity. So the dispensation of the gospel to Abraham, as it always is, was a dispensation of promise. Yet Joseph repeatedly reminded the Saints that the promises given to Abraham, and extended to Isaac and Jacob, were not to be theirs simply because they were given to the ancients.[36] Those blessings must be given to us by revelation as they were to the patriarchs and on the basis of the same covenants and faithfulness to the Lord.

Endowment means a gift, and President Joseph Fielding Smith taught that the Saints are given three gifts through the temple endowment: knowledge, power and blessing.[37] It is significant that Joseph Smith was inspired to bestow upon the newly married Boyntons the blessings of Abraham, Isaac, and Jacob, and those blessings have remained part of the marriage ceremony since that time. Latter-day Saints become candidates for the blessings of the patriarchs through the holy endowment and the sealing ordinances.

This brings us to Elijah. Section 110 does not specify the exact nature of the keys Elijah bestowed; it merely refers to Malachi 4:5-6 and then says, "Therefore, the keys of this dispensation are committed into your hands" (D&C 110:16). But modern prophets have taught that Elijah brought the sealing powers—the power and authority to seal or bind things eternally—the same authority promised to Peter, James, and John anciently (see Matt. 16:19). This is important because this sealing power is necessary for ordinances and covenants to have validity in eternity (D&C 132:7).

Thus three important elements relating to temples were restored by these ancient servants of the Lord. With these keys Joseph could gather Israel for the purpose of building temples, bestow in those temples the most sacred promises of the Lord unto his people, and seal or loose those covenants and promises for eternity. All of these principles were necessary threads in the tapestry of the gospel, but they were particularly important elements in that part of the gospel fabric dealing with eternal marriage.

Once in a while as the doctrines of the gospel were revealed some Saints and outsiders became confused as to how they were to be interpreted and implemented practically. The law of consecration and stewardship is one of the central doctrines relating to the establishment of Zion and an integral theme in the temple. But in the late Missouri period the practice of consecration was misrepresented by some who charged that the Mormons "not only dedicated [their] property, but [their] families also to the Lord." However, Joseph explained that Satan had put it into the hearts of men to pervert a sacred principle "into licentiousness." For "when a man consecrates or dedicates his wife and children," Joseph said, "he does not give them to his brother, or to his neighbor, for there is no such law: for the law of God is, Thou shalt not commit adultery."[38]

Revelations in the Nauvoo Period

When approximately 12,000 Saints were driven from Missouri in the winter of 1838–39, their lands, homes, buildings, and other belongings were taken over by their persecutors. That fall Joseph went to Washington, D.C., to petition the president and Congress for redress. When he encountered stony hearts he left Washington just before Christmas and took the train to Philadelphia. There he preached and visited friends and Church members in the vicinity for about a month. At the time, Parley P. Pratt was also in Philadelphia, and the two men spent several days together during which Joseph taught Elder Pratt some important principles pertaining to marriage. The doctrines of marriage had continued to be revealed "line upon line" to the Saints in Illinois, but as in Kirtland, some of the precepts taught by Joseph Smith did not appear in published revelations until late in the Nauvoo era. Parley's description of what he learned is among the classics of Latter-day Saint literature on the subject. His joy and enthusiasm at hearing the doctrine come through even though the account was written years later.

During these interviews he [Joseph] taught me many great and glorious principles concerning God and the heavenly order of eternity. It was at this time that I received from him the first idea of eternal family organization, and the eternal union of the sexes in those inexpressibly endearing relationships which none but the highly intellectual, the refined and pure in heart, know how to prize, and which are at the very foundation of everything worthy to be called happiness.

Till then I had learned to esteem kindred affections and sympathies as appertaining solely to this transitory state, as something from which the heart must be entirely weaned, in order to be fitted for its heavenly state.

It was Joseph Smith who taught me how to prize the endearing relationships of father and mother, husband and wife; of brother and sister, son and daughter.

It was from him that I learned that the wife of my bosom might be secured to me for time and all eternity; and that the refined sympathies and affections which endeared us to each other emanated from the fountain of divine eternal love. It was from him that I learned that we might cultivate these affections, and grow and increase in the same to all eternity; while the result of our endless union would be an offspring as numerous as the stars of heaven, or the sands of the sea shore.

It was from him that I learned the true dignity and destiny of a son of God, clothed with an eternal priesthood, as the patriarch and sovereign of his countless offspring. It was from him that I learned that the highest dignity of womanhood was, to stand as a queen and priestess to her husband, and to reign for ever and ever as the queen mother of her numerous and still increasing offspring.

I had loved before, but I knew not why. But now I loved—with a pureness—an intensity of elevated, exalted feeling, which would lift my soul from the transitory things of this grovelling sphere and expand it as the ocean. I felt that God was my heavenly Father indeed; that Jesus was my brother, and that the wife of my bosom was an immortal, eternal companion; a kind ministering angel, given to me as a comfort, and a crown of glory for ever and ever. In short, I could now love with the spirit and with the understanding also.

Yet, at that time, my dearly beloved brother, Joseph Smith, had barely touched a single key; had merely lifted a corner of the veil and given me a single glance into eternity.[39]

There is also an interesting connection between the Prophet Joseph's trip to Philadelphia and a beautiful passage from a lengthy letter he wrote from Liberty Jail which was canonized as sections 121–123 of the Doctrine and Covenants. Verse 45 of section 121 encourages: "Let virtue garnish thy thoughts unceasingly; then shall thy confidence wax strong in the presence of God; and the doctrine of the priesthood shall distil upon thy souls as the dews from heaven." Apparently during the month he was in the Philadelphia area, Joseph visited a family named Wilkinson. While with them he bestowed a blessing upon the family in the form of a written note in the front of one of their books. It is perhaps the most salient commentary on D&C 121:45 we have.

Virtue is one of the most prominent principles that enables us to have confidence in approaching our Father who is in heaven in order to ask wisdom at his hand therefore if thou wilt cherish this principle in thine heart thou mayest ask with all Confidence before him and it shall be poured out upon thine head and thou shalt not lack any thing that thy soul desires in truth.[40]

In the spring and summer of 1843 some of the concepts previously taught by Joseph Smith appeared in three important revelations. Additional information was also given which greatly expanded the Saints' understanding of how marriage fits into the eternal scheme of things. The first came early in April. According to verse 2 of section 130 we learn that in eternity "that same sociality which exists among us here will exist among us there, only it will be coupled with eternal glory." *Sociality* isn't precisely defined, but in light of other revelations, especially those recorded about this same time, it is not unreasonable to conclude that family relationships are included in the meaning of the term.

In the middle of May, Joseph visited Ramus, Illinois, a Mormon village twenty miles east of Nauvoo. There he visited with friends, specifically twenty-four-year-old Benjamin F. Johnson and his wife. Johnson had been a close friend for some time, and on the evening of May 16 Joseph said he wished to marry them according to the "Law of the Lord." At first Johnson thought it was a joke and made light of the situation. But Joseph chided his levity then, with the proper solemnity, sealed the Johnsons for eternity by the Holy Spirit of Promise. Afterward he gave further instructions. The celestial kingdom, he explained, had three heavens or degrees, and one must enter into the new and everlasting covenant of marriage to qualify for the highest degree. The doctrine was formalized in section 131; it takes man and woman united together in matrimony to achieve exaltation. Salvation is a family affair. And "if he does not" enter into this order of marriage, the revelation continues, "that is the end of his kingdom; he cannot have an increase" (D&C 131:3-4).

The meaning of the word *increase* is not totally clear in this passage, but it is easily understood from remarks Joseph made on that occasion (ideas which were later incorporated into section 132).

> Except a man and his wife enter into an everlasting covenant and be married for eternity, while in this probation, by the power and authority of the Holy Priesthood, they will cease to increase when they die; that is, they will not have any children after the resurrection. But those who are married by the power and authority of the priesthood in this life, and continue without committing the sin against the Holy Ghost, will continue to increase and have children in the celestial glory.[41]

The circumstances under which section 132 was recorded (not received) are of interest and have been detailed elsewhere, so they will not be reiterated here.[42] Suffice it to say that the tradition has long existed in the Church and is now supported by considerable evidence that this section of the Doctrine and Covenants is an amalgamation of several revelations that were given to Joseph Smith in the early 1830s. The revelation answers three questions which Joseph took to the Lord; two are explicitly mentioned in the revelation and knowledge of the third comes from a report of a statement from Joseph Smith in 1844.[43]

The first of Joseph's questions probably arose while he was revising the book of Genesis. According to verse 1 of section 132, Joseph wanted to "know and understand" why the Lord "justified" the ancient patriarchs in "having many wives and concubines." The second question was made known on 8 June 1844 when the Nauvoo city council debated the fate of the apostate newspaper *Nauvoo Expositor,* published the day before. As mayor, Joseph was deeply involved in these discussions. One of the central charges of the *Expositor* was that Mormon leaders were teaching and practicing polygamy, and the paper contained affidavits verifying that a revelation on the subject existed.[44] Someone in the council asked Joseph if there were such a revelation. He said there was and explained that it was a response to his question about the story of the woman with seven husbands (Matt. 22:23-30). The Sadducees' challenge—"in the resurrection whose wife shall she be of the seven?"—brought forth from Jesus the response that "in the resurrection they neither marry, nor are given in marriage, but are as the angels of God in heaven." This had piqued Joseph's curiosity. He told the council that upon asking the Lord about this passage, he learned that "men in this life must marry in view of eternity, otherwise they must remain as angels, or be single in heaven."[45] Joseph's knowing this as early as 1831 makes it understandable why glimpses of this doctrine show up in the writings of W. W. Phelps in 1835, the writings of Parley P. Pratt in reference to 1840, and the sealing of the Johnsons in Ramus in 1843—all before section 132 was recorded.

The third question is referred to in 132:41. It concerns adultery. Apparently when Joseph learned that under certain circumstances the Lord authorized plural marriage it spawned a question in his mind about the meaning of adultery.

The first portion of section 132 (vv. 1–40) answers the first two questions. The key word in Joseph's query about the plural marriages of the ancient patriarchs is "justified" (v. 1). Coming from a Puritan New England environment and growing up in a committed Christian family, Joseph's background evidently left him thinking plural marriages were sinful, yet the scriptures make clear that a number of polygamists, including Abraham and Moses, were special friends and powerful prophets of God. Joseph asked the Lord why, and in answer the Lord explained a general principle pertaining to *any* gospel covenant. He said that if such covenants do not meet four conditions—i. e., if they are "[1] not made and entered into and sealed by the Holy Spirit of promise, [2] of him who is anointed, [3] both as well for time and for all eternity, [4] and that too most holy by revelation and commandment [2] through the medium of mine anointed, whom I have appointed on the earth to hold this power"—then they "are of no efficacy, virtue, or force in and after the resurrection from the dead" (D&C 132:7).

The Lord then applied this principle to the covenant of marriage in three different cases detailed in verses 15–17, 18, and 19–20. In the first the Lord poses the situation of a marriage that is not performed according to these conditions—in other words, a civil or sectarian marriage. The revelation declares of those so married: "they are not bound by any law when they are out of the world" (v. 15). The second case concerns a marriage that is made for "time and for all eternity"—one in which the correct wording is used but otherwise does not meet the other three requirements. Again the declaration is that "it is not valid neither of force when they are out of the world" (v. 18). In the final situation the four conditions are met and the Lord declares that such a covenant "shall be of full force when they are out of the world" (v. 19).

The first case is particularly interesting because as part of his answer, the Lord, in language paralleling Matthew's gospel, says in verse 16:

Therefore, when they are out of the world they neither marry nor are given in marriage; but are appointed angels in heaven, which angels are ministering servants, to minister for those who are worthy of a far more, and an exceeding, and an eternal weight of glory.

Jesus' answer to the Sadducees—when he said "in the resurrection they neither marry, nor are given in marriage, but are as the angels of God in heaven" (Matt. 22:30)—is perhaps the most often cited passage in opposition to the Latter-day Saint doctrine of eternal marriage. Yet Joseph apparently caught the subtle implication in the verse that there is a difference in *status* in heaven between those who are married and the angels. So he inquired and learned that the "angels did not abide my law; therefore, they cannot be enlarged, but remain separately and singly, without exaltation, in their saved condition, to all eternity; and from henceforth are not gods, but are angels of God forever and ever" (D&C 132:17). Indeed, the Lord says, there is a difference in the two conditions: gods are married, angels are not. Regarding case three, the Lord said of those whose marriage is valid for both time and eternity:

They shall pass by the angels, and the gods, which are set there, to their exaltation and glory in all things, as hath been sealed upon their heads, which glory *shall be a fulness and a continuation of the seeds forever and ever.*

Then shall they be gods, because they have no end; therefore shall they be from everlasting to everlasting, because they continue. (D&C 132:19–20; emphasis added)

Thus, eternal marriage is linked with the definition of God, for only those so wed can qualify to become "gods." Part of God's very nature involves his ability to produce offspring eternally. Section 132 makes it plain that the absence of this power means one is not a god but an angel. One defining and supernal blessing of godhood is to have "increase," or what section 132 speaks of in other terms as having "a fulness and continuation of the seeds forever" (v. 19), having "no end" (v. 20), of "continu[ing]" (vv. 20–21), or having a "continuation of the lives" (v. 22). It is to have "eternal live*s*" (v. 24; emphasis added), which is in contrast to "the death*s*" spoken of in verse 25. Thus, the most profound and marvelous of revelations on marriage makes known that God's longevity and "continuation" and having "no end," as it were, is more than just living forever. It is to possess the ability to perpetuate his race forever and do the work of bringing to pass their immortality and eternal life. By contrast, those who do not render obedience to the new and everlasting covenant of marriage remain "separately and singly, without exaltation" (v. 17), and in them is the "deaths" (v. 25). The plural *deaths* heightens both the importance of the ordinance of eternal marriage and expands our theological understanding, for it defines the ongoing eternal and everlasting loss such people experience—the inability to perpetuate the "seeds" forever. In the words of Malachi (4:1), they are cut off "root and branch," having neither been sealed to ancestry (root) in the Patriarchal Order of the priesthood, nor possessing the ability to have posterity (branch) as numerous as the sands of the sea and stars in heaven.

We have seen that many of the principles of eternal marriage were revealed to Joseph Smith at an early date, and he gradually taught them to the Church. They made increasing sense as the full doctrines and principles of the gospel were revealed. By the end of Joseph's life the Church was in possession of sufficient revelations and teachings to clearly understand the purpose and importance of eternal marriage in the Lord's plan of salvation.

NOTES

CHAPTER ELEVEN

1. LeGrand Richards, in Conference Report, April 1969, 90. On another occasion Elder Richards said, "What life? They already had their lives here in mortality, but they are to become heirs together of the blessings of eternal life. How could it be written any plainer than that?" *Ensign*, January 1974, 59.

2. Kenneth Godfrey, "Joseph Smith As Husband and Father: The Roots of the Mormon Family" (unpublished paper in possession of the author).

3. A closer look at Mormon theology suggests a very liberal attitude toward women. For one example, from the beginning of the Church women were given a voice and "vote" in Church government through the principle of "common consent."

4. Joseph Smith, *History of The Church of Jesus Christ of Latter-day Saints,* 2d ed. rev., ed. B. H. Roberts (Salt Lake City: Deseret Book Co., 1959–60), 5:285; hereafter cited as *HC.*

5. Mary Anderson, ed., *Joseph Smith III and the Restoration* (Independence, Mo.: Herald Publishing House, 1952), 74–76.

6. "Last Testimony of Sister Emma," in Heman C. Smith, *History of The Church of Jesus Christ of Latter Day Saints,* (Lamoni, Iowa: Reorganized Church of Jesus Christ of Latter Day Saints, 1920), 5:358.

7. A. Karl Larson and Katharine Miles Larson, eds., *Diary of Charles Lowell Walker* (Logan, Utah: Utah State University Press, 1980), 1:349; emphasis added.

8. Relatively early in his work on the JST, Joseph was directed to "ask, and my scriptures shall be given as I have appointed" (D&C 42:56 [9 February 1831]). Many revelations in the Doctrine and Covenants were given during the period in which Joseph was working on the Bible, and a careful study demonstrates an undeniable connection between the doctrines in the revelations of this period and the themes being dealt with in the Bible.

While only those revelations dealing most directly with eternal marriage and the thesis of this paper are treated at length in the text, a number of the early revelations dealt with subjects relating to marriage and family, but not specifically eternal marriage. For example, D&C 25:5–15 was given to Emma Smith concerning her role in marriage with promises conditioned on her fulfillment of that role. In February of 1831 the Lord made binding upon the modern Church the ancient moral law and instructed leaders to keep the Church clean from sexual transgression. In doing so he placed what Kenneth Godfrey has called a "divine sanctity" on marriage. The Lord also instructed husbands to love their wives and to cleave to them and none else. He warned against lust and specified that a repentant adulterer should not be cast out of the Church, but did make provision for church trials, if necessary, for those guilty of adultery. (See D&C 42:22–25, 74–77, 80.)

9. Benjamin F. Johnson, letter to George F. Gibbs, 1902. Original in the LDS Church Archives, Salt Lake City, Utah. The spelling and grammar of the original have been retained.

10. See Danel W. Bachman, "A Study of the Mormon Practice of Plural Marriage Before the Death of Joseph Smith" (Master's thesis, Purdue University, 1975), 47–103; "New Light on an Old Hypothesis: The Ohio Origins of the Revelation on Eternal Marriage," *Journal of Mormon History* 5 (1978): 19–32.

11. For example, section 68 enjoins upon parents the teaching of fundamental doctrines to children before the age of accountability. Section 74 specifies that little children are holy, being sanctified through the Atonement and untainted by original sin. Section 75 places upon the husband and father the responsibility of providing for the family.

12. Verse 17 of section 76 is the JST version of John 5:29. The changes, seemingly minor at first glance, were profound in their implication. The word *unto* appears twice in John 5:29 in reference to the resurrection of life or damnation, but the Lord changed the word to *in* in section 76, and the words *just* and *unjust* replaced *life* and *damnation*. This completely shifts the emphasis from two final conditions or states as implied in John 5:29 to two resurrections specified in section 76:17. No wonder the changes caused Joseph and

Sidney to marvel and meditate. In changing those four words the Lord had prepared their minds and hearts to receive an entirely new concept about life after death. Now that he had their thoughtful attention the Lord gave successive visions of the degrees of glory which may be attained in the hereafter and the essential qualifications to obtain them.

13. This interpretation is suggested by stanzas 19–20 of Joseph Smith's "The Answer," *Times and Seasons* 4 (1 February 1843): 82–85. W. W. Phelps had written a poem to Joseph entitled "Go With Me," the message of which was essentially let us soar into the heavens and see what is there. Joseph's reply, a poetic version of D&C 76, suggested to Phelps that Joseph had already been there and this was a report of what he had seen.

14. Apparently some converts coming from other faiths wanted to know if their previous baptism was acceptable or if they should be baptized again. The revelation announced that all old covenants were "done away" and that converts must "enter... in at the gate" (D&C 22:1, 4).

15. *Chardon Spectator and Geauga Gazette,* 30 October 1835, as quoted in Max H. Parkin, "The Nature and Cause of Internal and External Conflict of the Mormons in Ohio Between 1830 and 1838" (Master's thesis, Brigham Young University, 1966), 176.

16. Dale Morgan to Fawn Brodie, 24 December 1947. Original in the Special Collections Department, Marriott Library, University of Utah, Salt Lake City, Utah. Morgan was explaining to Brodie the contents of an interview he discovered between a Mr. Deming and J. C. Dowman.

17. These episodes foreshadowed similar uses of authority regarding marriage in Nauvoo. See Bachman, "A Study of the Mormon Practice of Plural Marriage," 125–133.

18. Newel Knight, "Sketch," 5. Original manuscript in the LDS Church Archives.

19. Dean C. Jessee, ed., *The Papers of Joseph Smith Volume 2: Journal, 1832–1842* (Salt Lake City: Deseret Book Co., 1992), 2:89; see also "Homespun" [Pseud.], *Lydia Knight's History,* The First Book of Noble Women's Lives Series (Salt Lake City: Juvenile Instructor Office, 1883), 31.

20. Jessee, *Papers*, 89.

21. Knight, "Sketch," 6.

22. Knight, "Sketch," 6. It was perhaps this circumstance of which Benjamin Winchester spoke when he said that in the mid-1830s, Joseph taught that he was "God's prophet and God's agent" and that "he was responsible to God only." According to Winchester this doctrine "created a great sensation," causing a portion of the original Church membership to withdraw. See Benjamin Winchester, "Primitive Mormonism," *Salt Lake Tribune,* 22 September 1889. One of the reasons Winchester left the Church was over its authoritarian nature and Joseph Smith's use of authority in particular.

23. Homespun, *Lydia Knight's History,* 31.

24. *HC* 2:320; see also Jessee, *Papers,* 88–89.

25. Knight, "Sketch," 6.

26. Some early brethren made comments on the necessity of the priesthood to perform religious ordinances, including marriage, that illuminate this and similar episodes in Nauvoo. See the remarks of Hyrum Smith, discourse of 8 April 1844, original manuscripts in the Minutes Collection in the LDS Church Archives; Orson Pratt, discourse of 11 August 1871, in *Journal of Discourses,* (London: Albert Carrington, 1854–86), 16:175 (hereafter cited as *JD*); and as found in Wilford Woodruff's journal for 15 August 1847; and John D. Lee, *Mormonism Unveiled, or the Life and Confessions of the Late Mormon Bishop, John D. Lee* (St. Louis, Mo.: Bryan, Brand, & Co., 1877), 146–47.

27. *HC,* 5:135.

28. Jessee, *Papers,* 153–54; *HC,* 2:377–78. Actually this was not the first time Joseph had pronounced the blessings of Abraham, Isaac, and Jacob upon a couple he married. Six days earlier, at the wedding of John Webb and Catherine Wilcox, Joseph said, "I pronounced such blessings upon their heads as the Lord put into my heart ~~even~~ the blessings of Abraham Issac and Jacob" (Jessee, *Papers,* 138).

29. *HC,* 2:378.

30. The very next day Joseph signed a certificate of marriage for William F. Cahoon and Nancy M. Gibbs which read, in part, that the ceremony had been performed "according to the rules and regulations of the Church of the Latter-day Saints, in the name of God, and in the name of Jesus Christ" (*HC* 2:377–78). This same terminology

was used in the marriage of John Boynton and appeared in the article on marriage in the 1835 Doctrine and Covenants.

At the height of the Kirtland apostasy, the right to marry was again an issue. The day after Joseph Smith and Sidney Rigdon fled Kirtland, Joseph Smith, Sr., was arrested and charged with marrying a couple illegally. Apparently the elder Smith and other Mormons were continuing to deliberately violate the restrictive Ohio statute because they considered it unconstitutional and, more importantly, an imposition on their divine authority.

31. These remarks were made at the wedding of John Webb and Catherine Wilcox, 14 January 1836. See Jessee, *Papers*, 138. According to Joseph's journal, he conducted weddings on six occasions in the winter of 1835-36 (see Jessee, 88-89, 94, 103-4, 138, 149, 153-54). Four times he made "remarks" or gave an address. During the Boynton-Lowell wedding Joseph had a cold and Sidney Rigdon gave an address. On only one occasion is there no mention of any instruction relative to marriage, but this was on 17 January 1836 when Joseph married *three* couples. It is unlikely he would let such an important opportunity and such a large audience pass without giving some instructions about marriage, though it is not mentioned in his journal.

32. W. W. Phelps, letter to Sally Phelps (his wife), 26 May 1835, as quoted in Walter Dean Bowen, "The Versatile W. W. Phelps—Mormon Writer, Educator, and Pioneer" (Master's thesis, BYU, 1958), 68.

33. *The Latter-day Saints Messenger and Advocate* 1 (June 1835): 130.

34. Joseph Smith, *Teachings of the Prophet Joseph Smith*, comp. Joseph Fielding Smith (Salt Lake City: Deseret Book Co., 1967), 308; hereafter cited as *TPJS*.

35. Ibid., 183.

36. Ibid., 65–66. Incidentally, receiving the blessings of the patriarchs Abraham, Issac, and Jacob may be, in part, what the scriptures refer to when they speak of turning the hearts of the children to the fathers.

37. First Presidency, Letter to All Stake Presidents, Mission Presidents, District Presidents, Bishops, and Branch Presidents, 12 February 1971.

38. *HC,* 3:230–31.

39. Parley P. Pratt, Jr., ed., *Autobiography of Parley P. Pratt* (Salt Lake City: Deseret Book Co., 1938), 297–98.

40. Gerry Avant, "Collector Finds Rare Book, Autographed Statement by Prophet," *Church News,* 23 June 1985, 10.

41. *TPJS,* 300–301.

42. See Danel W. Bachman, "A Study of the Mormon Practice of Plural Marriage," 204–16; see also "The Authorship of the Manuscript of Doctrine and Covenants Section 132," *Sidney B. Sperry Symposium, January 26, 1980, A Sesquicentennial Look At Church History* (Salt Lake City: Church Educational System, 1980), 27–44; Bachman, "New Light on an Old Hypothesis," 21–22, especially note 6.

43. For a detailed analysis of this point see Bachman, "New Light on an Old Hypothesis," 20–32.

44. *Nauvoo Expositor,* 7 June 1844. See especially the "Preamble" and the affidavits of William and Jane Law and Austin Cowles on pages 1–2.

45. The minutes of this very important meeting were published in the *Nauvoo Neighbor,* 19 June 1844.

THE ETERNAL NATURE OF THE FAMILY

KEM T. CAZIER

DURING THE SUMMER of my eighth year, I discovered that my cousin Cleve had a serious health problem that would require open-heart surgery. I was very upset at hearing this, for not only were Cleve and I first cousins, we were also the same age and best friends. We lived on farms a short distance from each other, and we spent many hours together romping in the fields with my bum lamb, shooting marbles, playing with toy trucks and cars, and jumping in the haystacks. By nightfall our hands and faces were always dirty, and we usually had a new hole or two in our already patched jeans. Together we giggled and roughhoused and told each other secrets. We were practically inseparable.

I remember hearing my parents talk in hushed tones about Cleve's condition. I couldn't comprehend what I heard, but remember feeling frightened for my best friend and myself.

Arrangements were made for Cleve to go to the Mayo Clinic, hundreds of miles away in Minnesota, for his specialized surgery. The night before his departure, I was invited to spend the night with him. I recall Cleve's father, my father, and the bishop placing their hands on Cleve's head and giving him a priesthood blessing. Both my mother and Cleve's had tears in their eyes, and I knew that it was not a good sign. My heart leaped in fear. I never wanted that night to end, and Cleve and I played and whispered until the late hours of the night. Somehow, I think we both knew that this would be our last time together in this life.

Early the next morning, we traveled to the station to put Cleve and his parents on the train. I remember my father holding me up on his shoulders so I could see Cleve walk down the aisle of the passenger car. He proudly led his parents to their seats, and then we waved and waved at one another in a heartfelt good-bye.

A few days later I sang a solo, "I Am a Child of God," at my cousin and best friend's funeral. Everyone was crying except me. When I had looked at Cleve's still form, all dressed in white with his Primary Top Pilot pin fastened to his lapel, I knew he wasn't there inside that body. I wondered where he was, why he had to leave me, and why I couldn't see him. Sometime later, I wondered if Cleve would help prepare a way for his loved ones and be waiting for us on the other side. Just as he'd led his parents down the aisle of the train on his last earthly trip and waited patiently for them to take their seats, he would be waiting for us.

Challenges and Adversities of Life

Life is full of challenges and adversities for each individual and family. The gospel of Jesus Christ is our greatest aid in meeting the demands and trials that come to all of us. The Lord, through his infinite wisdom, has provided counsel and guidance for us. Our responsibility is to heed his counsel, whether it comes from him or his authorized servants. In the preface to the Doctrine and Covenants the Lord has said,

> What I the Lord have spoken, I have spoken, and I excuse not myself; and though the heavens and the earth pass away, my word shall not pass away, but shall all be fulfilled, whether by mine own voice or by the voice of my servants, it is the same. (1:38)

President Joseph Fielding Smith, in his address "Counsel to the Saints and to the World," taught that

> the family is the most important organization in time or in eternity. Our purpose in life is to create for ourselves eternal family units.... It is the will of the Lord to strengthen and preserve the family unit.[1]

To Lucy Mack Smith, the family unit was of utmost importance. She did all she could to strengthen and bless her family, alongside her good husband, Joseph Smith, Sr. She loved her husband and children and believed and trusted in them. When hardships came to her family, she relied on the Lord for counsel and guidance through prayer and faithful study of the Bible. She had many heartaches in her life which may have been hard for her to understand, especially before the gospel was fully restored. When her beloved twenty-five-year-old son Alvin was stricken with bilious colic, she recorded:

On the third day of his sickness, Dr. McIntyre, whose services were usually employed by the family, as he was considered very skillful, was brought, and with him four other eminent physicians. But it was all in vain, their exertions proved unavailing, just as Alvin said would be the case....

In the latter part of the fourth night he called for all the children, and exhorted them separately.... But when he came to Joseph, he said, "I am now going to die, the distress which I suffer, and the feelings that I have, tell me my time is very short. I want you to be a good boy, and do everything that lies in your power to obtain the Record. Be faithful in receiving instruction, and in keeping every commandment that is given you. Your brother Alvin must leave you; but remember the example which he has set for you; and set the same example for the children that are younger than yourself, and always be kind to father and mother."...

As I turned with the child to leave him he said, "Father, mother, brothers, and sisters, farewell! I can now breathe out my life as calmly as a clock." Saying this, he immediately closed his eyes in death....

Alvin manifested, if such could be the case, greater zeal and anxiety in regard to the Record that had been shown to Joseph, than any of the rest of the family; in consequence of which we could not bear to hear anything said upon the subject. Whenever Joseph spoke of the Record, it would immediately bring Alvin to our minds, with all his zeal, and with all his kindness; and, when we looked to his place, and realized that he was gone from it, to return no more in this life, we all with one accord wept over our irretrievable loss, and we could "not be comforted, because he was not."[2]

As the years passed, Joseph Smith continued to think about his brother Alvin. Would he be able to see him again and be with him and other family members? He pondered and repeatedly prayed for an answer. Finally, twelve years after Alvin's death, Joseph received an answer. On January 21, 1836, a vision was given to the Prophet in the temple at Kirtland, Ohio. He records:

> I saw Father Adam and Abraham; and my father and my mother; my brother Alvin, that has long since slept;
> And marveled how it was that he had obtained an inheritance in that kingdom, seeing that he had departed this life before the Lord had set his hand to gather Israel the second time, and had not been baptized for the remission of sins.
> Thus came the voice of the Lord unto me, saying: All who have died without a knowledge of this gospel, who would have received it if they had been permitted to tarry, shall be heirs of the celestial kingdom of God. (D&C 137:5-7)

This revelation must have brought much insight and comfort to the Smith family, as well as to people the world over. To Joseph Smith came the knowledge and consolation that families can be together forever when we do those things necessary to make family ties eternal.

Creating Eternal Families

Latter-day revelation on the family, found in our modern scriptures as well as from the mouths of our prophets, is important to heed, for Satan desires to destroy the family unit. President Ezra Taft Benson said: "There is convincing evidence that a creeping rot of moral disintegration is eating into the very vitals of this temple of American civilization. It gives cause for serious concern."[3]

Throughout time the Lord has warned us to safeguard our families and be aware of the power that comes from the home. President Ezra Taft Benson has noted:

> No nation ever rises above its homes.... We are no better as a people than are our firesides, our homes. The school, the church, and even the nation, I feel confident, stand helpless before weakened and degraded homes. The good home is the rock foundation, the cornerstone of civilization. It must be preserved. It must be strengthened.
>
> There has never been and there never will be a satisfactory substitute for the home established by the God of heaven. If this nation is to endure, then the home must be safeguarded, strengthened, and restored to its rightful importance.[4]

On May 6, 1833, the Prophet Joseph Smith received a revelation in which he and other leading brethren of the Church were instructed to set their own homes in order. They were rebuked for failing to teach their children correct principles. The Lord said:

> I have commanded you to bring up your children in light and truth....
>
> You have not taught your children light and truth, according to the commandments; ...
>
> And now a commandment I give unto you—if you will be delivered you shall set in order your own house, for there are many things that are not right in your house....
>
> Your family must needs repent and forsake some things....
>
> Pray always lest that wicked one have power in you, and remove you out of your place....
>
> [S]ee that they are more diligent and concerned at home. (D&C 93:40, 42, 43, 48–50)

Our responsibility as family members is to be diligent and concerned at home. If we desire to have an eternal family, we need to teach our children correct gospel principles, including prayer and repentance. The family is a divine institution established by our Heavenly Father, and we need to give it the attention and time it deserves. "The establishment of a home is not only a privilege, but marriage and the bearing, rearing and proper training of children is a duty of the highest order." [5]

We must never take lightly the eternal nature of families. We as parents have a grave responsibility to our children. We are instructed in the Doctrine and Covenants that

> inasmuch as parents have children in Zion, or in any of her stakes which are organized, that teach them not to understand the doctrine of repentance, faith in Christ the Son of the living God, and of baptism and the gift of the Holy Ghost by the laying on of the hands, when eight years old, the sin be upon the heads of the parents. (68:25)

What a solemn obligation we have! But we need to remember that it is also a privilege to teach our children "to pray and to walk uprightly before the Lord" (D&C 68:28), for as we strive to do those things the Lord wants us to do, we internalize those principles that are eternal in nature, and we become a happier people. President Spencer W. Kimball said that righteousness can create a heaven on earth: "We are true to our trust, to our companions, to our children, the Church, and our Lord, and being true and loyal and clean and worthy, we will constantly be in a heavenly atmosphere, or in heaven."[6]

The Lord does not want us to fail. He wants us to succeed, and he will help us. We should be optimistic about making our families eternal, for we have the Lord on our side. It can be accomplished if we strive day by day to follow his counsel. President Kimball has taught:

> You know the evil one has opposed us all the way from before the beginning. He has promised himself that he is going to disturb every person in this earth and try to get him to do evil. But remember that the evil one is a spirit only. He

has no body. Therefore, every one of you is stronger than Satan. If you will exercise your brain, your morals, your teachings, you can be superior to him.[7]

Because the family unit is so important to our Heavenly Father's plan, we are confronted with much opposition. Satan, realizing how precious the family is, will do all in his power to destroy it. President Kimball said:

Always remember that if this were not the Lord's work, the adversary would not pay any attention to us. If this Church were merely a church of men and women, teaching only the doctrines of men, we would encounter little or no criticism or resistance—but because this is the Church of Him whose name it bears, we must not be surprised when criticisms or difficulties arise.[8]

Spiritual Teaching in the Home

There is much we can do within our families to combat the evil one. *First of all, we need to remember that the most important teachings in the home are spiritual.* In a general conference, President Benson reminded us:

Parents are commanded to prepare their sons and daughters for the ordinances of the gospel: baptism, confirmation, priesthood ordinations, and temple marriage. They are to teach them to respect and honor the Sabbath day, to keep it holy. Most importantly, parents are to instill within their children a desire for eternal life and to seek earnestly that goal above all else.[9]

We need to remember also that parents are directly responsible for this spiritual training. President Benson tells us that "this responsibility cannot be safely delegated to relatives, friends, neighbors, the school, the church, or the state." [10]

As we strive to teach our children about important spiritual matters, we need to remember that the greatest teaching tool is example. Seeing an action leaves a lasting impression on the mind, whether for good or bad. President Kimball has emphasized:

> The child will carry into his own life much that he sees in his family home life. If he sees his parents going to the temple frequently, he will begin to plan a temple life. If he is taught to pray for the missionaries, he will gradually gravitate toward the missionary program. Now, this is very simple, but it is the way of life. And we promise you that your children will bring you honor and glory as you give them proper example and training.[11]

We are instructed in section 88 of the Doctrine and Covenants to "organize [our]selves; prepare every needful thing; and establish a house, even a house of prayer, . . . fasting, . . . faith, . . . learning, . . . glory, . . . order, . . . [and] a house of God" (v. 119). The Lord has given us commandments and programs to help us accomplish this, providing ways to strengthen the family unit and each individual.

The family home evening program is one such way. President Kimball stressed:

> We must not forget this home evening every Monday night. I say *every* Monday evening. . . . That is where we are going to save our nations. That is where we are going to have peace on earth, and it can come only through the family as the sacred unit that can be depended upon. So we have the home evening, and there we don't just have fun, we don't just have refreshments, and we don't just sit around and talk and play games. We have something serious in every home evening.[12]

As a prophet of God, President Kimball has additionally emphasized the important training family home evening provides:

> Immorality, drug addiction, general moral and spiritual deterioration seem to be increasing, and the world is in turmoil. But

the Lord has offered an old program in new dress, and it gives promise to return the world to sane living, to true family life, to family interdependence....

I wonder what this world would be like if every father and mother gathered their children around them at least once a week, explained the gospel, and bore fervent testimonies to them. How could immorality continue and infidelity break families and delinquency spawn?[13]

According to the Lord's counsel, *effective communication* is another way we can strengthen the family unit. Effective communication is more than a sharing of words. It is the careful and wise use of words in sharing feelings, concerns, and emotions. It requires thought and compassion. "Who is a wise man and endued with knowledge among you? let him shew out of a good conversation his works with meekness of wisdom" (James 3:13). Effective communication requires a willingness to listen, to avoid judgment, and to practice patience. "How forcible are right words!" (Job 6:25). Elder Marvin J. Ashton quoted Jones Stephens as saying: "I have learned that the head does not hear anything until the heart has listened, and that what the heart knows today the head will understand tomorrow."[14]

Too often as we communicate with family members we threaten, embarrass, beg, or command. Effective communication lines can close down entirely if we fail to use courtesy and respect during family discussions. Barriers put up at such a time may be almost impossible to take down later, when we want so much to convey a principle of importance. It is very discouraging for a parent to receive only a shrug of the shoulder or rolling of the eyes from a child after trying to communicate something of gravity.

The Lord has instructed us to follow a pattern when we communicate. Verses 122–125 of Doctrine and Covenants section 88 provide a guide for every parent and every child in all families:

...Let not all be spokesmen at once; but let one speak at a time and let all listen unto his sayings, that when all have spoken that all may be edified of all, and that every man may have an equal privilege.

See that ye love one another; cease to be covetous; learn to impart one to another as the gospel requires....

Cease to find fault one with another....

And above all things, clothe yourselves with the bond of charity, as with a mantle, which is the bond of perfectness and peace.

In April conference, 1976, Elder Marvin J. Ashton gave a powerful address on family communication. He stated:

When family members tune each other out, communication is not taking place. Words spoken are unheard, unwanted, and resisted when we fail to understand the basics for proper interchange. Each must be willing to do his part to improve, since the family unit is the basic foundation of the Church. Proper communication will always be a main ingredient for building family solidarity and permanence.[15]

Our living prophet, Ezra Taft Benson, has given us pertinent counsel on communicating with our children:

Praise your children more than you correct them. Praise them for even their smallest achievement....

Encourage your children to come to you for counsel with their problems and questions by listening to them every day. Discuss with them such important matters as dating, sex, and other matters affecting their growth and development, and do it early enough so they will not obtain information from questionable sources.[16]

Daily family prayer is another way we can solidify the family unit. The importance of having family prayer was taught by the Savior himself when he said, "Pray in your families unto the Father, always in my name, that your wives and your children may be blessed" (3 Ne. 18:21). President Kimball said: "In the family prayer there is even more than the supplication and prayer of gratitude. It is a forward step toward family unity and family solidarity."[17] He admonished us:

> O my beloved brothers and sisters, what a world it would be if the members of every family in this church were to be on their knees...every night and morning! And what a world it would be if hundreds of millions of families in the great land and other lands were praying for their sons and daughters twice daily. And what a world this would be if a billion families throughout the world were in home evenings and church activity and were on their physical knees pouring out their souls for their children, their families, their leaders, their governments![18]

President Kimball has also told us that *daily family scripture study* has long been suggested as a powerful tool against the temptations of Satan. He said: "This practice will produce great happiness and will help family members love the Lord and his goodness."[19] "Behold," said the Lord, "I stand at the door, and knock: if any man hear my voice, and open the door, I will come in to him, and will sup with him, and him with me" (Rev. 3:20).

Teaching our children of spiritual matters, setting a proper example, holding weekly family home evenings, having daily scripture study and daily family prayer will help strengthen our families. But there is another vital ingredient in making an eternal family, and that is the *obligation to be married in the temple and have children sealed to parents,* remembering that "whatsoever thou shalt bind on earth shall be bound in heaven" (Matt. 16:19). Within the walls of the temples of the Lord, those with the authorized keys can seal family members together for the eternities.

What we learn in this life will continue with us in the afterlife. The righteous things we do as individuals and as families will bring us eternal rewards and eternal progression. It is our responsibility to do all we can in this life to become more like our Savior. We need to prioritize the demands of everyday living. We need to govern our lives so we can give our families the time and consideration they need and deserve. If we are prayerful and careful in setting priorities, we can achieve great happiness in life. If we will follow the counsel of the Lord, we can literally build for ourselves celestial homes on earth and eternal kingdoms hereafter.

President Harold B. Lee said: "Remember that the most important of the Lord's work *that you will ever do* will be the work *you do within the walls of your own home*" (emphasis added).[20]

Conclusion

Thirteen years ago a young father of four was killed when the brakes went out in the big semi he was driving and he went over a steep embankment. The night before the funeral, the family met at the mortuary. A little five-year-old boy pulled a chair up to the head of the coffin in which his father lay. After the chair was situated just right, the boy climbed up on the chair so he could see his father. Tears welled up in the child's eyes. Gently, he placed his hand on his father's face, and then he smoothed his father's brown hair. Rising on his tiptoes, he whispered in his father's ear, "Daddy, can you hear me? Daddy, can you hear me? I love you, Daddy." Then with tears gathering in my eyes, I watched my little nephew touch my brother's cool face with his lips and kiss his daddy's cheek.

The challenge comes to each of us to accept those truths that are eternal and live them so that we can join our loved ones in the hereafter. Just as the Prophet Joseph Smith learned that he and Alvin would be able to see each other again, so I know that if I live righteously I will be able to see my cousin Cleve and my brother Roger again. That the family unit *continues* beyond the grave. That these blessings are available to all who seek and qualify for them.

NOTES

CHAPTER TWELVE

1. Joseph Fielding Smith, "Counsel to the Saints and to the World," *Ensign,* July 1972, 27.

2. Lucy Mack Smith, *History of Joseph Smith* (Salt Lake City: Bookcraft, 1954), 86–89.

3. Ezra Taft Benson, *This Nation Shall Endure* (Salt Lake City: Deseret Book Co., 1977), 99

4. Ezra Taft Benson, *God, Family, Country: Our Three Great Loyalties* (Salt Lake City: Deseret Book Co., 1974), 169.

5. Ezra Taft Benson, "Foundations for Family Solidarity," *Children's Friend*, April 1957, 26.

6. Spencer W. Kimball, *The Teachings of Spencer W. Kimball,* ed. Edward L. Kimball (Salt Lake City: Bookcraft, 1982), 157; hereafter cited as *TSWK*.

7. Ibid., 33.

8. Spencer W. Kimball, *Ensign,* May 1981, 79.

9. Ezra Taft Benson, *Ensign*, November 1982, 60–61.

10. Ezra Taft Benson, *The Teachings of Ezra Taft Benson* (Salt Lake City: Bookcraft, 1988), 499.

11. Kimball, *TSWK,* 342.

12. Kimball, *TSWK,* 344.

13. Spencer W. Kimball, "Home Training—The Cure for Evil," *Improvement Era* 68 (June 1965): 513–14.

14. Marvin J. Ashton, *Ensign,* May 1976, 52.

15. Ibid., 54.

16. Ezra Taft Benson, *Ensign,* November 1981, 107.

17. Spencer W. Kimball, *Children's Friend,* January 1946, 30.

18. Spencer W. Kimball, "Family Prayer," in *Prayer* (Salt Lake City: Deseret Book Co., 1980), 87.

19. Spencer W. Kimball, *Ensign,* January 1982, 4.

20. Harold B. Lee, *Decisions for Successful Living* (Salt Lake City: Deseret Book Co., 1974), 247–49.

NOTES ON THE AUTHORS

Kenneth W. Godfrey is director of the Logan Institute of Religion and has directed institutes in California and Ogden, Utah. He has been employed by the Church Educational System since 1958 and has served as an area director in California, Arizona, and Northern Utah. Brother Godfrey holds a Ph.D. from Brigham Young University, is a past president of the Mormon History Association, and has served on the board of editors of *BYU Studies*. He has published more than one hundred and sixty articles and six books. He is a former bishop and mission president and has served on the Instructional Development Committee of the Church. Married to Audrey Montgomery, he has five children and five grandchildren.

Robert J. Matthews was born in Evanston, Wyoming, and received his B.S., M.S., and Ph.D. degrees from Brigham Young University. He has been with the Church Educational System since 1955 and has taught in Idaho, California, and at BYU. For several years he was also assigned as a course writer, editor, and researcher for seminaries and institutes of religion. He served for eight and a half years as Dean of Religious Education at Brigham Young University and is professor emeritus of ancient scripture at BYU. Brother Matthews is married to Shirley Neves, and they are the parents of four children.

John K. Challis is a seminary and institute instructor. He was born in Salt Lake City and raised in Cedar City, Utah. He holds a degree in public relations and advertising from Southern Utah University, and he worked in those fields and in graphic design prior to joining the Church Educational System. He has taught in Cedar City, Utah, and currently teaches in Afton, Wyoming, and he has served in many Church capacities. He is married to Julie Maxwell and is the father of four daughters.

John G. Scott was born in Winnemucca, Nevada. He was baptized into The Church of Jesus Christ of Latter-day Saints in Pullman,

Washington, while attending Washington State University, where one year later he completed a four-year institute program. After serving in the Flordia, Ft. Lauderdale Mission, he received a B.S. in history and a secondary educational endorsement from Utah State University. He has also earned his M.Ed. degree from Brigham Young University and received a special certificate of achievement in post graduation studies from the Logan Institute of Religion. Brother Scott has taught in the Church Educational System since 1984 as a seminary and institute instructor. He and Valene Joyce Haralson are the parents of six children and currently own and operate a small farm in west central Wyoming.

Robert J. Woodford has taught in the Church Educational System for over 30 years. He has worked in the translation department for the Church and has served on the Church's curriculum committee. Brother Woodford earned his B.S. in math and science from the University of Utah and completed a masters in educational administration and a Ph.D. in Bible and modern scriptures studies at Brigham Young University. Currently Brother Woodford teaches at the University of Utah Institute of Religion and is the bishop of the Winder 3rd Ward. He is married to the former Narda Ehlers, and they have eight children.

Philip C. Wightman was born and raised in the Provo area. He was called as a missionary to the Great Lakes Mission, and is a graduate of Brigham Young University with a bachelor's degree in math and a master's degree in the history of religion. He has also completed his classwork towards a Ph.D. in junior college administration. Brother Wightman had been with the seminaries and institutes for 5 years when he joined the religion faculty at Ricks College. He has recently been released as the chairman of the religion department at Ricks and now serves as the chairman of the Division of Religious and Family Living. Brother Wightman has served in a number of Church callings, including high counselor and bishop. He and his wife, Pat, have six children—five sons and a daughter—and six grandchildren.

M. Catherine Thomas is a religious education instructor at BYU. She earned her Ph.D. in early christian history from Brigham Young University and has served as faculty on the London and Jerusalem study abroad programs. Sister Thomas has published articles in the

Ensign and several BYU publications and currently serves in her stake Young Women's presidency. She is married to Gordon K. Thomas, and they are the parents of six children.

Linda Aukschun was born and raised in Utah, and she graduated from Brigham Young University. She has taught release-time seminary for ten years and is currently assigned to the Brighton High School Seminary. Linda and her husband, Carl, have two grown sons, Ben and Bradley.

James A. Carver was born and raised in Nephi, Utah. He completed his education at Brigham Young University, obtaining a bachelor's degree in psychology and secondary education and a master's degree in religious education. He has taught in the Church Educational System for thirty-one years. Brother Carver has published in the *Ensign* and has written a pamphlet entitled *The Mormon Faith Un-Decker-ated* and *The New Mythmakers*. He and his wife, Merilyn, are the parents of ten children and currently live in Cedar City, Utah.

Richard H. Berrett, currently an instructor at the Logan Institute of Religion at Utah State University, has taught for many years in the Church Educational System. Previous assignments have included seminaries and institutes in Utah and Arizona, as well as BYU. In 1965, while teaching at the Orem Seminary, he initiated the first C.E.S. class at the Utah State Prison, and he continued to work with various programs there until moving to Arizona in 1971. He served a mission to North Central States and attended Brigham Young University, receiving an Ed.D. in 1972. He is married to JoAnn Judd, and they are the parents of five children. Their present home is in Providence, Utah.

Danel W. Bachman was born in Twin Falls, Idaho. He completed a bachelor's degree in psychology at Brigham Young University and a master's degree in history at Purdue University. He has taught in the Church Educational System for twenty-seven years. He and his wife, Pat, are the parents of four children. They currently live in Logan, Utah, where he is a member of the faculty at the Logan institute. Brother Bachman has published articles in the *Ensign* and scholarly journals.

Kem T. Cazier was born and raised in Star Valley, Wyoming, and served an LDS mission in Alabama and Florida. He graduated from

Rick's college with an associate's degree, earned his bachelor's degree from Utah State University in the college of family life, and received his M.Ed. degree from BYU in public school administration. He has taught elementary school for five years and has been employed by the Church Educational System for thirteen years. Brother Cazier has received specialized training in family education at the Johnson Institute, the Institute of Reality Therapy, and the Chemical Awareness Training Institute. He is currently principal of the Afton LDS Seminary and Institute and serves in the Afton Wyoming Stake presidency. He is married to Beth Pearson, and they are the parents of five children.

SCRIPTURE INDEX

PEARL OF GREAT PRICE

Moses

Abraham

SUBJECT INDEX